THE
CUTTING EDGE

STUDIES IN ANCIENT
AND MEDIEVAL COMBAT

THE
CUTTING EDGE

STUDIES IN ANCIENT
AND MEDIEVAL COMBAT

BARRY MOLLOY

TEMPUS

First published 2007

Tempus Publishing Limited
The Mill, Brimscombe Port,
Stroud, Gloucestershire, GL5 2QG
www.tempus-publishing.com

British Library Cataloguing in Publication Data.
A catalogue record for this book is available from the British Library.

ISBN 978 0 7524 4169 6

Typesetting and origination by Tempus Publishing Limited
Printed in Great Britain

Contents

Contributors

Christoph Amberger
jcamberger@gmail.com

John Clements
The Academy of Renaissance Martial Arts, USA
www.theArma.org

Jon Coulston
School of Classics, University of St Andrews, Fife, Scotland

Jeffrey Forgeng
Higgins Armory Museum, USA

Erhard Godehardt
Department of Thoracic and Heart Surgery, Heinrich Heine University, Duesseldorf, Germany
godehard@uni-duesseldorf.de

Dave Grossman
Killology Research Group, USA
www.killology.com

Thomas Hulit
tdhulit@telus.net

Jerzy Jaworski
Department of Discrete Mathematics, Adam Mickiewicz University, Poland

Barry Molloy
School of Archaeology, University College Dublin, Ireland
barrymolloy@gmail.com

Ronan O' Flaherty
Ballyhitt Lane, Barntown, Co. Wexford, Ireland
Ronan.OFlaherty@agriculture.gov.ie

Alan Peatfield
School of Archaeology, University College Dublin, Ireland
alan.Peatfield@ucd.ie

Peter Pieper
Department of Forensic Medicine, Heinrich Heine University, Düsseldorf, Germany

Allen Pittman
allenpittman@yahoo.com

Steven Pressfield
www.stevenpressfield.com

Thom Richardson
Keeper of Armour and Oriental Collections, Royal Armouries, Leeds, England
Thom.Richardson@armouries.org.uk

Hans Michael Schellenberg
Department of Ancient History, Heinrich Heine University, Düsseldorf, Germany

Piotr Taracha
Polish Academy of Sciences
taracha@iaepan.edu.pl

Richard Underwood
millennia@millennia-designs.com

Introduction:
the evil that men do …

Barry P.C. Molloy

INTRODUCTION

It is nearly three thousand years since Homer wrote of the epic war between the Greeks and the Trojans; that mighty struggle of heroes and gods in an age of raw passions and brutish short lives. The tide of battle was led by great champions, smiting lesser men by the dozen and rising to a crescendo as one hero faced another in bloody fracas where only one man was left alive. Whether these tales are true or myth, they celebrate flamboyantly deeds of valour and renown by great warriors. Even death itself on the field of battle brought prestige and praise. We can see in them the promotion of the masculine paradigm as a skilled and respected warrior, facing down death without compunction. It does not matter if these represent real people, it is immaterial if they are purely works of an ancient imagination; what is of fundamental importance is the belief within them and amongst their audiences of 'the way of the warrior'. This masculine warrior ideal can be traced throughout the millennia of recorded history, and stretches back further still into the world of prehistory.

In the ages of sword and spear, we find warriors who touched, tasted and grappled each other as they fought face-to-face in the mud, blood and filth of the battlefield. The might and influence of a polity rested with the celebration of the prowess of its fighting men, and there were many rewards for those who excelled in skills-at-arms. The passage of time has left us few written sources which give unambiguous tales of how these ancient and medieval warriors fought and died on the field of battle. What survives to this day are the countless artefacts of violence which bear testimony to this world of slaughter, along with a small group of cryptic texts and illustrations hinting at long forgotten warrior skills. These all have dramatic stories to tell.

We shall demonstrate in this volume that the ancient through to medieval worlds provide us with excellent case studies for the evolution of combat and weaponry, and their roles in human societies throughout the ages. The following papers will provide fresh evidence for the manner in which the ancient warriors of our past faced each other in the life and death environment of interpersonal combat. They dramatically bring to light recent findings in the field of combat studies, and in many cases challenge popularly held beliefs about the use of weaponry. Authors will demonstrate that medieval swords were far from being crude battering implements, that Roman gladiators were not condemned to certain death in the arena and that many of the supposedly 'ceremonial' weapons of prehistory were lethally effective tools for killing!

VIOLENCE IN HUMAN SOCIETIES

In our modern world, it is not permissible for us to respond violently when we feel wronged, offended or challenged, because the legal systems of our societies forbid it. Violence can only legally be undertaken by legitimate bodies of the state – the police and the army – on our behalf in the apprehension and punishment of those who infringe upon our rights. The social model fed to us from a young age in our media and educational systems relegates interpersonal violence to a 'wrong-doing' for which we may be punished by the state authorities. Retribution is undertaken by proxy through the legitimate forces of the state, and consequently modern civilians are denied the right to legitimately use violence in most forms of conflict resolution.

Is it any surprise that this viewing of violence as 'incorrect' or 'wrong' has frequently been translated to studies of past societies? Students of the past cannot and should not see episodes of violence and killing as culturally anomalous or a brief event characteristic of the breaking down of social order. Violence can be seen as part of the very social fabric in many societies past and present. It can be utilised in attempts to maintain order as well as cases of infringements of what is commonly regarded as 'order'. In this sense it represents a characteristic of social normality. As Pinker (2002, 336) notes:

> Many intellectuals have averted their gaze from the evolutionary logic of violence, fearing that acknowledging it is tantamount to accepting it or approving of it. Instead they have pursued the comforting delusion of the Noble Savage, in which violence is an arbitrary product of learning or a pathogen that bores into us from the outside.

Violence needs to be seen as a transformative occurrence which can affect the lives of many within society, yet it is not an aspect of the ancient world that has been explored in *its own right* in great detail to date (see Keeley 1996, Vandkilde 2003). In this regard there is an essential difference between broader studies of warfare and those examining the actions and tools of combat. Studies of warfare generally focus on the (nature and results of) events relating to armies/bands of warriors interacting on the field of battle. When investigating combat, we are engaging with agencies of violence focusing on the actions of past warriors.

Since the earliest artefacts were crafted by man, there has been the potential to turn these against fellow humans. While this should not be taken to infer that violence was endemic in human cultures of the past, its widespread development throughout space and time strongly infers that it is certainly intrinsic to our nature (see Turney-High 1949; Keeley 1996; Molloy & Grossman, chapter 15). In this sense, the explorations of violence in this volume neither condemn nor condone it, they simply seek to understand it for what it is – an activity which is as characteristic of our species as it is for many others in the animal kingdom.

Violence needs to be studied as a normal, and not an anomalous, social interaction being undertaken for set purposes. While it may be problematic to analyse violence bereft of social motives, we must still consider the physical mechanics of its manifestation when seeking to understand its social setting. To truly attempt to understand warfare in times past, we must explore the bloody actions of individual warriors striking or shooting a foe in violent confrontations. This is one of the central tenets of of what may be termed 'Combat Archaeoloy'.

EXPERIMENTAL AND EXPERIENTIAL APPROACHES

Publications dedicated to the study of ancient weaponry (as opposed to warfare) traditionally treat the shape of the weapon as its most useful trait. This provides us with the lingua franca necessary for making reference to the artefacts when engaging in discussions of their typological and technological context (Oakeshott 1960; Eogan 1965; and the important 'Prähistorische Bronzefunde' series, for example). These painstaking studies provide the backbone of archaeological literature on these artefacts, and their importance certainly cannot be overlooked or dismissed (Ramsey 1995). However, they are not, and were not, intended to be ends unto themselves (Bradley 2005) and it is necessary to build upon this literature and examine the interplay between the forms and the practical functions required of objects. In the case of weaponry in particular, it is wrong to simply view them as 'dead' pieces of matter – they come to life when wielded in human hands in the manner that they were designed for (Dobres 2000; Boivin 2005). This needs to be taken into account seriously when investigating the primary role of these artefacts as weapons of war.

The use of weaponry engages the physical body as much as (if not more than) the intellect, and it is therefore essential for us to investigate them through bodily experience (see Clements, Forgeng and Kiermayer, Molloy and Peatfield this volume). Hand–eye co-ordination cannot be found in any book, and the mechanics of striking or deflecting a blow, or shooting/throwing particular weapons comes from experience as well as instruction (Molloy 2006, Malafouris 2004). In many cases we must be dealing with designs of weapon derived from the expressed needs of those individual warriors who were trained in their use as *real weapons* designed to kill real human beings. These individuals would have learnt through personal experience the balance between speed, weight and strength that suited their own physique and fighting skills best in the prevailing combat environments. These issues are marked in the archaeological record by the significant variation in proportions of weapons even from a single typological group (see Pittman, Molloy and Clements, this volume).

As the mind *and* body are taught responses to combat situations, the body is transformed during this process by physical alteration to the musculature and bone structure, but also its instinctive response mechanisms (see Clements 1997; 1998; chapter 13; Molloy & Grossman, chapter 15). It will do as required of it within the constraints of its physical mechanics and is conditioned to do so with minimum delay between thought and reaction so that movement becomes virtually automatic. In this context, the physical characteristics of the warrior are truly a socially constituted construction (Treherne 1995). The body itself becomes a product of society and has material meaning in the world it inhabits, being both a symbol and celebration of the social processes that gave rise to it.

THE CUTTING EDGE

The time span covered by this volume ranges from around 4,000 years ago right up to 400 years ago, the common theme throughout the book being the efficacy and manner of use of combat techniques and weaponry. The material realities of the use of interpersonal combat weapons by past warriors is thus contextualised within a chronological setting stemming from their advent as the prevalent tools of war to their relegation to ceremonial weapons, or their utter demise in warfare. Chapters will be treated thematically below rather than sequentially.

Coulston's paper (chapter 4) considers the fighting prowess of the Roman army and gladiatorial schools. Combat on the battlefield was a corporate endeavour, with lines of battle working in close co-ordination produced through extensive drilling and training. This of course detracts neither from the requisite bravery nor combat prowess of the individual, but these are expressed through the ability to operate cohesively within a group or team effort. The gladiators of Rome were renowned as some of the most skilled 'warriors' of their time, yet their social position as *infames*[1] and potential fame meant that their status in society was a world apart from the soldiers of the army. Their craft at arms was very specialised and aimed at both efficacy and aesthetic/visual impressiveness. Coulston traces the evolution of both these parallel martial traditions – the individualist warrior and the drilled formation fighter (albeit from an 'individual' perspective).

At the very dawn of specialised combat weaponry, the emphasis rested heavily on the first of the above two traditions – the individualist (but elite ranking) warrior. For the Early Bronze Age in Ireland, O'Flaherty (chapter 7) argues that the specialised combat weaponry was intended for use in single-combats, which would have involved a significant display element, echoed in later times in elite Renaissance fighting schools (Amberger and Forgeng & Kiermayer, this volume). For the Middle and Late Bronze Ages in Ireland and Britain, the level of complexity of fighting appears to have increased and co-ordinated group combat appears to have grown in importance alongside single combats (Molloy, chapter 8), perhaps still being the preserve of the upper echelons of society. The complexity of fighting styles required to effectively wield Bronze Age swords indicates that there was a martial system in place which included deliberate training regimes amongst the warrior classes.

Peatfield (chapter 3) progresses the idea that the ancient Greeks not only had formal fighting styles, but also had a strong interest in the mechanics of the fight. Beginning back in the Bronze Age with a brief analysis of Minoan swordsmanship, he discusses the nature of the growing field of study focusing on ancient martial arts. Peatfield's work, along with Molloy (2006), represents a dynamic shift in how we approach this nascent field of research with innovative experimental and experiential methodologies. Moving on to the Greek Archaic period, he discusses issues of agonistic combat in the form of boxing and a form of ancient kickboxing better known as *pankration*. While the surviving sources are designed as 'works of art' rather than as a guide to combat styles, one can see in them the reflection of a complex and intelligent martial arts tradition. Peatfield teases out exciting new ways to analyse these ancient sources reflexively with modern combat arts knowledge and provides some truly innovative results.

In his paper on the use of swords (chapter 13), Clements traces the development of these weapons during the Middle Ages and the Renaissance.

As a martial artist with many years of experience in studying and instructing on the use of bladed weaponry, Clements critiques the validity of the historical debate of 'cut versus thrust.' The use of historically accurate replicas in reconstructing elements of medieval sword-fighting styles is espoused strongly, and the fruits of his experience in this field are brought authoritatively to bear. A timely reminder is also included that the evolution of weaponry in pre-gunpowder ages was not a linear development ever increasing in efficiency and quality towards an 'ideal form', a point also taken up in the contributions by Coulston and Molloy. The evolution of armour is often seen as being intrinsically tied to the developments in weaponry, but Clements critiques this 'Darwinian' progression arguing that there is a more deeply reflexive relationship.

This introductory chapter opened with mention of the Greek epic poet Homer. In his study of Aegean Bronze Age armour (chapter 11) Taracha investigates some aspects of the military equipment of the ancestors of the poet's warriors. In this period we first see the emergence of plate armour in Europe alongside a variety of offensive weapons. The rich martial milieu of the Aegean Bronze Age is discussed with the efficacy of these early trials in plate armour attested through experimentation.

It is made clear in Hulit & Richardson's contribution that contemporary Bronze Age scale armours in Egypt were of varying efficiency, especially in relation to the bow (chapter 5). A suit of armour manufactured from rawhide scales from the tomb of Tutankhamun provides evidence that this easily acquired material was in use alongside the more expensive material of bronze, even amongst the elite charioteers. This paper initially investigates the efficacy of sections of armour made from each of these materials, and one manufactured from a combination of the two materials, against high-powered bows and a replica Egyptian Bronze Age axe. The challenge is then taken a step further when they explore the use of such bows from a moving chariot on location in Egypt.

Godehart et al. also take up the argument of the efficiency of bows against defensive equipment, focusing on the penetrative power of later bows with iron-tipped arrows (chapter 9). These were tested against shields of various constructions. It is demonstrated that repeated arrow shots weaken the structural integrity of defensive equipment (primarily shields), considerably diminishing their efficacy. The many different ways in which this basic yet highly effective weapon could be manufactured had a direct bearing on intended modes of use. Thus we have variants of this weapon ranging from the heavy English longbows the height of a man to the short composite bows of the Scythians capable of being used with rapidity and accuracy even from a seated position on horseback.

The reconstruction of the Anglo-Saxon shield form is the subject of the contribution by Richard Underwood (chapter 10), with the great value of 'hands-on' experience in this process being emphasised. These shields represent a technology of manufacture which was widespread throughout north-western Europe at this time. Their use in a shield-wall is discussed as a defining characteristic of prominent modes of warfare in the Anglo-Saxon world and their effectiveness in this capacity is clearly demonstrated.

Testing of the combat applications of broadly similar large circular shields was undertaken by Pittman (chapter 6) which opens up the debate on the role of *othismos* or the pushing of massed ranks trying to break the opposing line in ancient Greek warfare. In this paper he examines how the individual and localised combat environment of the Greek phalanx was a complex and dynamic experience alternately moving from defensive fighting to the sometimes brutal stabbing and hacking when the opposing line provided an opening.

Amberger investigates the dynamic nature of combat arts of the later Middle Ages and Renaissance (chapter 14), arguing that many of the issues dealt with in them relate more to upper-class leisure activity than true combat arts of the battlefield. It is clear from this analysis that we must think clearly what we mean by 'combat arts' when we deal with these manuscript sources: is it civil or military in nature? Forgeng & Kiermayer have extensively analysed a great number of these sources and have been engaged in testing the efficacy of the techniques advocated (chapter 12). The most ancient of these documents (MS I.33), now housed in the Royal Armouries in Leeds, is the starting point for this discussion and it is clear that the swordsmanship described was both effective and representative of a vibrant, living tradition. The tradition of writing these fighting manuals, or *Fechtbücher*, had a long heritage thereafter with a number of great masters committing their secrets to writing, but in cryptic and coded expositions. While Amberger is clearly correct to question the context of the application of these martial traditions, it is also clear that one skilled in these arts can readily apply them to the battlefield, as highlighted by Forgeng & Kiermayer.

The dynamic event of killing fellow humans, that is the actual actions and experience of undertaking this, is discussed by Molloy and Grossman (chapter 15). In this paper it is shown that while warfare is essentially about killing, living or dying, these apparently straightforward acts must not be taken at face value. There are significant psychological consequences for combatants before, during and after combat, and these important factors are addressed as being central to the human experience of warfare.

Chapter 2 is an excerpt from Steven Pressfield's best-selling novel *Gates of Fire*, a story of the Greek stand at Thermopylae against the Persian invasion under the Great-King Xerxes. In academic discourse, there is neither room nor inclination to take flights of fancy and try to imagine 'what really happened;' the source information is typically too ambiguous to allow such extrapolations.

However, when we are seeking to understand weaponry as real-life tools designed to physically destroy the flesh and bone of another living being, fiction has the resources to bring to bear some of this emotion and experience of living beings on the field of battle.

The topic of this book is fixed in the realm of action and experience, and combat needs to be considered in these terms. Indeed, this reflects the growing interest in recent years in archaeological writings to address such aspects of investigating lived experiences in past societies (Treherne 1995; Tilley 1999; 2002; various contributions in Hamilakis *et al.* 2002; and in DeMarrais, Gosden & Renfrew 2004). In the storerooms and display cases of museums throughout the world we find weapons from the distant past, each of which were possessions wielded by living and thinking ancient warriors in the terror and tumult that is the realm of combat. We hope that our explorations in this volume will show the reader that the remains of this world of action and experience provide a dynamic resource for investigating the living reality of combat in past societies.

One day at Thermopylae: an excerpt from the historical novel *Gates of Fire*

Steven Pressfield

In 480 BC the Persian army of King Xerxes marched on Greece to annex it into his great empire which spanned vast areas of the modern Middle East and Turkey. The Greek world of this time was composed of numerous independent city-states, the most powerful of which were Athens and Sparta. King Leonidas of Sparta led a select bunch of 300 elite warriors and up to 4000 allies from other city-states to the pass at Thermopylae in northern Greece. Despite being outnumbered by as many as thirty to one, their objective was to hold this enormous force at bay until the other Greek states could organise a combined defence strategy. They held them for six days. Those that remained on the final day perished to a man. This excerpt from the novel *Gates of Fire* tells of one day in this bloody campaign and of their legendary heroism:

Only the dirt itself possessed clemency. Alone the stinking soup beneath the warriors' tread proffered surcease and succour. The men's feet churned it into broth ankle-deep; their driving legs furrowed it to the depth of the calf, then they themselves fell upon it on their knees and fought from there. Fingers clawed at the blood-blackened muck, toes strained against it for purchase, the teeth of dying men bit into it as if to excavate their own graves with the clamp of their jaws. Farmers whose hands had taken up with pleasure the dark clods of their native fields, crumbling between their fingers the rich earth which brings forth the harvest, now crawled on their bellies in this sterner soil, clawed at it with the nubs of their busted fingers and writhed without shame, seeking to immure themselves within earth's mantle and preserve their backs from the pitiless steel.

In the *palaistrai* of Hellas, the Greeks loved to wrestle. From the time a boy can stand, he grapples with his mates, dusted with grit in pits of sand or oiled with ooze in rings of mud. Now the Hellenes wrestled in less holy precincts, where the sluice pail held not water but blood, where the prize was death and the umpire spurned all calls for quarter. One witnessed again and again the battles of the second day, a Hellenic warrior fight for two hours straight, retire for ten minutes, without taking food and gulping only a cupped handful of water, then return to the fray for another two-hour round. Again and again one saw a man receive a blow that shattered his jaw or split the bone of his shoulder yet did no make him fall.

On the second day I saw Alpheus and Maron take out six men of the foe so fast that the last two were dead before the first pair hit the ground. How many did the brothers slay that day? Fifty? A hundred? It would have taken more than an Achilles among the foe to bring them down, nor solely in consequence of their strength and skill but because they were two who fought with a single heart.

All day Xerxes' champions came on, advancing in wave after wave with no interval to distinguish between nations or contingents. The rotation of the forces which the allies had employed on the first day became impossible. Companies of their own will refused to forsake the line. Squires and servants took up the arms of the fallen and assumed their places in the breach.

No longer did men waste breath to cheer or rally one another to pride of valour. No more did warriors exalt or vaunt their hearts in triumph. Now on the intervals of respite these simply fell, wordless and numb, into heaps of the unstrung and the undone. In the lee of the Wall, upon every hollow of sundered earth, one beheld knots of warriors shattered by fatigue and despair, eight or ten, twelve or twenty, dropped where they fell, in unmoving postures of horror and grief. None spoke or stirred. Instead the eyes of each stared without sight into inexpressible realms of private horror.

Existence had become a tunnel whose walls were death and within which prevailed no hope of rescue or deliverance. The sky had ceased to be, and the sun and the stars. All that remained was the earth, the churned, riven dirt which seemed to wait at each man's feet to receive his spilling guts, his shattered bones, his blood, his life. The earth coated every part of him. It was in his ears and nostrils, in his eyes and throat, under his nails and in the crease of his backside. It coated the sweat and salt of his hair; he spat it from his lungs and blew it slick with snot from his nose.

There is a secret all warriors share, so private that none dare give it voice, save only to those mates dearer than brothers by the shared ordeal of arms. This is the knowledge of the hundred acts of his own cowardice. The little things that no one sees. The comrade who fell and cried for aid. Did I pass him by? Choose my skin over his? That was my crime, of which I accuse myself in the tribunal of my heart and there condemn myself as guilty.

All a man wants is to live. This before all: to cling to breath. To survive.

Yet even this most primal of instincts, self-preservation, even this necessity of the blood shared by all beneath heave, beasts as well as men, even this may be worn down by fatigue and excess of horror. A form of courage enters the heart which is not courage but despair and not despair but exaltation. On that second day, men passed beyond themselves. Feats of heart-stopping valour fell from the sky like rain, and those who performed them could not even recall, nor state with certainty, that the actors had been themselves.

I saw a squire of the Phliasians, no more than a boy, take up his master's armour and wade into the manslaughter. Before he could strike a blow, a Persian javelin shattered his shin, driving straight to the bone. One of his mates rushed to the lad to bind the gushing artery and drag him to safety. The youth beat back his saviour with the flat of his sword. He hobbled upon his spear used as a crutch, then on his knees, into the fray, still hacking at the foe from the earth where he perished.

Night had fallen. Hellenes were reeling from casualties and exhaustion, while the Persians continued pouring in fresh champions into the fray. Those in the foe's rear were being driven onward by the whips of their own officers; these pressed with zeal their own fellows driving them forward into the Greeks.

Does His Majesty remember? A violent squall had broken then over the sea; rain began sheeting down in torrents. By this point most of the allies' weapons had been spent or broken. The warriors had gone through a dozen spears apiece; none yet bore his own shield, which had been staved in long since; he defended himself with the eighth and tenth he had snatched from the ground. Even the Spartan's short *xiphos* swords had been sundered from excess of blows. The steel blades held, but the hafts and grips had come undone. Men were fighting with stubs of iron, thrusting with shivered half-spears bereft of warhead and butt-spike.

Reliving Greek personal combat – boxing and *pankration*

Alan Peatfield

INTRODUCTION

It is rare in the study of the past to see a new field of studies emerging that is not driven by science and technology. I refer here to the increasing interest in medieval and Renaissance combat manuals. It is perhaps a little tendentious to refer to this as new, because as long ago as the late nineteenth century the trio of scholars Sir Richard Burton (1884), Egerton Castle (1884) and Alfred Hutton (1892) recognised the value of these manuals, but Burton and his fellows were themselves upper-class swordsmen with military backgrounds, and their students and successors mostly died on battlefields of the First World War.

A century on, the most striking thing about this reviving study is the way that the conventional distinctions between academic analysis and popular interest, in the form of re-enactment, are becoming increasingly blurred. Re-enactment has long had a valuable role in combat studies, particularly in relation to the Roman army (see Coulston, chapter 4) and the English Civil War. What is different about this current phenomenon, however, is that the focus is not on armies and the recreation of group-based battlefield tactics, but rather on recreating the techniques and concepts of *personal* combat. Striking too is the discipline and sophistication which is going into these technical recreations. It is not simply a matter of portly, bearded men sweatily bashing away at one another with poorly made replica swords and assuming that this was how combat took place in the past. Great care is going into the processes of translation of often obscure European dialects, interpretation of images and texts, and relating those to preserved weapons (see Forgeng & Kiermayer, chapter 12). As a result re-enactment groups are increasingly to be found engaged in debates with academic scholars such as Sidney Anglo (2000), or associated with museums (e.g. the Royal Armouries and the Higgins Museum). The range of authorship in this volume is also a testament to the value of such debate.

Individual conclusions aside, these activities have profound implications for archaeology. Given the current interest in the archaeology of the body, the experimental recreation of combat techniques in this way brings another dimension to experiential methodologies of interpretation. It is not just a matter of intellectually analysing image, text and artefact, but trying to *do* it engages the body into the process of analysis. Archaeology as a discipline has always had a strong tradition of sensory engagement: we see and touch soils, landscapes, artifacts, etc.; so it is important that we recognise in these combat studies that the kinesthetic methodology has its own fundamental analytical validity.

MINOAN SWORDS

It was with all this in mind that at the POLEMOS conference in 1998 I re-examined the swords of Bronze Age Crete (Peatfield 1999). My initial premise was that conventional handle-based sword typologies undervalued the functional aspects embodied in the sword blade, edge, point, weight and balance. These are the factors which determine the most effective delivery and recovery trajectories of a weapon's strike. When examined thus, it was clear that the swords of the high point of Minoan civilisation, the New Palace period (1700-1400 BC), were designed for long-ranged thrusts or sweeping cuts with a wide, open arc. They are long, straight, with thin edges supported by a central midrib. With these sorts of weapons it is easier to deliver a strike than it is to recover, which suggests that their users were not facing multiple opponents in a *melée*, but rather were engaged in more formal dueling combat situations. Fittingly, these sorts of formal combats are precisely those which are depicted on the contemporary gold seals and clay sealings found in Minoan and Mycenaean tombs and settlements.

Most of these weapons are to be found in elite contexts, particularly tombs from cemeteries (especially Zafer Papoura, Ai Iannis and Sellopoulo) around the Palace of Knossos; they are so full of weapons that they are known in the literature as Warrior Tombs. All of which goes to build up a picture of a Minoan palatial society, at least in its final phase, dominated by an elite whose identity was defined by martial prowess. In this social context warfare was more likely to be the semi-formal raiding process, which John Keegan suggests is characteristic of primitive warfare (Keegan 1994). This would certainly fit the sporadic but widespread nature of destruction deposits in Minoan sites of the palatial period.

By contrast, swords of the Postpalatial Minoan period, coming down to the end of the Bronze Age, are shorter and broader than their ancestors. Full-tanged, they are also distinguished by recurved rather than straight edges. These swords were designed for an action which has a more closed elliptical arc, a tighter, quicker recovery, using pull-cuts and short stabs, rather than long thrusts and wide sweeps. In other words, this sort of weapon is designed for the rapid direction changes of *melée* fighting, where one could face multiple opponents in the confusion of combat. Again this fits what we know of the destructive social and political conditions of the end of the Bronze Age in the Eastern Mediterranean.

Barry Molloy has developed these ideas further in his doctoral research under my supervision. This work, now completed, provides a foundation for the radical re-assessment of Bronze Age weaponry. His paper in this volume presents essential reading on the subject. But as an aside to acknowledge further the value of this experimental work in replicating ancient swords, I offer an observation here that arose specifically from my handling of his replicas of Minoan Type C and D swords. The main difference between the two swords is their guards. The Type C swords have horned guards, whose prongs point back towards the pommel of the sword. Type D swords have a smaller T-shaped guard. When handling the swords it was immediately apparent that the two swords were gripped in the hand differently. The handle and guard of the Type C sword suits a 'sabre' grip, whereby the wrist bends slightly to present the point of the weapon forward. This is enhanced by the design, allowing the forefinger to wrap comfortably around the ricasso. By contrast, the Type D sword prefers a more solid 'hammer' grip, which presents more of the edge of the blade toward the opponent. Although all swords with an edge and a point can be used for cutting as well as thrusting (see Clements, chapter 13), this distinct difference in the grip of the two Minoan swords suggests that they were designed for different styles of fighting. The Type C sword is clearly better for a more point-forward, fencing type of action, where the opponent is kept at distance. The Type D sword is more suitable for closer range cutting and stabbing actions. Clearly, Minoan warriors of the fifteenth century BC had the technical knowledge and expertise to develop different styles of sword-fighting and weapons appropriate to those styles.

GREEK MARTIAL ARTS — APPROACHING THE MATERIAL

The direction of my own research has gone on to examine the interactions of weapons fighting and empty hand combat; the present paper specifically addresses ancient Greek boxing and its kickboxing sibling, the art of *pankration*.

A great deal has been written about these subjects, most notably Poliakoff's *Combat Sports in the Ancient World* (1987). Most of this has, however, been derived from the point of view of Classical texts, rather than directly from archaeological evidence. There are problems with this approach.

First, many of the main literary sources for ancient Greek sport, most notably Philostratos, wrote in Roman Early Imperial times; consequently such discussions often suffer from a nostalgic idealism, or from an overt moralising tendency. The early Christian writer Dio Chrysostom further developed this process by using the story of the famous Greek boxer, Melankomas (who could win a combat bout by fighting for several days without suffering or giving a single blow) as a parable of proto-Christian ethical values, evident in the Classical period.[1]

Secondly, more contemporary sources, particularly Classical writers, tend to be very ambivalent about combat sports (see Poliakoff 1987). The philosopher Plato argued that the individualism fostered by personal combat was not conducive to the group spirit that was necessary in an ideal society. His contemporary, the artistocratic solder Xenophon, who shared Plato's right-wing politics, adopted the heroic notion that a real man should be born with skill at combat, and not have to learn it – the ideology of nature over nurture.

Nevertheless, it is clear that Greek empty hand combat was already sophisticated at an early date. Homer, composing his poems in the eight century BC, was aware of the advantages of exploiting vital points on the body; he allows Odysseus to win a boxing match by killing his opponent with a strike to the vulnerable point just below the ear. Although the *pankration* was not introduced to the Olympic Games until 648 BC, boxing seems to have been included early on. Onomastos of Smyrna reportedly established the rules for boxing in 688 BC. His system has not survived, but we know there were no rounds; bouts continued until one participant was knocked out, gave up, couldn't continue or was dead. Pythagoras of Samos is credited with the development of scientific boxing in 588 BC; presumably this refers to some systematisation of training methods and fighting techniques. But there is no mention in the sources of what these methods and techniques were.

We cannot however, assume that there were no manuals, ancient Greek equivalents of the medieval fight books. Indeed there is a single surviving papyrus scrap, which describes empty hand combat techniques (Poliakoff 1987), but the descriptions are opaque and confusing. Consequently, any attempt to recover the techniques of boxing and *pankration* is entirely dependent on static visual sources, the mute depictions on the Black- and Red-figure vase-painting of the sixth and fifth centuries BC.

To try and interpret movement from single, static images, is of course a difficult process, and at the very best it can only yield possibilities, not certainties. The experimentations that have produced such interesting and successful results with the medieval sword manuals does provide a model of analysis. There are, of course, essential differences between the medieval manuals and the ancient Greek vases. The manuals are overtly didactic, i.e. written to provide instruction, and the texts, even if occasionally concise to the point of obscurity, are there to support the illustrations.

By contrast, the Greek vase-paintings are only images. There is no overtly didactic intent. Indeed the impulse behind their creation seems to be essentially aesthetic. Much scholarly writing has tended to assume that these are merely generic images of combat, with the figures and scenes composed only for aesthetic impact. The inevitable question is, therefore, whether these images are at all appropriate for practical analysis. It is possible to create an intellectual argument to validate such an analysis, as I shall demonstrate below. But of itself, such a conventional argument is not enough. It has to be demonstrated, too, that images do present techniques which are practical, not merely aesthetic, which have an implicit knowledge, not just superficial beauty. It is out of this notion that the process of experimentation to the images.

PHYSICAL METHODOLOGIES

What is the physical basis of such experimentation? Most of the people involved in the recreation of the medieval manuals are martial artists who bring considerable physical experience to their processes of analysis. In other words, physical experience offers kinesthetic insight, which informs the intellectual analysis. This, of course, runs counter to conventional pure academic intellectualism. But, as I previewed in my introduction above, this is precisely the value of the exercise, that it engages the insight of the body as well as the mind in the analytical process. It does away with the Cartesian dichotomies and hierarchies of mind versus body, and offers a more balanced and harmonious perspective. This is fitting to the subject, too, because we should not forget that we are dealing with a physical activity and behaviour, i.e. something that was really done, not just thought about as an ancient Greek, quasi-Foucaltian mental/philosophical construct of 'The Body.'

The application of such methodologies to the ancient Greek material is not something new. It is clear for example that Gardiner & Harris' classic interpretations of Greek boxing owe something to their experiences of the amateur boxing of their school and college days, fitting to their class and educational background. Similarly Poliakoff is obviously influenced by the American tradition of college wrestling. This brings a greater depth to his analysis of Greek wrestling. In all these cases, however, such experiential sources for scholarly insight are left mostly implicit. By contrast, I state explicitly that the analysis I offer here of the Greek boxing and *pankration* vase-painting images is informed by 35 years of martial arts experience, including as a trainer of successful amateur full-contact fighters. In this, I have however, been sensitive to the accusation of subjectivity, which could be caricatured as 'ancient Greek boxing must have been like what I know how to do'. Thus subjectivity is necessarily balanced by objectivity arising out of my career as a professional archaeologist.

The physical analysis selectively previewed here is thus presented as an art of the possible, and an assessment of the implications of such possibilities. It is based on intense experimentation carried out with my students.[2] Given the essentially dynamic nature of this work, there are limitations in trying to discuss our results in writing. We have already offered physical demonstrations,[3] and are creating moving records of the techniques for a DVD to accompany the full written publication of the research.

ANALYSING THE MATERIAL — TECHNIQUES

The first premise of our research involves questioning previous assumptions about the generic nature of these images. In contrast, even allowing for stylisations within the artistic medium of vase-painting, we worked on the possibility that there are sufficient specific technical points to suggest that there are elements in the vase-paintings that were recognisable to the original viewers as familiar methods and techniques. I present here a selection of these technical points.

One of the most characteristic features of boxing and *pankration* was the high-guard posture. (*1*). It is often mentioned that the Greeks favoured head-strikes over body-strikes. This conclusion is derived from the frequency of images which show head-strikes. The famous Black-figure scene of boxers, one with a bleeding nose, from the sixth-century Nikosthenes Painter vividly reveals the damage. Both boxers hold a high-guard posture, with hands at head height, one hand extended in front of the face, the other pulled back behind the ear. This guard is the characteristic guard posture shown in Greek vase-painting, from the date of this vase (mid-sixth century) to at least the end of the fifth century, as can be seen too in the other illustrations. From this guard posture, strikes illustrated in the vase-paintings seem to be mostly direct thrusts, done with a flat fist or open palm, as I shall discuss below. The other hand was pulled back to protect the head; this seems to have been accomplished with a twisting action to judge by the way the elbow is lifted and the hand rotated outward.

The obvious exposure of the body resulting from this posture was recognised by the Greeks as a potential weak point. Consequently, many of the boxers in the vase-paintings are somewhat portly, the extra flesh providing padding, protection against body-strikes (*1* & *2*). Considering the Greek aesthetic preference for the body-beautiful, it is clear that here there is a sense of reality in their portrayal of the combatants.

1 Ankle trap. *Redrawn after original Red Figure vase by J. Kelder*

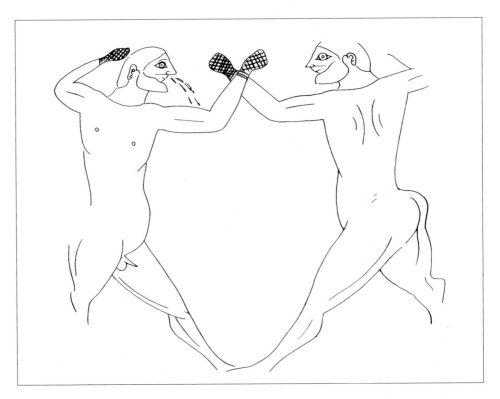

2 Bloody nose. *Redrawn after original Black Figure vase by J. Kelder*

It would be a mistake to regard this high-guard posture as purely a static defensive posture. This guard is also portrayed in solo shadow-boxing exercises (2), which suggests a more dynamic quality. Portrayals of strikes (3 & 7) also reveal that the posture was a platform from which to launch punches and hand-blows. Combining these possibilities, we therefore practiced switching the guard from side to side, while repetitively launching punches from this position. As we practiced this action repeatedly, several things became apparent. First, the thrusting punch with one hand combined with the pull-back and twist out of the other hand imparts a great deal of torque, which adds strength to the action. This clearly indicates that the Greek boxers and their trainers had a clear and sophisticated understanding of the body mechanics necessary to the effectiveness of their art – a science of skill and technique, not just brute strength.

The second major insight that emerged from this practice was an unexpected comparison with weapons combat. All Greek men were expected to fight for their city-state. Indeed, participation in athletic training, in order to be fit enough to defend the city, was part of the citizen's patriotic duty. The primary mode of warfare in Archaic and Classical Greece was hoplite warfare.

3 Drill punch. *Redrawn after original Black Figure vase by J. Kelder*

The heavily armoured hoplite's main weapon was a spear, used for thrusting over the top of his large round shield. The hand action and body mechanics of thrusting a spear forward (see Pittman, chapter 6) from head level would have been familiar to all Greek men from their military service. The action is startlingly similar to that of the Greek boxer's straight punch.

Writing several centuries later, Philostratos says that the Spartan hoplite soldiers originally fought bare-headed, so they developed boxing as a method of learning how to protect the head. He is, of course, wrong in this statement, because contemporary artistic and literary sources record the Spartans wearing helmets. Nevertheless, it does reveal a very clear awareness of the overlap between military and personal combat training, not just in terms of generic fitness, but also in terms of concepts and techniques. Again, this reveals considerable sophistication of knowledge and thought in Greek combat arts.

Comparison with other combat traditions may serve to emphasise this point. The fourteenth-century master-at-arms Fiore dei Liberi developed a progressive system of combat training for medieval knights, for which the essential foundation was empty hand combat leading into armed combat (Charron 2002). This progression is also widely attested in Asian martial arts (Draeger & Smith 1981).

Returning to the Greek material to look in more detail at the forward thrust action of the hands when striking, many of the images show that it was accomplished with a vigorous step into the opponent's space (5, 6 & 7). In modern western boxing this is called a 'drop step.' The great American boxer Jack Dempsey was famed for this strike action, and explains it well (Dempsey 1950). The 'drop step' dynamically commits the body weight behind the punch, thus adding considerably more weight and momentum to the force of the strike. Yet again, this reveals sophisticated understanding of kinesthetic mechanics.

The addition of kicking and grappling to these boxing actions is usually taken to be what distinguished *pankration* (meaning 'all powers') from boxing. Occasionally portrayed in vase-painting is a middle-height guard posture (oddly similar to the san-ti signature posture of Chinese *xingyi* – 'form and mind' – boxing) (4). The slightly raised or floating front foot clearly is preparatory to entering the opponent's space with combination kicks and punches (5).

As the illustration shows, when they connect, combinations of this sort can be devastating, but kicks can of course also be caught (6). In our experimentations this technique proved to be remarkably effective. We found that the strike under the thigh not only unbalanced the opponent, but also lifted him, thus destroying any rooting strength in the supporting leg. The catch of the leg too allows for a fluid transition to grappling (one of the hallmarks of *pankration*), specifically to a leg lock when the opponent had fallen.

4 Punch kick. *Redrawn after original Black Figure vase by J. Kelder*

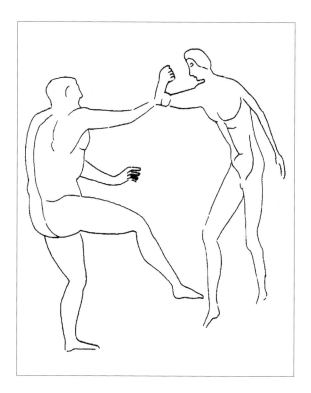

5 Guard kick. *Redrawn after original Black Figure vase by J. Kelder*

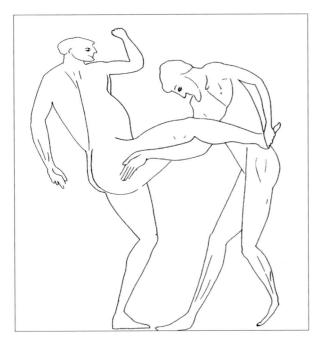

6 Catch kick. *Redrawn after original Black Figure vase by J. Kelder*

This clear and consistent preference for direct 'invasion' of the opponent's space also made sense of some small details in scenes that might otherwise be overlooked. The obvious detail here is the palm strike to the chin (7). Called a 'chin-jab' in Second World War Commando hand-to-hand combat (Fairbairn 1943), this simple but effective strike causes knockout by a whiplash effect to the neck. But portrayed here too is a step to the *outside* of the opponent's leg. Combined with the chin-jab, this is a setup for a throw, because the victor's body position exploits a weak angle in the opponent's body structure.

Such a sophisticated use of not just the fists but also the whole body may be apparent in other images too (8). A downed opponent is submitting to the dynamically advancing victor. The victor's forward foot clearly engages the rear ankle of the opponent. This rear ankle trap suggests a scissoring technique often called a 'back-lever.' Certainly the outstretched arms and turned torso as well as the leg position of the victor recall representations of this technique in medieval and Renaissance manuals. Indeed this is a universally effective technique favored in many martial systems widely separated in time and space.

The final technique illustrated here is a shoulder lock (9). The defender on the left has evaded a punch and slipped his own arm under the outstretched arm of his opponent, to lock it in place in order to apply leverage to break the arm or to throw the opponent. The subtlety of such evasion and reactive counter-attack is suggestive of both technique and skill.

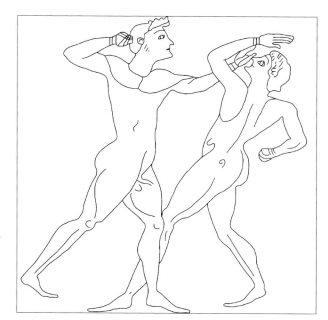

Right: 7 Chin jab. *Redrawn after original Black Figure vase by B.P.C. Molloy*

Below: 8 Punch step. *Redrawn after original Black Figure vase by B.P.C Molloy*

31

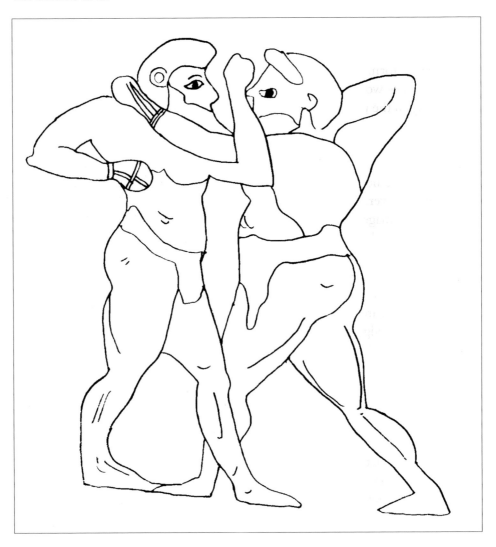

9 Shoulder lever. *Redrawn after original Black Figure vase by B.P.C. Molloy*

IMPLICATIONS

The essential point to emerge from the technical experimentations sampled above is that ancient Greek boxing and *pankration* were considerably more sophisticated arts, in terms of training, technique, conceptual and practical body knowledge, than is commonly interpreted in conventional academic accounts of ancient athletics. That is to say, Greek sport combat involved a sophisticated understanding of body mechanics, not just a brutal slugging by the participants. There are implications that arise from this.

On a technical level, the clarity of many of the portrayed actions, which can be effectively recreated, establishes the probability that represented here are specific, even formal techniques. The question inevitably arises whether the Classical Greeks would have perceived of combat in this formal technical way. Significantly, in the play *The Phoenician Women*, Euripides describes how Eteokles defeats his brother Polynikes in battlefield combat through the application of the 'Thessalian stratagem.' Even if this stratagem was itself entirely of Euripides' imagination, the fact that he applied a name to it suggests that his audience was familiar with the notion of categorising combat techniques and strategies.

Perhaps, however, the most important implication addresses the context of the vases and their images in terms of artefact and social relations. Most of these vase-paintings are found on Panathenaic amphoras, created as prizes for the Athenian Games, or on vases used in the symposium drinking parties that were essential to the social life of Archaic and Classical Athens. The people who used these vases and admired their images were exactly the same group of males whose education and lives revolved around gymnasiums and athletic endeavours. They would have shared the knowledge of sport combat and its vocabulary. It is already recognised that the mythological themes portrayed on these vases were often reflective of contemporary political issues (Boardman 1991; Osborne 1998). It is not a great step into the realities of the human processes involved in the creation of these athletic combat images to argue that they could have been commissioned specifically for symposiums celebrating boxing or *pankration* victories. The social impact of depictions of *specific* and *recognisable* techniques, which may have been favourites of the victors or even those with which they won their contests, would have been far more intense and personalised for guests on these occasions than would vague, generic scenes, however aesthetic. If this is true, it indicates an even greater sense of interaction between artist and viewer, potter/painter and customer than is generally accounted for in studies of vase-painting.

AFTERWORD

One of the great attractions of the study of violence and warfare is the appreciation of the beautiful if terrible functionality of the artefacts, and the visual splendour of bright armour and uniforms in concentrated formation. But as archaeologists we should recognise too that humankind's most fundamental tool of violence is the human body itself. And it is only through understanding how cultures and civilisations have chosen to mould the human body to express their concepts and visions of violence that we begin to understand one of the great universals of human experience.

4

By the sword united: Roman fighting styles on the battlefield and in the arena

Jon C.N. Coulston

INTRODUCTION

In many periods up to the present, warfare and other elite activities have involved the carriage of swords as weapons and as indicators of social status. However, scholars have generally lavished more attention on the weapons and their accoutrements than on practical considerations of use (but cf. Cope 1989; Robson 1997; Amberger 1999; Cohen 2002). The latter may be taken to mean how a sword was wielded, what style of fencing was employed, how the sword was used in conjunction with other equipment, especially armour, and how these practicalities interacted with the dangers posed and opportunities presented by particular contemporary opponents. The obvious exceptions are cases in which the pathology of conflict activities can be studied through skeletal evidence (e.g. Thordemann 1939; Shackley 1986; Fiorato 2000; *Gladiatoren* 2002, 43–8, 70-2).

For the Roman period there has been a massive surge of military equipment research in the last twenty years, including some simulations of both military and gladiatorial weaponry, although reconstruction work has been as much for public show as for academic research (exceptionally see papers in *Journal of Roman Military Equipment Studies* 11, 2000; Sim & Ridge 2002). There is not only a rich artefactual record for the study of Roman fighting styles but also a varied and numerous body of iconographic evidence. Soldiers appear in many artistic contexts (*10*; Bishop & Coulston 2006, 1-20). Moreover, there are thousands of representations of gladiators, much of whose equipment and training methods were related closely to military practices (*11*; Coulston 1998; Junkelmann 2000b; Connolly 2003, 90). Of course the compositional conventions of any genre must be fully understood, but many soldiers were certainly involved in the creation of military iconography whilst the gladiatorial subjects were studied closely by artists and audiences alike. The evidence is diachronic and geographically widespread, making the coincidence of detail in numerous cases rather more reliable. In this connection the writer is very impressed by the work of Alan Peatfield, at University College, Dublin, who has combined a detailed study of Archaic and Classical Greek ceramic painting with a varied knowledge of martial arts to convincingly reconstruct the moves, throws, attacks, defences and flowing combinations of the *pankration* (chapter 3, this volume). The ancient paintings appear to be well observed, realistic and reliable.

The following paper is intended to construct a picture of Roman fighting styles as used by infantry in the main battle line in formal conflicts. Virtually nothing will be said about mounted fighting other than some comments made about mounted opponents (see Bivar 1972; Coulston 1986). Particular attention will be paid to the interactions between arms and armour, the two coming together in design and practical application, whilst due regard will be taken of parallel evidence from the context of Roman 'display' combat in the arena.

MILITARY FIGHTING STYLES: THIRD CENTURY BC TO SECOND CENTURY AD

In the Classical Greek and Hellenistic worlds armies relied upon a main battle line of close-order, more or less armoured infantry with shields. The main offensive arm of these troops was always a shafted weapon, the single-handed spear (*doru*) of Greek hoplites, or the two-handed pike (*sarissa*) of Macedonian and Successor phalangites (Connolly 1981, 63, 77-9; 2000b; Hackett 1989, 57-8, 66-7, 105-7, 118-19; Snodgrass 1999, 57-9, 115, 118-21; Hanson, 1989, 83-8). From at least the third century BC Roman infantry relied upon an entirely different weapons combination. These men fought using a short sword as the primary arm, combined closely with a large shield. Javelins of various weights were thrown at a short range before infantry lines came into contact. These javelins (*pila*) were specially designed to be heavy and to use a small, pyramidal or barbed head and a long iron shank to punch through shields and body-armour (Bishop & Coulston 2006, 50-3; Connolly 1997; 2000a). Any opposing infantry would take casualties immediately, but would also have been badly disordered through having *pila* awkwardly stuck through shield-boards. Men would fall, others would trip over *pilum*-shafts or wrestle with transfixed shields. Others still would discard their precious shields, all this seconds before the charging line of Roman swordsmen cut into their formation (in general see Bell 1965; Wheeler 1979; Connolly 1981, 129-248; Keppie 1984; Hackett 1989, 149-221; Junkelmann 1986, 236-48; Goldsworthy 1996; Gilliver 1999, 89-126; Sabin 1996; 2000; Santosuosso 1997, 150-98; Zhmodikov 2000; Campbell 2002, 51-65).

10 Detail of legionary soldier adopting the 'first position', on a metope relief from the Tropaeum Traiani, Adamclisi, Romania. *Photograph: J.C.N. Coulston*

11 Detail of a gladiator adopting the 'first position', on an on-site pedestal relief at Ephesus, Turkey. *Photograph: J.C.N. Coulston*

At this time the Roman soldier of the third century BC to second century AD fought with a pointed, double-edged sword. The early form was adopted from experience in the Iberian peninsular and an increasing number of published examples now allows a sequence of evolution through the period to be reconstructed. The proportionally narrow *gladius Hispaniensis* had a blade *c.*0.65m long and *c.*0.045m wide (Connolly 1997, 49-56). By the first century BC the tapering 'Mainz'-type sword was in widespread use, *c.*0.4-0.55m long and *c.*0.054-0.075m wide (Bishop & Coulston 2006, 78-9). During the second half of the first century AD this was joined, and ultimately superseded, by the 'Pompeii'-type sword, *c.*0.42-0.5m long and *c.*0.042-0.05m wide (ibid., 71). The latter differed from its predecessors in having parallel sides and a short, triangular point. All these swords had in common blades which were proportionally short and with a heavy pommel; they were well balanced for delivering thrusting blows. Of course, a swinging cut could be delivered because both long edges of the blade were sharp, but they were not weighted towards the point in the manner of earlier Greek single-edged (*kopis, machaira*) or double-edged, short, slashing swords (Snodgrass 1999, 97-8, Pl. 50, 52). The Pompeii-type was better suited to this than the Mainz form, especially against unarmoured opponents, and a swinging blow intended to deliver a cut with the diagonal edge of the triangular point would have been ideal (Connolly 1989, 27; 1991, 362).

Throughout this long period of 450 years the shields carried by Roman legionary troops were designed as variations on a tight theme. The board was large and curved on its lateral, short axis. It was always carried by a horizontal wooden handle or bar set at the very centre, holes for the fingers being cut through, and the whole covered by a domed metal boss (Bishop & Coulston 2006, 61-3, 91-4, 137-9). Starting as a proportionally narrow oval, this could cover the bearer from shoulder to lower shin with the long sides curved around the soldier. This latter feature may have made it difficult to draw the sword from a scabbard hung on the soldier's left side, explaining why the overwhelming majority of iconographic and archaeological evidence shows the sword suspended on the right side (see Fraia & d'Oriano 1982, 20-1). There was no difficulty in drawing the short sword from a right-side position with one, fluid vertical or diagonal forward motion, as has long been conclusively demonstrated by experimental reconstruction. Early shields were bound along their top and bottom rims with metal, along the top specifically to protect against downward slashing blows (Polybios 6.23). Shields were constructed of three layers of glued wooden strips also specifically designed to prevent splitting (Bishop & Coulston 2006, 61-3, 179-82; James 2004, 162-63). They varied though time in exact shape by having the top and bottom cut away horizontally, and/or the sides cut away vertically to give an ends-truncated oval, a sides-truncated oval or a true rectangular form.

Shields were always curving, but never square. Even the shorter, cut-off forms covered the bearer from shoulder to knee.

Thus, once the *pila* had been thrown, the soldier drew his sword and adopted a stance with his left foot and shield forward. During the third to second centuries BC a variety of body-armour was worn according to the soldier's personal wealth, from a small square or round chest-plate (*pectorale*) to a plate or scale cuirass with extending textile lappets over thighs and upper arms. The wealthiest wore a ring-mail cuirass with a long skirt and reinforced shoulder panels (Polybios 6.23; Bishop & Coulston 2006, 63-4). From the first century BC onwards it is likely that ring mail or scale cuirasses were worn by all legionary troops to be joined, but not wholly replaced, by the plate armour known since the Renaissance as *lorica segmentata* (ibid., 85-90; Bishop 2002). The earliest positive evidence for this mild steel armour form, articulated on internal leathers, comes from *c.*AD 9, but it is likely that it had Hellenistic antecedents (ibid., 18-30). It covered the torso down to the waist, but not below. The projecting lappets (*pteryges*) of a textile undergarment could again have extended protection over thighs and upper arms. There was particular emphasis on protection of the shoulders with sets of overlapping plates, in similar fashion to the shoulder-pieces on mail cuirasses, for reasons discussed below.

Protection of the head and limbs likewise changed over time. Into the second half of the second century BC the soldier wore a greave on his left, forward leg. Thereafter artefactual finds of greaves are difficult to attribute, but by the later first century AD some legionary troops are depicted as wearing greaves on both legs (Florescu 1965, Fig. 190, 195, 198, 202). These cover the shin, but not the knee. A logical correlation between 'fields' of protection offered by cuirass, shield and greave(s) would suggest that the longer Republican shields made up for variable torso coverage and were supplemented by one greave, even for the lower wealth brackets of soldier (Polybios 6.23). State subsidy of equipment coupled with a broader social range of recruitment meant improved cuirass provision. Longer shield-forms could still protect much of the legs if greaves were not worn, but cut-off boards could work well with knee-less greaves to give full frontal armour coverage. Clearly the body and left arm was well protected by the curving shield, but all along the northern Roman frontiers there is cumulative evidence for additional protection of the exposed right sword-arm in the first to second centuries AD. This took the form of a segmental, metal sleeve of *manicae*, terminating perhaps in a guard for the back of the hand and upper thumb (Florescu 1965, Fig. 189, 195, 197-201, 212, 217, 221; Bishop & Coulston 2006, 98-101; Richardson 2001; Bishop 2002, 68-72).

Helmet forms changed radically over the period but several features remained constant. Particular attention was paid to protection of the back and, increasingly over time, the sides of the neck. The front of the bowl routinely had an additional 'peak' from the first century BC onwards, then embossed 'eyebrows' which served to corrugate, thus strengthen protection to the frontal cranium. By the later first century AD additional reinforcing bars were often riveted over the bowl, fore-and-aft, and side-to-side. Ears were uncovered so as to facilitate reception of aural commands, but they were protected from downward-slicing blows by increasingly prominent flanges on the sides of the helmet bowl. Cheek-pieces covered as much of the face as possible without restricting sight and their edges were progressively flared to direct blows out from the face and edges of the jaw and away from the vulnerable neck and throat (Robinson 1975, 13-85; Waurick 1988, 327-38; Bishop & Coulston 2006, 65-6, 100-1, 173-4; Feugère 1994, 37-50, 77-97; Junkelmann 2000c, 52-85, 93-153). Overall, the weaknesses of 'spun' copper alloy bowls were increasingly compensated for by reinforcement measures and deflective design (a point made to the writer by Graham Webster many years ago).

The increasingly wide and deep neck-flanges of helmets were still in the second century AD high enough not to restrict head-movement, especially were the soldier to crane his head backwards, or to lean his body forward keeping his head upright. This latter stance is what many artworks depict: the soldier leading with his left foot and shield, leaning forward into the latter with it held vertically to cover his knee, the sword-arm drawn back with the forearm near-vertical, and the short sword held point forward with the blade horizontal (e.g. Cichorius 1896-1900, Scene CXV; Espérandieu 1907-66, No. 7763, 5822; Florescu 1965, Fig. 198-200, 205, 217; Frenz 1992, No. 6, 10. See Junkelmann 1986, 184-86; Connolly 1991; Coulston 1998, 4). This stance afforded the greatest armour protection from blows delivered by an opponent to the front (see *10* & *14*). It was a solid 'first position', well balanced, buttressed against impact and suited for a progressive advance, shuffling forward behind the shield, yet providing a solid base for an attacking thrust forward, straightening the sword-arm and extending the blade horizontally at shoulder height. At full extension the arm would be well protected if *manicae* were worn.

The long point of the 'Mainz' sword could burst through body-armour. The heavier, triangular point of the 'Pompeii' sword would have been formidable in this respect, but, with training and correct timing, it also allowed for different cuts to be made on an opponent. Soldiers and gladiators are depicted with upraised sword-arms, and occasionally with the arm extended forward over the shield (Arm up: Robert 1940, No. 213; Florescu 1965, Fig. 195; Junkelmann 2000a, Fig. 74. Arm over: Florescu 1965, Fig. 197; Pfuhl & Mobius 1977, Pl. 18; Junkelmann 2000a, Fig. 173). The latter sometimes involves a twist of the wrist and/or a downward thrust to bypass the opponent's board. Thus, cuts to the top, front and sides of the head, the neck and the shoulders were all possible, as well as to the chest if left open. With his shield close to his body, and with his arm sheathed in *manicae*, the soldier would still have been well protected from the opponent's attack. He would also have been able to fluidly parry a downward cut, or meet individual missiles by raising the shield (Florescu 1965, Fig. 201, 212).

The 'first position' stance is figured in gladiatorial iconography (see below) most commonly in paired combat contexts, but also in one mosaic scene from Flacé-les-Mâcon, France, it is adopted by a swordsman in training (Golvin & Landes 1990, 156; Junkelmann 2000a, Fig. 21). The literary sources mention the use for sword exercises by both soldiers and gladiators of a six-foot (2m) wooden post (*palus*) set in the ground (Vegetius, *Epitoma rei militaris* 2.23; Juvenal, *Satirae* 6.247-48). Several gladiatorial gravestones appear to depict the *palus*, sometimes with a smooth shaft, sometimes as a tree-trunk with roughly lopped-off branches (Sabbatini Tumolesi 1988, No. 106, Pl. XXIII; Grant 1971, Pl. 34; Gregori 1989, No. 50, Pl. XIX.2; Junkelmann 2000a, Fig. 19). Moreover, both military and gladiatorial sources record the use of double-weight shields and swords in training exercises (Vegetius, *Epitoma rei militaris* 1.11, 2.23; Suetonius, *Caligula* 32). Thus a regime of hard, continuous sword exercises can be envisaged for new recruits and maintained for more experienced soldiers, building up and reinforcing the specialised musculature which has been detected in the skeletal record for soldiers and gladiators (Bisel 2002, 468; *Gladiatoren* 2002, 19-20). Use of artificially heavy equipment further built up stamina and would have allowed swordsmen to fight for longer. Various points on the *palus* may have been targeted in order to simulate specific parts of an opponent's equipment and anatomy. Training emphases may have varied according to the arms, armour and fighting techniques of known opponents. There would have been a formal series of attacks and defences, cuts and thrusts, drilled into the recruit (Vegetius, *Epitoma rei militaris* 1.11). Although sword exercises were part of the elite education in urban gymnasiums across the Roman world (cf. Cicero, *pro Caelio* 11), there is little direct evidence for teaching 'manuals' or competing 'schools' of fencing style characteristic of Renaissance and later practices. One style of fighting with curved shield and short sword was current, thus it is unsurprising that on occasion, usually in times of crisis and the need to build up military forces quickly, gladiatorial instructors were employed to train soldiers (Valerius Maximus 2.3.2; Coulston 1998, 2-3. Cf. Pliny, *Panegyricus* 13.5).

The iconographic record makes it clear that the shield was not used solely in passive defence. Held at the centre of gravity, it could have been raised or lowered to meet targeted blows, but it could also have been used to sweep aside an opponent's weapon and open up his defence. The soldier's body behind his shield could be used to barge an opponent to knock him off his feet or at least to unbalance his stance, leaving him vulnerable to subsequent attacks (cf. Hanson 1989, 28-9, 169, 172-77). Careful timing might also allow the soldier to thrust forward with his shield arm, aiming the boss at the opponent's face. Disconcerting this would be as a feint, potentially incapacitating if the boss connected with his face (cf. Livy 30.34; Tacitus, *Annales* 14.36-7; *Agricola* 36; Vegetius, *Epitoma rei militaris* 1.11). Another move shown in the artworks is the horizontal extension of shield-arm and shield at shoulder level (Cichorius 1896-1900, Scene XL; Espérandieu 1907-66, No. 5822; Frenz 1992, No. 6). On the face of it this would seem to expose the soldier's lower torso and legs. The same move is also depicted in gladiatorial artworks (Robert 1940, No. 213; Junkelmann 2000a, Fig. 10, 32, 34-5, 132, 139, 153, 181). However, exactly timed, this move doubled the soldier's reach by half the length of the board, and it could have used an attacker's momentum to deliver a blow with the metal-rimmed lower edge of the shield. Caught in the chest, or, worse, the face or throat, the opponent would have been abruptly stopped, stunned, and again vulnerable to a follow-through attack.

A Roman legionary style of infantry fighting for the period down to the late second century AD may thus be reconstructed. Over time the soldier's protective equipment improved, both in terms of coverage and design. Increasing emphasis was placed on protecting the front and sides of the head and the shoulders, notably by presenting metalwork strengthened by corrugation and additional bars, and by providing angled, deflective surfaces. Faced with deep formations in disciplined ranks of spearmen or pikemen, the soldier threw his *pila* creating casualties, but, more importantly, confusion and gaps, into which the soldier with his fellows cut their way, protected by a large shield and, hopefully, getting past the multiple points of shafted weapons (Keppie 1984, 33-44; Goldsworthy 1996, 191-227; Santosuosso 1997, 150-98; Sabin 1996; 2000). Once inside the opposing formation, the Roman swordsman was at a tremendous advantage over opponents with unwieldy primary arms, very secondary training with swords, and, in the case of pikemen, small shields not really suited to swordplay. Such opponents became rare after the first half of the second century BC. Increasingly Roman armies fought northern and north-western European opponents: Illyrians, Celts, Dacians and Germans. These presented formations of 'warrior' infantry armed with flat, central-grip, bossed shields, javelins and spears, and a variety of short and long slashing swords (Connolly 1981, 113-26; Ritchie 1985; Rawlings 1996; Goldsworthy 1996, 42-60; Ilkjaer 1997; Randsborg 1999; Zhmodikov 2000, 72-3; Jørgensen 2003; Coulston 2003b).

Perhaps grouped in formations based on geography, war-leader following, tribe, clan and/or familial groups, the warrior opponent would have had less coherent arms training and perhaps less longer-term stamina, despite a background of heavy, repetitive agricultural tasks. He might also arrive at the Roman line enthusiastically, but initially as an individual or as part of a clump of warriors ahead of the main mass, raindrops before the storm as it were (Polybios 2.33; Hill 1986, 1-3; Rawlings 1996, 88). Even taking into account Roman stereotypes of unarmoured and metal-poor 'barbarian' cultures, it is clear that after the defeat of Hellenistic and Carthaginian armies, Rome's northern opponents were for the most part far less well provided with defensive equipment than the Roman army (Ferris 2000; Coulston 2003a, 428). The latter was efficiently served by armour workshops and the careful recycling of valuable metal resources (Bishop & Coulston 2006, 233-40). The warrior opponent would have been attempting to use his shield in similar fashion to the Roman soldier, but with a longer sword his stance would have been less compact and more reliant on momentum, the first warriors hoping to break open a gap in the Roman line for followers to exploit.

The Roman soldier stood or advanced in a braced stance ready to react to the nature and direction of an opponent's attack. He may have stepped forward at a moment judged by the combination of instinct and trained timing developed in any fencing style, to catch the warrior with his shield and follow through with his sword, lunging in search of a vulnerable point exposed by the shield or the slashing style of the warrior swordsman, the sword-point taking the warrior perhaps in throat or armpit. He might of course hope for a moment of exposed face, stomach, thigh or even knee, targets presented by an enthusiastic but inexperienced opponent. Thrusts at the face would have been particularly intimidating, as any modern broken-bottle or knife-fighter knows (Polybios 2.33.6; Tacitus, *Annales* 2.14; *Agricola* 36; Vegetius, *Epitoma rei militaris* 1.11). Such actions would be repeated cyclically, smash with shield, thrust with sword, between opponents if the individual combat was not immediately decisive, or with successive warrior opponents, and repeated right along the Roman line. The soldier could advance with each move or maintain a braced position. If the former, then the Roman line might become increasingly ragged, depending on how closely the soldiers were spaced. A looser formation would make the line of contact between the two opposing formations more a series of individual combats (on spacing see Polybios 2.69.9, 18.30.6-7; Caesar, *Bellum Civilum* 1.44; *Bellum Gallicum* 2.25; Livy 28.2.8-9; Asklepiodotos, *Techne taktike* 4.1-4; Tacitus, *Annales* 2.14; *Historiae* 2.22; Arrian, *Techne taktike* 11; Vegetius, *Epitoma rei militaris* 3.14-5; Junkelmann 1986, 238-39; Goldsworthy 1996, 176-82; Sabin 1996, 70-4; 2000). A closer formation, shoulder-to-shoulder, would not suit the Roman fighting style so well, although more than one soldier might be better able to concentrate on a single warrior opponent in cooperation, especially on the first to 'arrive' (cf. Prebble 1967, 74). A one-to-one basis of combat is an artificial model perhaps after the lines met fully in the confusion of individuals choosing their opponents, hacking and thrusting opportunistically in frenzied confusion. However, the Roman soldier would normally have enjoyed more effective armour coverage and design than his warrior opponent (Polybios 2.28-30; Tacitus, *Annales* 2.14; Herodian 6.7.8). One-to-one the margin might not have been very great, but along a battle line of thousands with a multiplier effect the disparity in successful woundings would have been significant. The Roman would have been better and more specifically trained, have greater stamina and longer staying power, and would have been accustomed to fight in regular, ranked formation.

So far the Roman soldier's fighting style has been considered with reference to infantry opponents. However, there were two theatres in which Roman armies regularly came into conflict with mounted adversaries: across the Middle and Lower Danube there were Asiatic steppe nomad Sarmatians (Iazyges and Roxolani. Sulimirski 1970; Coulston 2003a); in Mesopotamia, and sometimes raiding into Armenia and Syria, there were Iranian Parthians (Bivar 1972; Coulston 1986; Goldsworthy 1996, 60-8). Both sets of opponents specialised in armies of mounted archers, which led them also to deploy the maximum provision of armour for both horse and man, and to develop heavy penetrative and concussive weapons, such as long, heavy swords, axes, maces and lances. The traditional, short Roman sword may not have been well suited to these theatres, although seldom in history have cavalry horses been persuaded to charge home on formed, resolute infantry. The development of Roman armour with its emphasis on head- and shoulder-protection, was very appropriate when facing the opponents' weaponry wielded from horseback, as was the large shield and limb-defences for protection against arrows (cf. Plutarch, *Crassus* 25; *Marcus Antonius* 45, 49). Rome further countered the threat of archery by recruiting archers from the east in the same archery tradition, and by modelling the armour and weaponry of some Danubian cavalry regiments on Sarmatian practices (Coulston 1985, 282-98; 2003a, 429-30).

MILITARY FIGHTING STYLES: THIRD TO FOURTH CENTURIES AD

From the later second century AD the beginnings of a radical evolution in Roman infantry fighting style are detectable in both the artefactual and iconographic records. By the mid-third century a new infantry style had largely replaced the one already discussed. The *lorica segmentata* went out of use, although future finds might prolong its known period of currency (Bishop 2002, 91). Curving rectangular shields were replaced by oval, slightly concave boards, that is curving slightly on both lateral and longitudinal axes (Bishop & Coulston 2006, 179-82; James 2004, 159-70). The old helmet forms developed even deeper and wider neck flanges, and it seems that a helmet ('Niederbieber/Heddernheim') type which extended low down on the back of the neck was adopted widely by both infantry and cavalry (Robinson 1975, 96-103; Waurick 1988, 338-41; Feugère 1994, 97-100; Coulston 1990, 146; Connolly 1991, 362-63; Bishop & Coulston 2006, 173-8; Junkelmann 2000c, 85-7; James 2004, 101-3). Although the short sword never entirely died out (Vegetius, *Epitoma rei militaris* 2.15; Bishop & Coulston 2006, 192), it was largely superceded by much longer blades. These generally occur either as proportionally broad and heavy weapons ('Hromowka/Lauriacum' type, *c.*0.557-0.633m by *c.*0.062-0.075m), or proportionally long and slim ('Straubing/Nydam' type, *c.*0.65-0.8m by *c.*0.044m). These were suspended from a broad baldric and scabbard-slide, now on the soldier's left side (Ulbert 1974; Bishop & Coulston 2006, 154-63; James 2004, 140-41). The *pilum* also continued in use, but thrusting spears (*hastae*) and longer-range light javelins (*lanceae*) came to dominate (Bishop & Coulston 2006, 150-4).

These changes were closely interconnected, and did not stand alone in cause and effect. Certain types of equipment were best suited to the battlefield function of close-order, battle-line legionary infantry, and for use against specific opponents. Shields were still large, covering the soldier from shoulder to knee, but because they no longer curved on one, lateral axis, they did not obstruct the unsheathing of the sword from the left side, across the body, a sword which was now much longer and requiring this long draw. The comparatively flatter shield may have been connected with the phasing out of the segmental plate armour in favour of cuirasses with longer leg-coverage. Oval shields were not constructed in the old three-ply manner but of vertically aligned, glued planks with a rawhide rather than metal edging. On the face of it these would seem to have been less effective against heavy downward sword-blows than earlier boards (James 2004, 160-62. Cf. Ammianus Marcellinus 21.2.1). However, in the east the concern for infantry may have been more for protection from arrows than from enemy swords. There was a continuing emphasis on limb defences, and also a new third-century appearance of plate or scale gorgets, and coifs of scale or mail (presumably instead of a helmet: Coulston 1990, 145, 151; but see James 2004, 102). In the eastern theatre these presumably likewise indicate concern about archery.

There were two overall implications of all these evolutions and innovations. The first is that it was precisely the more restrictive forms of arms and armour, battlefield function-wise, which were phased out, or, put another way, the forms which allowed soldiers to operate flexibly were maintained and developed. The *pilum*, for example, which was so effective at short range against infantry, and still potentially as disruptive against northern, Germanic warriors (Franks, Alemanni, Goths, etc.), may have been hopelessly out-ranged by horse-archery. Moreover, although skirmishing, javelin-armed light infantry (*lancearii*) were always present in some form within the legions, there was more marked emphasis on this function in third-century legionary formations, together with the provision of integral archers (Speidel 1992, 14-21). The legal and cultural distinctions between citizen legionary battle-line troops and non-citizen auxiliary forces had in any case been eroded away by the early third century.

The second implication is that the soldier now assumed a much more upright fighting stance. This is clearly demonstrated by the evolution in helmet design which prevented the soldier from craning back his neck and hunching forward in the old manner. The more rapier-like long sword would have been suited to both thrusting and cutting, whilst the heavier sword lent itself to slashing attacks, brutal on an unarmoured opponent, at least concussive against an armoured adversary. Arguments for both types having been used both on foot and mounted may be made, especially if the foot-soldier faced a mounted enemy. Again this may be a key to explaining change, in that these swords could have be used in a wider variety of contexts than the short sword. This could also be seen as a logical progression on from the Pompeii-type sword, lengthening it and making its cut far more effective. Continued emphasis on delivery of the blow with the point might indeed mean either a thrust or a contact between the last few centimetres of the blade and the target with a cut (Vegetius, *Epitoma rei militaris* 1.12).

These are 'practical' explanations for change which may have been fuelled by the crucial Danubian and Mesopotamian 'Schools of War'. The undeniably greater success during the third century AD of Rome's opponents, northern Germanic peoples and the eastern Sassanid Persians who replaced the less aggressive Parthians, may have played a part (see now Potter 2004). However, ancient equipment design and employment was not only, or even predominantly, determined by technical considerations. The shift from Italian traditions towards a more Danube-dominated army culture, already underway in the second century, may have played as important a part in changing Roman infantry fighting style. This is not a question of a more or less 'aggressive,' or more or less 'defensive,' Roman military ethos, but one of regional imperial cultures coming to the fore. The 'celtic' style decoration of military equipment which flourished over the same period as the fighting style changes may be another indicator of culture-play (Bishop & Coulston 2006, 144). Long swords, suspension-methods and other features may have been predominantly central European adoptions, more suited to the Danubian troops who came to dominate and re-invigorate the army throughout the third-century empire.

GLADIATORIAL FIGHTING STYLES: FIRST CENTURY BC TO FOURTH CENTURY AD

As indicated at the beginning, a study of fighting styles exercised in the context of gladiatorial games may aid by lateral reflection in the understanding of military arms, armour and combat methods. This is partly because of the overlap in equipment designs, terminology, training methods and personnel, and partly because the arena is so richly represented in surviving Roman artworks. Put bluntly, legionaries and legionary veterans loved watching gladiatorial combats because they trained in the same manner and identified with the cultural values on display (Suetonius, *Divus Iulius* 31; Nardoni 1989, 51; Wiedemann 1992, 45; Barton 1993, 16-9; Welch 1994, 80; Futrell 1997, 75; Coulston 1998; Junkelmann 2000b). The thousands of representations of gladiators in a great range of media (sculptures, paintings and mosaics; bronze, bone, wood and terracotta figurines; metal and ceramic decoration; graffiti; and *dipinti*) are now accessibly published in monographs and catalogues, not all unconnected with public interest surrounding the AD 2000 film *Gladiator* (Aurigemma 1926; Robert 1940; Pfuhl & Mobius 1977; Sabbatini Tumolesi 1980; 1988; Gregori 1989; Köhne & Ewigleben 2000; Junkelmann 2000a; La Regina 2001; Connolly 2003; Jacobelli 2003. See also Winkler 2004). To save space here only Junkelmann's illustrations are referenced in full.

Nevertheless, the vast social gulf between soldiers and gladiators must not be ignored and it plays a part in the discussion below. Soldiers were respected and somewhat feared free men with a proud military ethos and in the legions, the core of the army, full Roman citizenship and all the accompanying cultural baggage. Gladiators could win great public acclaim and celebrity status. Being highly trained, they were a valuable commodity, so not all bouts ended in fatality and popular individuals could be spared if defeated after displaying the proper qualities. The best could have a long career of multiple victories and eventual retirement (Cicero, *Tusculanae disputationes* 2.17.41; Seneca, *de ira* 1.2.4-5; *de vita beata* 15.5; Petronius, *Satyricon* 45; Martial, *Liber spectaculorum* 29; Pliny, *Panegyricus* 33.1; Dio 51.72; Tertullian, *de spectaculis* 21). However, they were also members of one of the 'untouchable' professions which carried social disrepute (ibid., 21; Barton 1993, 12-5, 25-31; Plass 1995, 65, 72-7, 254).

There were many types of gladiator which modern scholars have attempted to categorise using weapons, armour and ancient epithets as criteria (e.g. Lafaye 1896, 1583-90; Grant 1971, 55-62; Nardoni 1989, 65-85; Golvin & Landes 1990. 161-68; Wiedemann 1992, 117; Junkelmann 2000a, 96-128; Köhne & Ewigleben 2000, 45-64; La Regina 2001, 153-73; Connolly 2003, 71-81). Some did not use swords at all but shafted-weapons or bows, most acted on foot, but some fought on horseback or even from a chariot. In the present context the main concern is with *gladiatores* in the literal sense of the word, men who fought using the sword (*gladius*) as their principal weapon, either the short Roman sword discussed above, or other forms such as the curved, supposedly 'Thracian' *sica* (Robert 1940, No. 151, 209; Pfuhl & Mobius 1977, No. 1237-38, 1240; Sabbatini-Tumolesi 1988, No. 92; Junkelmann 2000a, Fig. 31, 93, 110, 131; *Gladiatoren* 2002, 78-9. cf. Schnurbein 1979). Of these, the swordsmen with large, curving rectangular, central-grip, bossed shields came closest to military infantry in fighting style (*12 & 14*). These are shown in exactly the same 'first position,' leading with the shield or using the shield offensively (*13*), sometimes training at the *palus* (Junkelmann 2000a, Fig. 21, 38, 51, 61, 76, 96, 136, 148, 152, 169, 178, 213, 222). Gladiators also frequently fought using a smaller, less curved rectangular shield, or a concave round shield (ibid., Fig. 20, 29, 31, 33, 50, 59, 92-3, 110, 183-6, 189-91, 221, 234). In most cases where the men's legs are clearly depicted there is a close correlation between length of the shield and the protection it afforded to the lower limbs, with length of greaves worn. Long shields correspond with kneeless greaves, whilst moulded greaves which come up over the knees are figured with shorter shields (ibid., Fig. 51, 63, 76, 96-7, 103-4, 107, 127, 145-47, 216, 229-30, 234, 326-31). Both in the iconography and amongst the finds of gladiatorial equipment made at Pompeii (Italy, pre-AD 79) there are also greaves like high riding-boots in that they come up to cover the wearer's lower or mid-thigh (ibid., Fig. 16, 20, 31, 33, 59, 92, 102, 105-6, 145, 183-85, 234, 321-24). These worked with the smallest shields to give full frontal coverage. Protection from a smashing blow direct to a patella, or indeed an oblique impact glancing off the lower part of the shield, was clearly of great concern. Most swordsmen also wore *manicae* on their sword arm; some were equipped with a *pectorale* (e.g. Sabbatini Tumolesi 1988, No. 101; Junkelmann 2000a, Fig. 67). However, except for the comparatively rare instances of all-over cuirasses being worn, most men fought with an unprotected abdomen (cf. ibid., Fig. 42).

Gladiatorial helmets fall into four main design types: enclosed, combed, undecorated; very wide-brimmed, decorated with embossed motifs, metal-crested for feather or horse-hair display; more narrow-brimmed, embossed decoration, and a figural metal griffin crest; frontal peak, wide neck-flange, embossed or undecorated, with plume-fittings (Ridder 1915, Fig. 90; Pflug 1988; Nardoni 1989, 66, 88, 42, 96, 104, 120; Junkelmann 2000a, Fig. 56, 69, 72-3, 83-4, 86-8, 90, 100-1, 119-26, 270-320; Köhne & Ewigleben 2000, 38-45; La Regina 2001, 370-80; Connolly 2003, 92-7). In the artworks the first type is generally worn by the men with largest shields, thus those closest to the military fighting style, but normally paired against a trident-and-net gladiator (*retiarius*). The most flamboyant helmets are associated with other larger-shield men ('*samnites*'?) who normally paired off with small-shield fighters (e.g. Aurigemma 1926, Fig. 86, 93-4; Sabbatini-Tumolesi 1988, Pl. III, XII.2; Junkelmann 2000a, Fig. 92, 221, 234). The latter often wore the griffin helmet type and fought with a *sica*, so may have been defined as a 'Thracian' ('*thraex*'). All the types of helmets bore hinged, multi-part face masks with jaw-line deflective flanges and grills over the eyes, although the fourth, most military type sometimes appears unmasked in earlier artworks (e.g. Sabbatini Tumolesi 1988, No. 101; Junkelmann 2000a, Fig. 20, 27, 29, 42, 60, 67, 78-80).

12 Detail of a gladiator adopting the 'first position', seen from the man's left, on a pedestal relief from Antioch-in-Pisidia, Yalvaç Museum, Turkey. *Photograph: J.C.N. Coulston*

13 Gladiatorial monument depicting gladiatorial combats with an armoured gladiator attacking with shield held horizontally. Museo Nazionale delle Terme, Rome, Italy. *Photograph: J.C.N. Coulston*

The embossed decoration of helmets, including those of military form (with additional mask plates), actually acted to strengthen copper-alloy helmets and there is no reason to think that even the most highly decorated gladiatorial helmets were used solely for display and not for combat (Junkelmann 2000a, 70-3, 161-63; 2000b, 113; Köhne & Ewigleben 2000, 38-45, *contra* Nardoni 1989, 48, 120). The richness of decoration was part of the display and one of many elements of the games which advertised the munificence of the donor (*editor*). Helmets are depicted being carried ahead of gladiators in the pre-games procession (*pompa*) but everything about their design indicates protective practicality (Tertullian, *de spectaculis* 7. See Nardoni 1989, 35-6; Wiedemann 1992, 93-4; Junkelmann 2000a, 130-31, Fig. 207-8). A close parallel may be drawn with highly decorated army equipment, breast-plates for mail and scale cuirasses, and cavalry 'sports' helmets used in training and display exercises (Robinson 1975, 107-35; Garbsch 1978; Feugère 123-40; Petculescu 1990). Both were functional, not merely decorative. The Roman army did not have 'parade' equipment as such, and nor did gladiators (Bishop 1990).

As a principal adversary of large-shield gladiators, the *retiarius* also deserves some attention. He wore a greave on his left leg, *manicae* on his left, forward arm and a flanged plate (*galerus*) attached to his left shoulder to shield his face and neck. He was armed with a shafted trident and a knife, and carried a net (Nardoni 1989, 73-4; Junkelmann 2000a, 124-27). Faced with the classic Roman fighting style discussed above, the *retiarius* had a clear range of options. The net was a crucial tool for enmeshing the opponent, slowing him down and restricting defensive movement, hopefully making him vulnerable to a thrusting attack with the trident (Sabbatini Tumolesi 1988, No. 114). A heavily weighted net could also be used as a flail to knock the opponent off balance with a lateral swing, to wrap around his legs and yank him over, or to entangle his helmet and yank him forward off his feet. The smooth, combed helmet form was evidently designed to counter the latter move, and its small eye-holes prevented damage incurred from the barbed trident points (Junkelmann 2000a, Fig. 10, 13, 16, 22, 34-5, 51, 61, 76, 127, 146-47, 149, 199, 213, 218, 222, 228-30, 233, 235; Connolly 2003, 94-5. cf. *Gladiatoren* 2002, 72). Loss of the net resulted in the *retiarius* fighting two-handed with the trident, holding both shaft and knife awkwardly in one hand. At this point artworks show the *retiarius* thrusting powerfully at the opponent's forward knee, hoping to land a crippling blow (Robert 1940, No. 227; Junkelmann 2000a, Fig. 127, 213, 216; *Gladiatoren* 2002, 88). Loss or damage of the trident reduced the man to reliance on his last weapon, the short knife (Aurigemma 1926, Fig. 86a; Sabbatini Tumolesi 1988, No. 114; Junkelmann 2000a, Fig. 216, 228-30).

Retiarii were despised in public opinion (except by people who specialised in supporting them) even more than other gladiators because they were lightly armoured and they fought in a specifically 'non-Roman' manner whilst leaving their faces unmasked. Their reliance on mobility was thought to be cowardly, even unmanly (Juvenal, *Satirae* 6.143, 8.199-210). Here there is a clue to why gladiatorial helmets were masked. Scholars have frequently commented on this feature, positing a range of explanations. The suggestion that gladiators were masked to disguise members of the same troop from each other in combat, thus not make them reluctant to kill close colleagues, is untenable. After months, even years of training together, every man would have known his colleague's bodies, body language and fighting style intimately and no mere covering of the face would have disguised them. The higher-status swordsmen, and perhaps even the higher-ranking volunteers who flirted with gladiatorial fighting at grave risk to their own good name (*famia*), perhaps welcomed masking. Overriding all these considerations was the 'artificial' nature of gladiatorial armour provision, in the sense that too much armour might prolong a combat to the point of audience boredom. Too little in crucial areas might end the bout virtually before it had begun. Limbs were well protected, required for fighting and mobility. Abdomens and upper thighs were generally not protected so as to provide a decisive target for skilled delivery of blows. Considering the number of modern boxing-matches halted because of eye and scalp cuts resulting in copious bleeding and accompanying blindness, it seems safest to conclude that helmets were masked primarily to avoid these messy and incapacitating wounds (Wiedemann 1992, 119; Coulston 1998, 6; Junkelmann 2000a, 53, 70-1; Köhne & Ewigleben 2000,46-7). Moreover, an all-enclosing helmet with eye-protection would have engendered confidence, just as today a plastic hard-hat or a motorcycle helmet act psychologically as well as physically to armour the wearer.

Despite his low social status, the gladiator on display was an admired model of Roman virtue, the term '*virtus*' literally meaning 'manly' quality in the sense of bravery, military skill and public service. This quality, especially when exhibited by a swordsman, became a Roman cultural example to the urban masses who seldom took any part in real military activities after the first century BC (Barton 1993, 16-22; Wiedemann 1992, 3, 35-6, 39; Welch 1994, 80; Plass 1995, 30-2, 39-40, 44; Futrell 1997, 8, 49-50; Coulston 1998, 1-2). The legionary short sword and curving rectangular shield current in the Augustan period were closely associated iconic features in the multi-layered meaning of the Roman games. The classic Roman fighting style lived on in the arena because, unlike on the imperial frontiers, the nature of the opponents did not change, and because its cultural meaning did not lose its relevance. Thus short swords and curving rectangular shields persist in fourth-century gladiatorial artworks, such as the Villa Borghese arena mosaic, which nevertheless faithfully record contemporary attire (Sabbatini Tumolesi 1988, No.113; Nardoni 1989, 179-209), long after the combination had disappeared from use in the army.

14 Two legionary soldiers, one adopting the 'first position', the man behind with shield raised, on a pedestal relief from the legionary fortress principia, Mainz. Landesmuseum Mainz, Germany. *Photograph: J.C.N. Coulston*

CONCLUSION

This paper has been concerned with the fighting methods of the Roman battle-line infantryman as an individual. It has not addressed larger and still unresolved questions about unit organisation and the wider functioning of such formations on the battlefield. The soldier's equipment and training regime changed over time and to suit various opponents. It was not the result of central planning or even necessarily of a guiding rationale, other than the technical considerations discussed above. The picture presented here may indeed seem to be a technically 'deterministic' one, but this is inherent in an enquiry which concentrates on equipment and its uses. In actuality, technical considerations were not necessarily dominant, or indeed always a conscious factor. The culture of Roman society, regional cultures of the Roman world and the internal military culture of the army were equally significant, as were these societies' social makeup, economic systems and technological capabilities.

ACKNOWLEDGEMENTS

The writer would like to acknowledge the help in the form of discussion received in the research for the present paper from Mike Bishop, Peter Connolly, Cathy Coleman, Hazel Dodge, Simon James, Thomas Wiedemann(†), and a number of lecture and seminar audiences. Opinions and any mistakes contained herein are the responsibility of the writer alone.

5

The warriors of Pharaoh: experiments with New Kingdom scale armour, archery and chariots

Thomas Hulit and Thom Richardson

INTRODUCTION

In 1994-5, during the preparation for the new Royal Armouries Museum in Leeds, the academic team of the museum worked closely with Yorkshire Television in the production of some 43 in-gallery films. The films were a central feature of Guy Wilson's, the then Master of the Armouries, vision of the museum, and their success can be judged by the fact that they are almost all still running at the time of writing. John Waller as Head of Interpretation (now Creative Director) of the museum worked closely with Guy on the films, many of which featured the re-enactment of historical combats for which he is justifiably famous.

The combined expertise of the two organisations in making the films for the new museum led them to attempt a commercial sequel after the opening in 1996, and this bore fruit as a series of five hour-long documentary films for the History Channel, the *Arms in Action* series in 1998 (*Slings and spears, Mail and plate armour, Castles and sieges, The sword* and *The first firearms*). Their success in turn led to a further series of five programmes in the series in 2000 (*Bows, Knights, Hunting, Self defence* and *Artillery*). The first film of the second series featured a replica ancient Egyptian composite bow which was used to shoot bronze-tipped arrows at a replica bronze scale armour made by Tom Hulit.

In 2004 the Royal Armouries and Tom Hulit were approached by National Geographic to replicate and elaborate on the New Kingdom archery shown in the *Arms in Action* film and the experiments conducted by Tom Hulit during his PhD research, for the production of the documentary *Behind the Mysteries: Egypt's Warrior King*, which involved the history of Thutmosis III and the Battle of Megiddo (*c*.1481 BC). Originally the team who were to travel to Egypt and demonstrate the bow in action was intended to be Graeme Rimer and Tom Hulit, with Thom Richardson doing a piece on slinging, but in the event Graeme was unable to go and the archery was left to the two Toms.

The thesis was that the combination of a whole set of components, the composite bow, bronze-tipped arrows, scale armour and two-horse chariot, was essential for the *maryannu* charioteers of the Mitanni, which were introduced to Egypt by the conquering Hyksos and came to characterise the New Kingdom Egyptian armies.

SCALE ARMOUR

In 1997 Tom Hulit began his PhD research at Durham University in England. The research focused on the construction, manufacture and effectiveness of Late Bronze Age scale body armour from the Middle East. The hypothesis revolved around the fact that the armour is very rare in archaeological contexts in the Middle East; however, it is almost the same across the whole region; from Mycenae in Greece to Thebes in Egypt. The armour is made of scales of bronze or, as it was discovered, rawhide (untanned leather), which are laced together in rows, and these rows are then stitched to a backing material (*colour plate 1*). Each scale has a pattern of holes for lacing, usually five or seven, and a raised medial strengthening ridge.

This form of armour is primarily associated with the elite chariot troops of the Late Bronze Age Middle East. The armour, chariots and short composite bows (made of horn, wood and sinew) were a three-way association in this time period. Scale armour was not issued to the regular infantry troops, and was probably not even issued to all of the chariot troops. There are a variety of different types of chariots in the ancient world (several different types have been found in Egypt, particularly those from the tomb of Tutankhamun), and it is quite feasible that there were different types of chariot troops. Most of them would have been in un-armoured units which roamed the edges of battle, loosing arrows into the enemy ranks, while an elite section of the charioteers would have been heavily armed and armoured and capable of fighting in any capacity, perhaps not terribly dissimilar to modern commando forces who are trained and equipped to handle any eventuality. It is most likely these elite charioteers would have been the ones issued with the scale armour.

The number of individual bronze armour scales found across the Middle East totals about 500 (from more than 20 sites), and it would take at least 1,500 of average size to make a single coat of armour. There are several hypotheses which may account for this:

1 very few coats of armour were ever made, and even fewer made it into the archaeological record,

2 the coats of armour were very rarely buried/discarded and the bronze was recycled, and/or

3 the armour was made of perishable materials.

In actual fact, Tom Hulit's research suggests that it is a combination of the last two hypotheses.

Scale body armour appears in the Nuzi texts from Iraq (1475-1450 BC, see Starr 1939, Kendall 1974), the annals of the Battle of Megiddo (c.1481 BC, Kendall 1981: 222, 1974: 263), and the dowry set by Tushratta, King of Mitanni to Amenhotep III (text EA 22, el Amarna Cochavi-Rainey1999: 71). Depictions of armour appear in the tomb reliefs of Ramses III in the Valley of the Kings (Lorimer 1950: 198, Wise 1981: 21) and in the tombs of Paimosi (Figure 15, Lepsius 1842–45: Vol. 5, Pl. 64) and Kenamun in the Valley of the Nobles (see Yadin 1963: 197). As noted above, remains of armour have been found at more than 25 sites across the Middle East. Several of the Nuzi texts (Kendall 1974) note many complete coats of armour in the inventories of the palace armouries, and the texts note that they were checked out by notable soldiers, so they were items that saw actual use.

The rarity of the armour prompted the author to engage in a series of experiments in order to better understand the use, materials and construction of the armour. The rarity of the armour also suggested that the armour may have been an item of conspicuous consumption; nothing more than a very expensive dress uniform. As such, several sections of scale armour were to be produced. To begin with, it was necessary to examine some of the existing armour. It was possible to examine the armour found at Nuzi (held at the Harvard Semitic Museum; see Starr 1939), and the coat of armour found in the Tomb of Tutankhamun (*16*, held at the Egyptian Museum, Cairo). Furthermore, one of the best collections of scale armour found to date (at Kamid el-Loz, Lebanon) has been well presented by Walter Ventzke (1986). With these three sources, the size and construction of the sections of replica armour were planned.

The shape of the armour scales were based on the armour from Kamid el-Loz. Scale types IIb and III were chosen as they were the most plentiful of the nine types found at this site. Furthermore, they shared the same pattern of lacing holes as some of the armour scales from Tutankhamun's armour and the armour scales from Nuzi. Overall, compared to the armour from all of the archaeological sites, this pattern of lacing holes was most common. The size of the replica scales manufactured were 65mm by 22mm and approximately 1.5mm in thickness. This adequately represented the average size of scales across the Middle East, although it must be noted that some scales from the archaeological record are as small as 5mm by 9mm (from Tutankhamun's armour) to as large as 40mm by 120mm (Malqatta, Egypt).

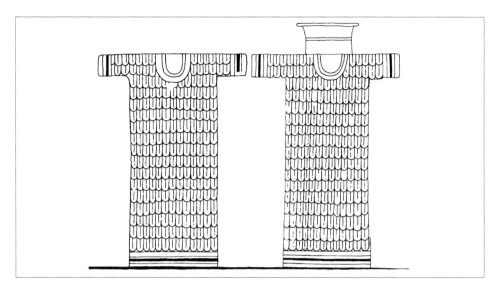

15 Illustration of scale armour from wall painting in tomb from Paimosi. *After Davies 1930. Redrawn by Jenny Doole*

16 Coat of rawhide scale armour from the tomb of Tutankhamun. *Courtesy of the Griffith Institute, Oxford*

Scales were made in two materials; bronze and rawhide. Most of the armour scales found in the archaeological record are of bronze, and those from Tutankhamun's armour were rawhide, therefore it was deemed necessary to make both types. The bronze was kindly donated by EIP Metals of Birmingham, and was delivered already the right thickness and cut to the right width. The scales were formed into blanks 130mm in length with both ends correctly pointed using a metal guillotine. The lacing holes were drilled in the appropriate places, and then the scales were cut in half. The resulting drilled scale blanks were then placed between the dies on a fly-press and the medial ridge was pressed in. A similar method of manufacture was used for making the rawhide scales. Long strips were cut from a cow-hide and the 130mm long blanks were cut by hand with heavy shears. The holes were drilled and medial ridge was pressed in the same manner as for the bronze scales.

Once a quantity of scales were manufactured, they were laced together into rows of 25 using the pattern shown in *colour plate 2*. The lacing pattern was derived from the examination of Tutankhamun's armour, and as the pattern of the holes in the Kamid el-Loz scales was the same, it was taken as suitable method of lacing. Three variants were manufactured: one entirely of bronze, one entirely of rawhide and third in which rawhide and bronze scales alternated. Ten rows of scales were then selected and stitched to a backing of six layers of linen (also based on the backing material from Tutanhkamun's armour). The single remaining empty hole at the top of each scale served to be the point at which the rows were stitched to the backing. Three sections of armour were produced, one in bronze, one in rawhide, and a third composite section.

In many instances the Nuzi texts note coats of armour which are composite (e.g. HSS XV: 11, Starr 1939: 541 and HSS XIII: 195, Kendall 1974: 351). It is not possible to tell from the texts how the coats of armour are actually constructed; for instance, there is reference to armour that has the back in bronze and the front in leather, and another which has the body of leather and the sleeves of bronze. It may be that these coats of armour had whole sections entirely in the material mentioned, or they may have had sections (e.g. sleeves) which were composite with alternate rows in bronze and rawhide or alternate scales in bronze and rawhide (as in *colour plate 3*). For the replica section of composite armour, alternating scales were used as this proved, as will be noted below, to be as effective as armour made entirely of bronze.

THE ARCHERY EQUIPMENT

It was decided that the best test of the armour would be to see if it was proof against replica New Kingdom Egyptian archery equipment. It was necessary to devise a suitable target for the testing, as a flat board would not allow the armour to move correctly. A martial arts punch-bag was selected as it would provide both swing and compression and thus better represent a human body (*colour plate 4*). It was suspended from the ceiling and also tied to weights on the floor to limit the amount of swing upon being struck with the arrows. A light arming jacket was put over the bag (some form of padded garment is worn beneath almost all forms of armour), and the sections of replica armour tied to the target and tested in turn.

The museum purchased a replica of an ancient Egyptian composite bow from Edward McEwen. Actually, it was originally intended as a replica Assyrian bow, with duck-billed nocks copied from reliefs such as those at Khorsabad and Nineveh (Yadin 1963: 418-9, 453), but is of the same angular form characteristic of Egyptian composite bows of the New Kingdom period (and was decorated by Mr McEwen with inscriptions from two of Tutankhamun's bows to make it look even more Egyptian). It is constructed of wood, horn and sinew, and covered in birch bark. The bow has a draw weight of 40-45lbs at 30-33ins (18-20kg at 760-840mm), to which both authors drew consistently. It is 1455mm in length (1420mm when strung). Although not vastly powerful, it is a nice bow to shoot, quite gentle to draw and quick on release. Although the Tutankhamun composite bows are all a good deal smaller than this (885-1315mm ignoring the tiny and possibly votive bow no. 1598, which is 720mm in length), these were all made for the young king as a child and a youth. The Balfour bow in the Pitt Rivers Museum on Oxford is 1445mm measured along its belly, and the Brooklyn bow is 1452mm measured in the same way, both of comparable size to our replica and probably more representative of adult bows (McLeod 1960, 1964).

A considerable number of cane arrows with hardwood feet and bronze heads were made for the filming. Some were made by John Waller with bronze points cast by John Mainwaring (www.bronzeedge.co.uk), others by Ted McEwen and others by Tom Hulit. Owing to the nature of the materials, these varied somewhat in weight and dimensions. Examples of four survivors are given in *Table 1* below. In addition, Tom produced numerous ramin-shafted arrows as expendables. The Middle Kingdom group analysed by Hart (1994), with reed (identified there as common reed, *phragmites communis*) shafts, hardwood feet and flint heads ranged from 840-885mm in length. The Tutankhamun group vary widely, like the bows, but the larger ones, mostly of reed footed with hardwood, range from 805-905mm, averaging about 865mm (McLeod 1982: 13-26). No weights are recorded for any of the arrows, and it is possible that most original ones are much lighter than the replicas we used.

	Overall mm	Shaft mm	Foot mm	Head mm	Weight g
McEwen 1	930	735	140	55	54
Waller 1	995	775	150	80	76
Waller 2	1020	800	150	80	80
Hulit 1	955	775	100	80	64

Table 1: replica New Kingdom arrows

The arrows that were used had three types of points. Some were made by Ted McEwen and some by Tom Hulit. Mr McEwen's arrows were made of Japanese cane with hardwood foreshafts. He used two types of points: long tapered ebony bodkin points and cast bronze points based on a generic ancient style. The author also made a series of arrows for the tests which used bamboo shafts with hardwood foreshafts and leaf-shaped points made of cast bronze based on those from Tutankhamun's tomb. These points were made of hard alloy (88% copper, 10% tin, 2% zinc) and work hardened. However it is possible that our bronze heads were larger, and most probably heavier, than contemporary Egyptian ones such as Tutankhamun 62 (McLeod 1982), and none of these have been weighed.

THE BALLISTIC TESTING

The original tests were conducted at a distance of 7m. This distance was chosen as it is the theoretical minimum distance that an archer would ever be from his target in battle. Furthermore, it allowed a certain increase in accuracy which would allow several shots at each target in different, undamaged sections, and should allow any yaw in the arrow as it is shot from the bow to settle (though our later work in Egypt, described below, suggested that it may not have settled before 10m). This distance would also be a maximum test for the effectiveness of the armour and arrows, as with increasing distance the arrows begin to lose velocity.

Five shots were made at the replica section of bronze armour. In no case did the arrows penetrate the armour. In each case the armour was somewhat damaged, usually involving bent scales and occasionally scales were torn from the backing material. The bronze arrow-heads were bent or curled with the ebony bodkin points being cracked and dulled. Interestingly, the most significant damage to the bronze armour was in the lacing. As the armour was struck by the arrows the sharp holes in the bronze scales tended to cut the lacing, causing one or two scales to fall away from the armour. The missing scales would leave a gap, which would have compromised the effectiveness of the armour.

Three shots were made at the composite bronze/rawhide section of armour, and as with the bronze section noted above, no arrow penetrated the armour, and the arrows were not as badly damaged. This is quite significant as this section of armour weighed 42% less than the bronze section but was just as effective at stopping the arrows. Any soldier in battle would choose the armour that was lighter but just as effective. Furthermore, the rawhide scales had a buffering effect, fewer laces were damaged and no scales fell away from the armour. Some of the bronze scales were bent, but this did not severely compromise the effectiveness of the whole.

In the third test three shots were made at the rawhide armour. This section of armour stopped the arrow with the tapered ebony point, but both the bronze-pointed arrows penetrated the armour. The generic point cast by Ted McEwen penetrated to a depth of 15mm and the sharp leaf-shaped point made by the author penetrated to a depth of 63mm. Both of these would have been dangerous wounds, particularly the latter, which would likely have been fatal. Despite the apparent decrease in effectiveness, very few of the laces were broken and the armour was not seriously damaged. Although this may seem a moot point, it is important as the armour would certainly have been reclaimed to be re-issued to another soldier in another battle.

For the experiments in Cairo, we did three archery sessions: distance shooting, shooting at armoured and unarmoured targets, and shooting from a chariot.

The distance shooting session took place in the evening of the first day of filming in the dunes outside Saqqara. Both Toms were able consistently to shoot the replica Egyptian arrows 100-150m, and modern aluminium arrows 150-175m. Shooting was curtailed by the rapid population of the dunes towards sunset; no less than two games of football were going on around the base of a very early pyramid, and parties of walkers, camel riders and cyclists abounded, to say nothing of the large audience the National Geographic film crew had attracted.

For the ballistic testing on the morning and afternoon of the second day of filming we obtained a martial arts bag stuffed moderately firmly with straw, and cleared an enclosure used for storing and stripping palm fronds (the staple industry of the village is palm-frond basket manufacture). A tall mud-brick wall at one end ensured range safety, and an arrangement of wooden poles provided a convenient suspension point for the bag (*colour plate 5*). Weights were attached to the bag so it was reasonably firmly tethered at the bottom and not free-swinging, and it was about 1m away from the wall.

First we shot at the unprotected bag. At a range of 5m arrows penetrated 470mm, at 7.5m they penetrated 650mm, and at 10m they passed right through the bag. This is most probably because at shorter ranges the yaw of the arrows altered the angle of strike, and the yaw had evened itself out by 10m. All arrows at the start of their flight have to bend to pass around the bow, and their springiness, or 'spine,' has ideally to be matched to the bow in order for them to do it effectively (see Godehart, Schellenberg, & Jaworski, this volume). Once in flight this bend, or yaw, gradually reduces until the arrow flies straight, and the effective transmission of the arrow's energy to its head on impact is much greater when it is in straight flight. Most of the shooting we did for the filming, however, was at 5m for accuracy, to maximise the usable footage.

The bag was then clad in replica rawhide armour. At 5m, arrows penetrated 70–90mm consistently, but did not significantly damage the lacing of the armour (*colour plate 6*). Next the bag was clad in replica composite rawhide and bronze scale armour. Arrows consistently penetrated a rawhide scale and were stopped by the bronze scale underneath, or, if they contacted a bronze scale first, bounced off. The tips of these arrows curled on impact, making them unusable. Next the bag was clad in replica bronze scale armour, which resisted all arrows. Cane arrows shattered on impact, while the ramin-hafted arrows broke at the junction of the head and shaft.

The apparent ineffectiveness of the rawhide armour was unexpected. The tests were conducted at a very close distance, and still the rawhide armour stopped the ebony-tipped arrow. In the Late Bronze Age most of the arrows would not have had bronze points because they were expensive and because most of the intended targets would not have been wearing armour. Ebony tipped arrows form a substantial proportion of even the royal Tutankhamun assemblage of arrows (McLeod 1982). The scale armour in the Late Bronze Age Middle East was exclusively used by the elite chariot crews. The infantry usually fought with short single-handed weapons (axes, swords or spears), with a free hand to use a shield, and this is what appears in the ancient depictions of infantry ranks.

Unfortunately the tests could not include testing at any great distance, so it is not yet clear how much more effective the rawhide scale armour would have been at a distance of 25, 50 or 100m. It is likely that with the reduction of arrow velocity at longer ranges the rawhide scale armour would have been more effective, but we have been unable to test this so far.

Another problem with this (and most other) ballistic testing of armour is the nature of the target. Although the straw-filled martial arts bag we used was fine from a filming point of view, it did not really provide the armour with a resilient enough backing to test it fairly. At the end of the afternoon session the National Geographic crew obtained a lamb carcass, skinned and dressed (and given to the village for their evening meal later). This was suspended in place of the martial arts bag and shot at. The bronze arrows penetrated lethally unless they contacted bone, where they penetrated up to 10mm and stuck fast. When the carcass was clad in the replica rawhide scale armour the characteristic of the animal carcass underneath caused the good shots we succeeded in making to bounce off, rather than penetrate as they had through the same armour on the bag. Pressure of time coupled with the difficulty of hitting an armoured lamb carcass consistently prevented us from doing as much research in this area as we would have liked.

THE AXES

After the experiments with the archery equipment, Tom's original experiments were expanded upon by testing the armour with axes. The National Geographic generously commissioned John Mainwaring to produce a selection of replica New Kingdom Egyptian axes with bronze heads and rosewood hafts. The section of bronze armour was re-attached to the archery target and repeatedly struck with the axes. The author had sharpened two of the axes to razor-sharpness, and the results were really somewhat unexpected.

The bronze scale armour suffered considerable damage from the blows of the axes, with many laces being broken and many scales, including whole rows, becoming detached from the backing. After this experiment, another axe was selected and the linen backing itself was struck. What is quite interesting is that the linen itself proved to be exceptionally good armour. Only the first of the six layers was cut. While the severity of the blows would certainly have resulted in severe internal damage to anyone wearing the armour, the skin itself would not have been cut. This clearly serves to demonstrate that fabric armour would have been quite effective by itself without the use of additional defences. Furthermore, it suggests that perhaps there was more textile armour used in the ancient world than is acknowledged. As textiles are organic they rarely survive in the archaeological record and as such we rarely have any evidence of them. We also attempted to test the axes to destruction on a palm log, and failed dismally; the axe was undamaged at the end of the test, the log in tatters.

THE CHARIOT

Time was running out for us in the desert, and we still had the third phase of our work to do. A film prop chariot with a pair of horses, who seemed highly unimpressed with the entire proceeding, was organised, and we set up a set of three targets in a line in the desert about 30m apart. The chariot was heavy and clumsy, and had quite serious problems with its harnessing. Most problematic of all was its all steel construction and complete lack of suspension, which magnified every bump in the ground and meant balancing, let alone shooting from the chariot, was difficult. Neither Tom had ever ridden on a chariot before, either. Both Toms had a run in the chariot and shot off a series of arrows at the set of targets. Neither of us braved the shot shown universally in depictions of Egyptian pharaohs shooting from their chariot (straight over the horses' heads), but found standing at the left side of the chariot car and shooting to the left or behind it relatively easy (*colour plate 7*). Given a little more practice with bow and chariot we could certainly have shot straight ahead at the wider, steadier target offered, but even with this brief experience of the art were both able to hit the targets from a moving chariot with a substantial number of arrows.

Primitive though the demonstration was, it was quickly evident that the light two-horse chariot of the New Kingdom was a highly effective mobile shooting platform, and that the elevation given even by a chariot was a position of dominance on the Late Bronze Age battlefield. The relatively short length of the composite bow enabled it easily to be handled within the confines of the chariot car, in a way that a comparable self bow was not (we did not, unfortunately have a replica Egyptian self bow with us, but the inference was quite obvious). The original chariots, five of which from the tomb of Tutankhamun are preserved in the Egyptian Museum in Cairo, are all of light wooden construction. Though none of their leather floors has been preserved, slots for the rawhide straps in the side members make the woven construction of these floors obvious. Sprung floors were crucial to the effectiveness of the chariot in action, and a solid floor is too bouncy to use at any speed.

None of the Tutankhamun chariot bodies has any provision for a rear support, but another example, from the tomb of Tjuyu and Yuya, found by Maspero and Davis in 1905, has a rear panel for the left side of the chariot body (Partridge 2002; Yadin 1963, 190-1). It has been suggested that this chariot was a training vehicle for a youth, and both of us felt we could have used such a feature. While pharaohs are regularly depicted shooting forwards from the chariot with the reins tied behind their backs, lesser mortals are shown hanging to the left side rail of the chariot for grim life, bow in hand.

CONCLUSION

Despite our collective inexperience and ineptitude (we were, after all, new to this, and had not spent our lives training in war chariots with bows), we were both able to shoot from a moving chariot with reasonable accuracy from the start. It was quite clear to us that the whole package – the composite bow, bronze and leather scale armour and the two-horse chariot – were all essential for the chariotry of Egypt in the New Kingdom.

These experiments have shown that the scale armour of the Late Bronze Age Middle East was an effective item of equipment. It may have seen little use due to the complexity of construction, but it was used by the elite chariot troops to protect them from harm and ensure that they brought their valuable equipment (the chariot and horses) home after battle. It is not surprising that the armour is very rarely found in the archaeological record. Coats of rawhide armour would not survive very long when buried, and the bronze scales would be very easy to melt down and reuse.

They have also shown how a costly item of equipment, used across the ancient Middle East, can easily vanish from the archaeological record. Scholars, historians, archaeologists and others must always remember that even if the material they study seems to be rare, it may not have actually been so. There are always cultural, natural and other unforeseen factors over the centuries and millennia that can affect the remains we have to study.

6

'With your shield or on it': combat applications of the Greek hoplite spear and shield

Allen Pittman

INTRODUCTION

When one thinks of the world of ancient Greece, images that immediately spring to mind are the proliferant scenes of warriors fighting either mythological beasts, strangely dressed 'barbarians' or most frequently other similarly armed warriors. The Greek world was comprised of independent city states or *Poleis* which were constantly at each other's throats and warring with each other. The warriors so often illustrated in the art of the period were known as hoplites, citizen-soldiers whose duty to fight was due to the privilege of citizenship of their home Polis. From our earliest records up until the time of the Macedonian ascendancy these citizen-soldiers fought as infantry in the massed ranks of the phalanx. Despite all of the great changes and achievements of the ancient Greek world, the field of battle remained one of the greatest constants of the culture. While equipment changed over time with regard to visual appearance, the tactics on the battlefield remained remarkably simple – two lines of men clashing together on a hot summer's day seeking to drive each other from the field. However, there has been remarkably little scholarship about the actual activities of the warriors right at 'the coal face' of combat – how did they actually physically interact with each other using their famed weaponry?

The purpose of this article is to introduce and explain the structure, significance and basic usage of the hoplite spear and shield in warfare in Archaic and Classical Greece from *c.*600 to 380 BC. Considering the hundreds of thousands of hoplite warriors who fought in this long epoch, it is perhaps surprising that so few offensive weapons survive in museum collections today. Indeed, it is the articles of defensive weaponry which best survive. This is at least in part due to the fact that they were frequently dedicated at religious sanctuaries to mark victories in battle.

There is a parallel bias in most modern written works dealing with the hoplite military panoply, and little focus has been placed to date on the offensive weaponry which was used in these lines of battle (Connolly 1998; Warry 2001; Snodgrass 1999). For several hundred years the spear was the primary weapon of the Greek hoplite, with the sword functioning more as an auxiliary weapon which was used when the spear was shivered or when the lines of battle were broken and fleeing opponents were to be cut down. From the defensive weaponry of the hoplite, one of the most characteristic features was the shield or *aspis*, a large concave structure of wood, sometimes faced in thin, polished bronze or fixed with a blazon depicting mythological creatures or more simple motifs.

The shield and spear functioned in harmony in the hoplite system, creating a robust wall of wood with spear thrusts coming from above the shield to drive the attack against the enemy lines. Many studies examining hoplite warfare deal with the larger 'whole' of the battlefield, such as tactical innovations and developments, but this paper will present an interpretation of the more localised combat environment of the frontline warrior and his immediate environment. To this end, I have been involved in the reconstruction of a number of these centrally important weapons of hoplite warfare. These have been used to investigate potential modes of use with the help and participation of some of my students from martial arts class. Training and drilling with these was undertaken on both a single and a group basis in order to examine potential uses of these against swordsmen, spearmen and persons equipped with similar spear and shield, including fighting in formation.

THE EQUIPMENT

Hanson (2000, 83–88) makes a brief study of the hoplite spear, estimating a width of 1in. (25mm) and a weight in the range of 2–4lbs (*c.*1–2kg) for spears made of cornel or ash wood, and they would typically be of 2–3m in length (Connolly 1998, 63). Hanson (following Polybius) suggests that spears of this thickness would have a tendency to shiver on collision with the initial impact of opposing phalanxes, a possible reason for the carrying of two spears in much Black-figure artwork of the Archaic period. Spears would have had an iron point and in most cases a bronze ferrule or butt-spike which would have served as a counter-balance to the spearhead, which allowed more of the spear to be held forward of the user, hence increasing its range. It would also have served as a secondary means of offence if and when the spear was broken and the spearhead was lost in the *melée*. The suggestion that most of the spearheads of the front-rank warriors would have been lost in the first few moments of combat resulting in a jostling match, while possible, is not well reflected in contemporary sources dealing with hoplite warfare such as Herodotus or Thucydides.

THE HOPLITE'S SPEAR

Modern commercial reproductions of the Greek spear usually present a weapon with a 1in. (25mm) diameter shaft. That is the diameter used in my own experiments detailed below, although future work will include examination of accurate replicas of thinner shafted weapons of ¾in. (18mm) diameter. Some of the 'mock-up' spears with steel cuffs used in my testing program are of this smaller size and proved illustrative of some aspects of their potential uses. When the 1in. diameter spears get to lengths of 6ft (c.2m) or greater, issues of speed and maneuverability as well as arm strength start to amplify. The kind of arm and shoulder development necessary for handling a 1in. diameter 6ft spear with ease are not well depicted in Greek art. Based on close examination of the artwork and the diameters of surviving ferrules, a diameter of ¾in. (18mm) for Archaic and Classical spears can be considered a realistic estimate (*17*). In this regard, it is best to envisage a level of heterogeneity in the weapons of the hoplite warrior, as the role of personal preference in the self-armed citizen-soldier allowed for a warrior to purchase weapons which best suited his physical strength and dexterity. While the thinness of Greek spears as illustrated in the art may be simply convention, the archaeological findings support this, and they appear this diameter even on very well-executed images.

Aspects of practical necessity are also most pertinent as the light weight of these spears allowed considerable accuracy when thrusting. When confronting a heavily armoured opponent who may only have his throat or eye as a target, this is extremely important, especially in the press of bodies which characterise this form of warfare. The image of orderly lines of hoplites stretching along the field of battle all coming face-to-face in neat array and pushing each other while seeking to stab an adjacent foe is dramatically over-simplistic, as will be discussed below.

The Masai tribesmen of Africa use spears of similar thinness as appears to be the case for the Greek hoplite, and in spite of their spears' thin structure, they are still sufficient to kill a lion at close quarters. Two spears could be carried into battle, as is frequently depicted in the artwork from Geometric (*18*) through to Classical Red-figure vase paintings. However, one of our earliest sources, the Chigi Vase, makes the intriguing possibility that, at least in this early period, these weapons were of different lengths, one short or about man height, and the other about 1ft (300mm) longer – see for example the famous vase by Exekias depicting Achilles

17 Archaic Grave stele with spear-bearing
warrior. *National Museum, Athens*

and Ajax, now in the Vatican museum (Woodford 1994, 24). The differential spear
lengths on the Chigi Vase in particular are not simply artistic convention trying
to get them to fit into a tiny space, as there are spears placed upright by non-
combatants and these are also of differential length (Connolly 1998, 38-39). It is
clear from the artistic sources available (given that we have no extant wooden
shafts from the period) that the use of spears of equal length was also relatively
common. Anderson's statement is instructive for assessing the use of this second
spear in the mature phalanx: 'Yet the second spear may have sometimes been
found as part of the hoplite's equipment after the development of the regular
hoplite phalanx, from which light armed or unarmoured missile throwers were
excluded' (Anderson 1993, 18).

Stress is laid by Classical authors on the effect of the Greek phalanx, a shield
wall overlapping, which hit the enemy with such a resounding force it often
knocked the first line into the second line. The integrity of 'the line' was as
legendary as it was essential. Most of the surviving art shows the first blast of the
line with the spears held over arm, as shown in figure *19*.

18 Late Geometric warriors on vase from the Keramaikos. *Keramaikos Museum*

19 Black–Figure vase depicting typical Hoplite martial stance. *National Museum, Athens*

It is interesting that in this position a spear can not *only* be thrust down but that one can throw a spear or if it is sufficiently heavy, 'drop' or slide the spear downward by releasing and re-tightening the grip. This can be done in a similar way to a throw, but without losing the weapon. It is a sharp, quick slide and is aided by the palm up grip. With a light spear it can be done accurately and it can compensate for sudden shifts of distance which within 6in. to 1ft (150mm-300mm) can be the difference between hitting or just missing the target with a spear-point. Spear-throwing as the lines closed could also be undertaken, with projectiles released as a shower on collision or before, similar to the Roman *pilum*, especially if one had a second spear (probably shorter and more effective for close combat) and a sword or dagger as a back-up weapon. While the historical sources do not refer to this use of spears in hoplite combat, we must remain cautiously aware of the Athenocentric nature of Classical written and artistic sources and bear in mind that regional and temporal variations would have been highly likely. It is most frequently believed that the spear was used solely in an over-arm or above head fashion, but there are innumerous depictions of it being used under-arm also in the artwork.

THE SHIELD IN PERSPECTIVE

The shield of Classical Greece was a remarkable piece of engineering in many regards. It differs significantly from its predecessors, most of which were lighter constructions, possibly of wicker and rawhide. The hoplite shield was manufactured from carved wooden planks abutted at the edges which created a broad bowl-shaped shield. These were often faced with bronze blazons or devices, and in many cases were entirely faced in bronze. The shield of the ancient Greek hoplite also made use of a new and innovative method of holding and managing its weight in combat. The central handle is replaced by a brace which accommodates the forearm just below the elbow of the left arm, and the hand grips a thong close to the perimeter of the shield (*20*). This has many significant implications, the first being weight management. Many heavy shields from the Mycenaeans to the Vikings made use of a telamon or shoulder strap to take the weight of the shield, yet this is absent on the Greek shields, some of the heaviest forms used in ancient warfare. The innovative method used to overcome the need for a shoulder strap on the Greek shields was placing the elbow at the center of gravity of the shield, bearing much of the weight. Essentially, this transformed the upper arm into a 'strap,' in that the weight was suspended directly from the shoulder, placing little strain on the forearm in carrying the mass of the object. This meant that the forearm and hand could be used to manipulate the heavy shield tactically, rotating it and also being able to swing the front of the shield out to strike with the shield rim itself (*21*), or more practically to allow for sword-strikes or underarm spear-thrusts without compromising one's own defense to too high a degree.

Held in this manner, the user could also push their shoulder comfortably into the bowl of the shield and use it for pushing forward offensively, an essential component of the actions of *othismos*, or attempting to break the opposing line by sheer pressure and force. While there were clear advantages to the Greek shield, a problem which arose from this manner of gripping it was the potential to push against the left hand 'over-hang' in the press of battle, which would apply leverage, consequently reducing the area of the shield covering the user. This opening of a slight weakness on the right-hand side of a warrior's defence would cause each warrior to seek shelter behind the overhang of the shield of the warrior to his right, thus causing a shifting of the entire line of battle towards the right, risking a flanking attack. To this end, it was common to place the toughest and most experienced troops on the left wing so that they would hold their ground, as described by Thucydides.

The shields used in the experiments weighed about 20lbs (*c*.9kg). When the *Porpax* (wrist brace) and other metal/bronze accoutrements are added the weight is raised to as much as 30lbs (*c*.14kg). At the time of photography the hoplite team was using a leather elbow brace on some shields and steel braces on other examples (later all replaced by metal braces). Once held up, the first thing that both I and my students noticed about the shields is that it was extremely difficult to see over or around. Once you get moving it is very disconcerting and you find you use your ears as much as your eyes, and one can feel it effecting the way one can move forward comfortably. It was a bit like having an open umbrella pointed in your face!

As discussed above, the overlapping of the shields is essential for the shield-wall to maintain integrity and cohesion. I am not aware of any in-depth analysis of this 'locking the shield wall,' and therefore I will do so in this section. When the interior of hoplite shields is depicted in artwork, it is clear that a rope ran around the interior of the bowl. A portion of this was sometimes used (in the absence of a specific handle) to grip the perimeter of the shield, but this does not explain why the rope continued around the rest of the interior. After experimenting with the inner rope of the shield it began to become clear that it was possible for one's fellow hoplite to hold one's rope through their hand-grip or possibly their elbow. The slack in the rope can be easily adjusted until the shield edges overlap neatly and the hold is strong with taught rope. The overall effect on shield/wall movement is astonishing. The entire shield wall becomes a unit and one can sense every shift of shield movement on either side. Moreover, the entire wall can be articulated – shields lifted or shifted horizontally – through this linkage.

Above: 20 The interior of a hoplite shield on sculpture. From the Siphnian Treasury at Delphi. *Delphi Museum*

Right: 21 Upper thrust/striking with the edge of a hoplite shield

It is notable that on the unprovenaced shield in the Museo Gregoriano at the Vatican (illustrated in Connolly 1998, 53) there is no evidence for a rope encircling the entire interior of the shield. However, there is room for a rope grip on both the right and the left of the shield, and, as we know from artwork, these shields most often had a very specific top and bottom, making the left-hand handle essentially redundant unless it was utilised in some other manner, the above linking being a most viable interpretation.

It was not possible to investigate practically tactical considerations based on this linkage, as we lacked enough equipment and men. It is possible that, thus linked, smaller groups of hoplites such as those from a broken line or pursuing/being pursued could also link up to form a defensive unit, potentially closing around an opposing force in a lasso-like pincer move. This would give a further range of options for perspectives on marching arrays and footwork patterns. I expect there was a synchronised art to 'locking' and 'unlocking' or gripping and loosening the grip on one's fellow's shield-cord. This would be useful particularly after the enemy line was pounded back or the line itself started to break and needed to retreat, disperse or be replaced from the rear.

There are two vision obstruction/suppression strategies with the shield and spear combination. One is simply to push the huge shield in the face of the adversary. The other is that the spear is held so that it is descending at an angle of 30-45 degrees. Since the opponent has to look up and over his own shield, whatever its size, he ends up looking directly at the point of the spear which, if held properly, presents very little of the shaft. This throws off judgment as to thrusting speed, which is incredibly hard to evaluate when looking at a point. The optical phenomenon is much like that encountered by aircraft pilots when viewing an oncoming plane on the horizon line.

DOWN CUT/THRUST

The double-edged spear can cut on thrust and draw. This is particularly noteworthy since this means an opponent can be cut on both the thrust and the retraction of the spear. One need only get the spear-head down amongst the enemy's legs for it to cut (see *colour plate 8*) as little motion is needed and here one realises that greaves were a necessity rather than an option. In this capacity the leather skirts which sometimes were attached to the bottom shield-edge make sense beyond simply defence against archery or projectile attack.

The idea of the 'running wall,' that is, the line of men actually running towards the enemy attempting to close the distance to reduce the casualties caused by archers, was even intimated in the Olympic events, which included foot racing in armour and holding shields. The running also gives impact to the shield wall. Experimentation I have carried out has proved that, if standing, the antagonist's first line can be thrown back well into the second line. This would make them temporarily vulnerable to the spear throw at or after initial impact. And a spear throw can be effective two to five lines deep into the enemy's ranks. The first lines receiving the impact of the shield wall could easily release a volley of spears into the second and third lines of the enemy with maximum effect prior to impact. And if the first line is carrying a second spear – as rendered in many Greek art remnants – it could be worth the loss of the first spear. Hanson (2000, 162) has argued that the spear was held underarm for this initial clash; however, the risk of the spear sticking into an enemy's shield and thus grounding a 2m spike facing back into one's own crowded and pushing men would be extremely dangerous and must negate this suggestion. Rather, we should envisage the spear as being held aloft, either for throwing or stabbing on the initial impact. After the two opposing lines have engaged following this first crash, learning a sense of group 'rhythm' in training can be shown to teach the 'line' how to synchronise movement. With regard to this corporate movement and group training of hoplites Thycydides (6.68) tells us of the Argive 'select force of one thousand, who were given long training in warfare at public expense' and less than a century later we know that the thousand strong Theban Sacred Band were an elite force afforded great resources in their training. The historic sources make it clear that, for at least certain key elements in the army, much time and effort was spent on teaching them how to fight effectively as an army, the Spartans of course being the most famous advocates of this extensive system of training.

For the Phalanx to optimise its wall-like pressure it can adopt a 'pulse' or rhythm so the mass of men moves as a unit. This is analogous to a battering ram or a team playing the game of 'tug of war.' This can best be achieved through a drum or vocal chant. Placement of the shield precisely along the back of the man in front with emphasis of pressure below the right shoulder blade is most effective (*22*). The men on the front line can physically push forward grounded robustly behind their shields, and can make use of their head and thigh to push forward as well as their shoulder, thus restricting their vision but presenting little by way of target to the opposing line by keeping the head below attack line, especially if helmeted. The body angle of each man in front of a fellow's shield is well matched to its own curvature and size, eliminating any space between body and shield which could serve to increase percussion on impact. A row (as opposed to line) of men can thrust and retract simultaneously or in a staggered pattern. This creates a lateral alignment or 'disalignment' of the spears from the front, allowing a higher frequency of offensive moves by a multi-row phalanx. In this context it is extremely important that the spear-heads and their angles are carefully maintained to avoid weaknesses in the line or, worse still, injury to one's own comrades.

22 Nestling the shield into the back of the line in front to add strength to a line

If the shields of the wall unlock and open and a hoplite goes to 'free fighting' out of line (notably as a line collapses or during a rout) the technique of rotation to use the butt-spike is highly efficient. The smaller spear here, less than the height of the man carrying it, allows for fast spinning or pivots on a vertical plane and can be brandished with amazing efficiency, as it can literally be used in a fencing style. However, as long as battle-line formation is maintained the spear should not be moved in laterally/horizontally sweeping motions as there is a high chance of spearing one's own men. This more versatile mode of spearmanship is best suited to when the '*melée*' begins and line formation is lost, then the spear can be used effectively under-arm and the sword and dagger become useful.

The shield as an offensive weapon is another consideration. The bronze facing sometimes added to the shield could be carried to the edge and effectively act as a blade of sorts, and the thinness of the shield edge itself makes an excellent impact weapon. This opens up a whole new series of studies on techniques. Pictured in figure *21* is a shield technique using a kind of 'uppercut' or palm-up strike. Here, the shield is used to 'stop – hit' as they say in fencing parlance or 'hit in time.' As the opponent (with his back to the camera) winds up to with an overhand thrust, his adversary (facing the camera) launches his own attack with his shield edge, which not only stops the spear attack but also holds the shield at bay while hitting the throat. In spite of the weight of the shield this can be done quiet easily due to the elements of its balance along the elbow.

Because the hoplite shield is curved, only 2ins or so of actual contact surface is maintained with the opponent's shield at any one time. This makes it difficult for the hoplite's enemy to know and feel just which way the hoplite is pushing. The continual disorientation during contact can be used to create a tactical advantage by an experienced and skilled warrior. Flat shield against flat shield would be much easier to 'read' and sense the pushing direction of the opponent. This factor of disorientation of pressure must have been extremely frustrating for the hoplites' antagonists, should they have had flat shields, notably during the Persian wars. Moreover, in action the convex surface distributes pressure in such a way as to prevent the enemy's shield from sliding over the top of the shield. The inner curved surface of the hoplite shield allowed the hoplites to 'sit' inside the shield and push back against the enemy, where the legs are used more efficiently, like a recumbent bicycle. The problem with this is that it cannot be used in the mass shield press. It is possible to jump into the shield with the hip or thigh while holding the spear aloft.

CONCLUSION

It has been argued that *othismos* or mass pushing of the hoplite lines of battle was intended to literally smash through the lines of an opposing army (Cawkwell 1978). When we consider the versatility of the hoplite weaponry and some of the variety of modes of attack discussed in this paper, it becomes clear that these contests of force had considerably more variables. If we consider a hoplite battle as lasting around one to two hours (Hanson 2000; Cawkwell 1978), and that the lines of battle could stretch for hundreds of yards/metres, then the idea of a simple pushing match becomes difficult to maintain. This issue of the lengths of the combat lines and the various discrete 'micro' battles along the lines is of great importance and must be stressed emphatically. While there was a clear necessity to break or destroy the opposing lines, it is certain that priorities between offensiveness and defensiveness would have swung as the cohesion of each (interlinked) section of the lines alternated. There is little doubt that the many methods of pushing through brute force described above could be used during *othismos* to seek to smash the enemy line, but this would have been at discrete areas of the line as opposed to along its entirety. This again ties in with the varying priorities of warriors, whether they would ground themselves behind their shield and try and push home an advantage gained at spearpoint, or whether they would push into the opposing rank to open up room for more effective spear-work (or sword-work) to gain a strategic advantage. One must stress again the heterogeneity of the lines, both with regard to quality of troops and combat fortitude or even luck, as it is essential to remember the line of battle was not a monolithic, self-conscious entity, but masses of individuals. In this regard, it was frequently the case that different areas of each army's line might break through the opposing army's simultaneously. Without sufficient reserve troops, this could not be driven home as an immediate end of the conflict, and the lines could be re-formed through looser formation hand-to-hand fighting as described in this chapter. Conversely, a line could indeed collapse entirely as a single break-through successfully spread along the line causing a snowball effect.

The hoplite warrior needed a wide range of skills to fight in this dynamic combat environment, and he could certainly expect to switch from pushing to kicking to stabbing to cutting over the course of a single engagement. As I have described in the preceding pages, the weaponry which he possessed was well suited indeed to many modes of interpersonal combat and could be used with lethal precision as well as brute strength. Hopefully these ideas and demonstrations will give a more living quality to the many studies on Classical Greek warfare already in place.

ACKNOWLEDGEMENTS

Thanks go to carpenter and student of mine, Teak Perrin and Master Wood Turner Nick Cook, for all the work they have done on the construction of shields and spears, as well as to the folks at Museum Reproductions Limited for being kind enough to give me a break on equipment costs. Also thanks to Blake Dalton of Several Dancers Core and students John Moulton and Diane O'Donnell who, along with Teak, continue to work with me many hours each week on Greek weapon construction and practice. Thanks also to Barry Molloy for his helpful advice in writing this chapter and for the use of figures 17-21. I would like to further add that I am compiling footage of the techniques as still photographs do not actually convey the actual workings of the weapons as well as I would like. If you would like footage on DVD it is available from www. apittman.com, also known as Physical Training Traditions.

The Irish Early Bronze Age halberd: practical experiment and combat possibilities

Ronan O'Flaherty

INTRODUCTION

Halberds have been the victims of some of the most colourful epitaphs in archaeological literature. Macalister writing in 1928 comments that they have 'all the interest of mystery, for they present more problems than might be expected on a superficial glance at a museum case containing them'. They are, in the words of Peter Harbison (1969, 35), 'possibly the most puzzling and problematic *Leitfossil* of Early Bronze Age Europe'. O'Kelly (1989, 164) describes them as 'one of the most remarkable and perhaps enigmatic artefacts of the first half of the EBA.' John Waddell (1998, 131) also sees them as 'puzzling objects', 'large, extravagant and unwieldy'.

Despite the aura of mystery surrounding them, the halberds of the Early Bronze Age are in reality fairly simple objects, at least at first glance. In most cases, the halberd consists of a long, stout blade with a strong midrib, attached at right-angles to a shaft of wood. In parts of central Europe, the shaft is of metal. They seem to date fairly consistently across Europe to the Early Bronze Age, flourishing from around 2200 BC to 1700 BC. The distribution of these blades is interesting, displaying a tendency to concentrate heavily in particular areas, often at some remove from each other. The key-zones for the production and use of halberds are Ireland, Central (Aunjetitz) Europe and southeast Spain. Despite increasing finds elsewhere, Ireland remains the most important of these regions, alone accounting for just over 30 per cent of all known halberds. However, the *idea* at least of the halberd must have been more widespread, as it is depicted in the contemporary rock-art, statuary and miniatures of regions and societies where no actual halberds are known. Just what halberds were actually used for has been hotly disputed for many years. However, the evidence suggests that they are weapons whose function changes over space and time to embrace both combat-use and prestige display. Certainly, the Irish examples show considerable evidence for wear, as a recent analysis of the Iberian halberds also shows to be the case there (Brandherm, 2003); on the other hand, the central European metal-shafted types seem designed primarily for display.

This paper focuses on the Irish halberds, of which there are at present some 186 known examples (177 described in Harbison, 1969; balance in O'Flaherty, 2002). It describes the results of experimental work using a replica Irish halberd and then moves to consider the nature of combat in the Early Bronze Age and how the halberd might have been used in that context. It draws heavily upon material published elsewhere by the author (see in particular O'Flaherty, forthcoming), but takes the opportunity to amplify some of the contextual discussion surrounding the combat possibilities.

MAKING AND USING A REPLICA HALBERD

The Irish halberd has tended to be seen as non-utilitarian, with archaeologists pointing to a perceived weakness in the hafting technique, as well as a presumed clumsiness in the hand (e.g. Macalister, 1928; Ó Ríordáin, 1937, 241; Herity and Eogan, 1977, 137; O'Kelly, 1989, 164-5; Waddell, 1991, 70; Mallory and McNeill, 1991, 102). The interpretation of the continental halberds has been more mixed; a recent analysis of the Iberian halberds now identifies many of these as practical weapons (Brandherm, 2003). In order to test this assumption, it was decided to design and construct a replica halberd and test its effectiveness in practical trial.

A full account of the design and construction of the replica is published elsewhere (O'Flaherty, Rankin and Williams, 2002). However, for the purposes of this paper, suffice it to say that the blade is a Type Cotton, which is the most common Irish type and whose distinguishing feature is the slight curve to the midrib and, in many cases, to the blade itself. It is not a replica of any particular blade in any of the various collections, but instead its dimensions have been created from a careful analysis, in the hand, of some 69 Type Cotton halberds, or about 74 per cent of the total known population. It is cast from arsenical copper, the usual metal of the Irish halberds.

However, the major problem in reconstructing an Irish halberd is not with reproducing the blade, for which we have plenty of models, but with designing the shaft to which it was originally attached. Out of the 186 blades known from Ireland, just two were found with the shaft attached, and only one (the eponymous 'Carn Halberd') survived long enough for a replica to be made (Raftery, 1942). The story is similar elsewhere in Europe and the extreme paucity of direct evidence means that we have to look to other sources for the information necessary to reconstruct the shafts of Early Bronze Age halberds. Again, the basis used for the reconstruction of the shaft is fully discussed in O'Flaherty, Rankin and Williams (2002). In brief, however, the proportions of the haft-head were based on careful measurements of rivets surviving *in situ* on Irish halberds, while the dimensions of the shaft were based on assumptions drawn from a combination of sources, including the Carn Halberd, rock-art depictions and the metal shafted halberds of Central Europe. The shaft is of oak, which was the timber used in the original shaft found with the Carn Halberd.

The dimensions of the finished replica (*colour plate 9*) are as follows:

- Shaft length: 1220mm
- Shaft thickness: 24mm
- Shaft width: 33mm
- Shaft head: 14mm top, narrowing to 6mm at back
- Length of blade: 250mm
- Thickness of blade: 9mm
- Rivet lengths: uppermost – 20mm, central – 22mm, lowermost – 22mm
- Rivet head diameters: 11.5-12mm
- Total weight: 1.5kg

The replica halberd deviates from the 'norm' in a small number of respects only. The central rivet would usually be the shortest of the rivets, which is not the case here, but that said, there are many Irish halberds with a middle rivet of this length. More significantly, the arsenic level of the copper in the blade is only 0.2 per cent rather than 2 per cent, which would be more usual and which would give a stronger blade.

In terms of the rivets, enormous difficulty was encountered in producing the high domed heads so characteristic of Irish halberds and these were eventually simply closed over. If it had been possible to reproduce the domed heads accurately, this would probably have achieved a stronger fix of blade to shaft.[1] It should also be pointed out that the blade received no annealing or cold-hammering after removal from the mould, nor were the edges sharpened. Both these processes would probably have been applied to the original halberds (and indeed metallographic analyses of some have proved this to be so – see Allen, *et al.* 1970), producing harder, sharper blades. Without such post-casting treatment and with an arsenic content fractionally that of most Irish halberds we can only conclude that however well the replica performs under trial, an actual Bronze Age halberd would perform better.

PRACTICAL TRIAL

Having created the replica, the next step was to see how it would perform in practical trials. A full account of the trials is published elsewhere (O'Flaherty, forthcoming) but the principal points are reproduced here.

For a variety of reasons, which are discussed later, the Irish halberd seems best designed for impact on bone rather than muscle. To be fatal, the target would most likely be the skull, although other areas of the body (notably the rib cage) would also be likely candidates, or indeed the throat (Brandherm, 2003). In the event, it was decided to test the effectiveness of the halberd against the mass of bone in the skull. Obviously, trying it out against human heads was not an option, so the question was to identify a source of animal heads which offered the best parallels. After discussion with veterinary personnel from the Irish Department of Agriculture, it was decided that it would be best to work with sheep-heads, preferably fairly young animals. Contact was made with Mr Liam Walsh of ICM Camolin, a specialised sheep killing plant just north of Ferns, Co. Wexford, who readily agreed to help and I am most grateful to the company for their assistance in this matter.

ICM Camolin kill up to 3,000 sheep a day, so supply of the heads was not a problem. What was a problem, however, was that as part of national controls to prevent the spread of BSE, these heads are officially classified as Specified Risk Material (SRM). After killing, the heads and other risk material are collected for separate, secure disposal so there could be no question of removing the heads from the plant. In addition, after any trials were concluded, the heads would have to be returned to the production chain for safe disposal as SRM.

The trial was set up for 30 August 2002. I arrived at the plant shortly after 10a.m. accompanied by a colleague, Mr Christy Philpott, who had agreed to assist and to record the proceedings.

The ICM plant is uniquely designed on three levels. The animals are killed on the uppermost level and then the usable and non-usable product is segregated and passed to the relevant lower levels for processing. The SRM material, including heads, is passed down a chute to the lowest level where it travels along a short conveyor belt before being dumped into designated bins for disposal. While it was originally intended that we should collect the heads we needed from these bins (which contain a great many things even less pleasant than the heads of dead sheep), plant management were fortunately persuaded to let us 'borrow' the heads from the conveyor belt stage and return them to the belt once more when we were finished.

The heads were obtained directly from the kill-line only minutes after slaughter and so can be considered, effectively, as 'live' subjects. They were quite intact, unskinned and came from a mixture of yearlings and older ewes. Twenty heads were collected in all and transported outside to a grassy area where it was proposed to carry out the trials. To avoid unintended damage to the halberd, the heads were simply placed on the grass rather than being fixed on to some form of structure. This meant, of course, that the target was 5-6ft lower than might perhaps have been the case in combat, but since the purpose of the trial was to test the robustness of the halberd in the face of repeated impacts, the location of the target was not deemed critical.

The design of the halberd, which involves attaching a heavy copper blade at right angles to a relatively slender shaft, means that when held in the hand the weapon has a natural inclination to lie with the point of the blade facing downwards. This influences the way it must be handled: the rock-art of the period in continental Europe clearly shows halberds being raised high above the head, presumably delivering the blow completely within the vertical plane (*23*). This makes perfect sense – travelling in the horizontal plane the halberd always seeks to return to its natural position, point downwards, and it seems that this is the logical way to wield it. The evidence of wear on Irish halberds would support this, suggesting that the most vulnerable point is in fact at the back of the hafting plate (O'Flaherty, 2002). All this is consistent with delivery of heavy, direct, punching blows with the impact directed along the length of the blade and ultimately absorbed where the back of the hafting plate meets the wood of the shaft.

The heads were placed one by one on the grass and struck with the halberd in the centre of the forehead, using a short chopping motion. The expectation, conditioned by the received wisdom regarding the fragility of the hafting, was that the halberd would break relatively soon. However, this did not happen. In fact, the halberd proved itself to be remarkably effective and resilient. A short, chopping blow, raising the weapon no more than a couple of feet from the head and delivered with confidence rather than brute force was sufficient to pierce the skull, often very deeply indeed (*colour plate 10*).

The small rounded end of the blade ensures that the full force of the blow is administered to a tiny area of the skull first, virtually guaranteeing a puncture each time. The fact that the end of the blade is rounded rather than a sharp point adds strength to this area, which otherwise might bend or even snap on first impact. It also suggests that the blade is designed for impact on bone rather than muscle, where a sharp pointed weapon would seem more appropriate than a blunt-nosed one. Once the skull is pierced, the degree of force behind the blow determines the depth to which the blade will be driven, while its expanding sides then widen the cut in either direction in a clean slicing motion. The blade cut through the bone of the skull with remarkable ease, producing a clean, narrow puncture wound, up to 5-6cm long depending on the depth to which the blade penetrated (*colour plate 11*). The ease with which the blade could be withdrawn from the wound, in most cases, was also noteworthy.

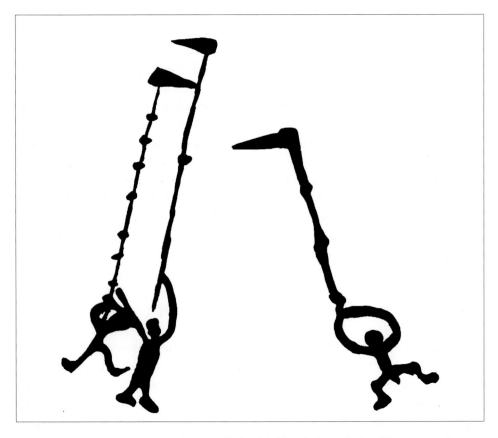

23 Figures from rock art depicting the use of halberd held aloft above the head from Monte Bego. *Redrawn by B.P.C. Molloy after Chenorkian 1988*

The halberd was examined periodically over the course of the trial, but appeared to be suffering no damage. After disposing of all 20 heads, a closer examination was carried out which confirmed that the halberd was apparently unharmed. There was no buckling of the blade, apart from a very slight, almost indistinct 'ripple' to the edge. In addition, there had been some slight expansion of metal at the point, obviously resulting from impact with the skull – I had noted but not remarked on this type of damage on some of the Early Bronze Age halberds in the course of museum work and it seems clear to me now what this results from. The blade, however, remained secure in the haft; there appeared to be no loosening of the rivets whatsoever and the haft head was also quite undamaged. There being every appearance that the halberd might continue in effective use indefinitely and in the interests of minimising further interference with SRM, the trial was concluded. The pierced heads were returned to the conveyor belt for disposal. Gloves and headgear were discarded, boots disinfected and the halberd itself thoroughly cleaned and disinfected.

On the basis of this trial, the only possible conclusion is that the traditional view of the Irish halberd as incapable of practical use is without foundation. It is quite clear that the halberd could have functioned extremely as a weapon and, in fact, aspects of its design (such as the choice of a blunt-nose and strong midrib) seem best explained in this context. We should not forget that the trials were undertaken with a halberd which was in some respect deficient when compared with Early Bronze Age originals, having received no post-casting treatment and having a lower arsenic content. We can only presume that a Bronze Age original would perform even better and for longer. In fact, contrary to what Treherne (1995, 109) asserts, it is arguably the halberd, if anything, and not the sword which is 'the first object clearly designed for combat instead of simply being adapted from an existing tool form' (see also Molloy, this volume). Just how it might have been used in combat is something we consider next.

COMBAT AND CONFLICT IN THE EARLY BRONZE AGE

Debate about the role and nature of warfare in human society has often centred on whether it can be explained in functional terms, whether it is adaptive, and why some societies undertake it frequently while others do not (Fried, Harris and Murphy, 1967; Keegan, 1994). Notwithstanding such virtuous affirmations as the 1986 Seville Statement from UNESCO (in which all characterisations of man as naturally violent were condemned), it remains a fact that violence is endemic in human society (see Grossman & Molloy this volume).

Over the last 10 years or so, there has been a considerable increase in the volume of archaeological literature dealing with warfare in prehistory (e.g. Edmonds and Thomas, 1987; Sharples, 1991; Drews, 1993; Louwe Kooijmans, 1993; Treherne, 1995; Carman, 1997; Osgood, 1998; Carman and Harding, 1999; Osgood and Monks, 2000; Guilane and Zammit, 2001; Kristiansen, 2002). Much of this has reflected on later prehistory, or on aspects of combat in the classical world, and so is not directly relevant to the period or society under consideration here. However, it is widely accepted now amongst archaeologists that small-scale raiding and feuding was a common feature of Early Bronze Age society, what Osgood and Monks (2000, 7) have described as 'opportunistic and sporadic, unplanned and … [with] no obvious or consistent motives'.

From an anthropological perspective, there are a great many accounts and references which might be considered for the purposes of a consideration of the pursuit of combat and war amongst pre-state societies (e.g. Chagnon, 1967; Divale, 1973; Väyda, 1976; Ferguson and Whitehead, 1992). Space does not allow for a detailed consideration of these here but Divale's descriptions (1973, 21) of warfare amongst the mountain peoples of New Guinea summarises a number of points common to several, including the fact that there was little or no military effort, a concentration on individual duels, much posturing and a tendency where possible to conduct affairs at long distance by hurling spears and firing arrows.

In terms of case studies, however, Väyda's account of the Maring of New Guinea is worth considering in a little more detail for the light it casts on the degree to which pre-state societies can use ritual to define and control the nature of the combat.

Väyda (1976) points out that fights among the Marine passed through several carefully regulated phases, moving from ritualised combat to much bloodier encounters. These last were invariably followed by thanks-offering feasts, where surplus pigs were consumed in honour of ancestor-spirits. However, because pigs were only in surplus every 10 years or so, it was incumbent on major conflict to follow and respect a similar timescale. To attempt warfare without the basis for thanking the ancestors was to court disaster. As a result, the Maring developed a policy of actually *creating* excuses for serious warfare every 10 years or so, to coincide with their surplus of pigs. Väyda points out that as the 10-year cycle reached its end, the neighbouring clan clusters began to offer each other the type of slights and insults designed to occasion war and eventually honour demanded satisfaction.

What is fascinating about the Maring approach is both the degree to which warfare was controlled and the degree, as a result, to which deadly weapons of war might only be put to real use once every few years. However, the fact that they were only sporadically used does not in any way lessen their 'reality' as weapons. This could be quite significant for our interpretation of Bronze Age weapons, not just the halberds, since the evidence of wear that has been identified along the blades may have been accumulated over a long, long time, during which the weapon may have enjoyed extensive periods of non-use. It might still have been brandished, displayed or employed as a threat, but not actually used in the conventional sense. This does not make it an exclusively non-functional object any more than the existence of use-wear makes it exclusively non-ceremonial. The tendency on the part of archaeologists to define 'ritual' in terms of whatever appears irrational or non-functional has been identified and criticised by Brück (1999) and her arguments are particularly apposite in this regard. Brück points out that the distinction drawn by modern researchers is a product of post-Enlightenment rationalism and has little to do with how prehistoric societies viewed their behaviour. It is not so much that the symbolic and the practical are two sides of the one coin, she argues, but rather that they are the same thing (ibid, 325).

There is of course another form in which violence manifests itself in many societies and that is 'ritual murder'. The importance of this to societies such as the Aztec is well-known (eg Clendinnen, 1991) but it was also important to earlier societies such as the Egyptian where it is sometimes depicted in the artwork of the period. Ritual slaughter of captives was well-established amongst the North American tribes such as the Pawnee or the Huron, and it was not unknown in fact for the captive to willingly participate in his own sacrifice (Turney-High, 1949; Clendinnen, 1991). The reasons behind this practice are complex but tend to relate to the need to sustain the community by appeasement of the gods. We cannot exclude the possibility that such activities may also have been practised by certain Bronze Age communities and that the surviving weaponry may also have been used to this end. The skull recovered from Drumman More Lake, Co. Armagh, which had a dagger driven through it, may well fall into this category (Waddell, 1984). With the evidence that already exists for this practise during the Late Bronze Age Ireland (Cooney and Grogan, 1994, p.147), it is worth bearing in mind that the halberd would have provided an excellent means of execution. However, until we find the hard evidence of a skull bearing the diagnostic long, narrow wound suggested by the experimental work described earlier, the possible use of the halberd as an executioner's tool must remain even more speculative than its manner of use as a combat weapon.

In fact, if we are to consider just how the Early Bronze Age halberd might have been used, we need to look at the use of a weapon much closer to home, chronologically speaking. This is the 'historical' halberd, the pole-arm which was used extensively in Europe during the Middle Ages. There is only one treatise surviving from the period which is devoted exclusively to the technique of halberd combat. This is *Le Jeu de la Hache*, written down sometime in the fifteenth century and published for the first time by Sydney Anglo in 1991. This text is particularly valuable because it describes in great detail how pole-arms of this sort might be used in *single combat*, rather than as the weapon of massed infantry. This may shed some light as to how the Early Bronze Age halberd, which so many commentators have regarded as clumsy and ineffective, could in fact be used very effectively in the hands of a skilled warrior.

Anglo (1991: 115) makes the important point that in fighting hand-to-hand with pole-arms, the technique adopted was much like that used in quarter-staff play. 'Long handled swinging strokes', he comments, 'were easily countered and were not greatly admired … '. In fact, the author of the *Jeu* specifically recommends that combatants should lead with the *queue* or shaft of the weapon and a striking feature of the whole treatise is the extent to which this part of the weapon is relied upon for both attack and defence. Anglo points out that the *queue* is mentioned more than three times as often in this text as the *dague* (the spur projecting from the back of the axehead) while the 'business-end' proper appears to have been rarely used. This observation is of immense interest as it reminds us that what has survived from the Early Bronze Age is only *part* of the whole weapon – we are missing the shaft (rarely considered as more than a prop for the blade) which may have been the most important part of the whole weapon, particularly for those types with reasonably long shafts.

In particular we might imagine considerable use of the shaft as a precursor to creating the opportunity for a killing-blow. Pole-work like this would also provide an opportunity to display skill and expertise in the handling of the weapon, without endangering the copper head, and indeed, if the ethnographic examples are anything to go by, this type of encounter may have been sufficient in itself to conclude some conflicts. Contemporary Bronze Age depictions often show halberds with large bulbous ends to the shaft, or protruding spurs (24), and if these are in fact accurate depictions they also hint at substantial use of the shaft to deal blows or perhaps trip or disarm the opponent. If a kill was required, it seems likely that the primary target would be the head of one's opponent – aiming elsewhere runs the risk of trapping the halberd without hope of recovery and without inflicting a fatal wound. In addition, as pointed out earlier, the fact that the Irish halberds are blunt-nosed rather than sharply pointed seems better designed to impact on bone rather than muscle. The practical trials described earlier have shown that a blow to the head, correctly delivered, is virtually guaranteed to penetrate the skull deeply and kill.

The experience of sword-play in medieval Europe also helps us flesh out a picture of how the Early Bronze Age halberd may have been used. Oakeshott (1960: 158-9) comments as follows:

> To begin with, one combatant would strike at the other. … a good deal of preliminary manoeuvring and feinting took place before one combatant or the other saw his opportunity and smote. The other would then defend himself either by taking the blow on his shield, or by evasive action … It was only when the shield had been so cut up that it was useless that one used one's sword to parry with, and then one would try only to use the flat of it, for if sword-edge clashed with edge much damage resulted.

The extent to which combatants sought to protect their blade from impact against an opponent's is notable. Our perceptions as to how blades are used in combat have, to some extent, been coloured by the interpretations presented by Hollywood films, which delight in the clash of steel upon steel (see Clements this volume). The fact of the matter is that, when engaged in this type of hand-to-hand combat, the last thing you want to hit with your blade is your opponent's blade – you are, after all, trying to connect with a somewhat softer target. We should not be surprised if in the Early Bronze Age, combatants were to take even more care of their expensive metal blades and only strike with that portion of the weapon when they were reasonably confident of hitting the target. We need

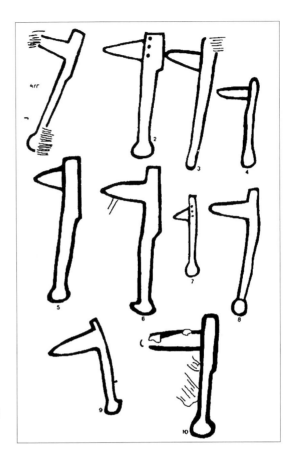

24 A variety of halberd forms (including shafts) from European rock art. *After Chenorkian 1988*

to think in terms of the halberd as being used judiciously, not in wild, swinging strokes that could be easily avoided and which were risky to both blade and user.

It is quite possible, however, on the evidence presented by some of the surviving blades, that halberds did clash, as the nicks and notches suggest. Broader denting may well have resulted from a blow being parried by the wooden shaft of the opposing weapon.

We need to remember, of course, that serious conflict may only have occurred at intervals of many years (Väyda, 1976) and that the evidence of wear that is seen on many Irish halberds may represent extensive use over a long period of time. Sue Bridgford has pointed out (pers.comm) in relation to the swords, that burrs and notches would probably have required re-honing, since otherwise they could catch in the scabbard. That would not necessarily be the case for a halberd, however, and so the nicks and dents that they display could well have been accumulated from many sporadic fights, interspersed with periods of non-use. Again, the lesson for us is to avoid the extreme assumptions: too often we tend to think in terms of weapons as either functional or ceremonial when they can fulfil both roles simultaneously. Bridgford (1997: 95) touches on much the same point when she says:

> A sword may *simultaneously* be, or have the potential to be, a beautiful object, an efficient killing tool, a symbol of power and wealth, an implied or actual threat, a sacrifice, a gift, a reward, a pledge of loyalty and/or an embodiment of the idea of conflict.

The same is true of the halberd and one is minded of Bruck's arguments about the artificiality of the distinctions drawn by modern researchers between what is symbolic and what is practical (1999).

There are other matters to be considered in relation to the use of the halberd. It is certainly true that, however effective it may have been as a weapon, it enjoyed only a relatively brief floruit during the Bronze Age. Much the same seems to have been the case with its namesake in the medieval period which gradually began to be replaced by the pike after the fifteenth century, and later still by the rifle-and-bayonet. Both these replacements would seem to indicate that the advantages in combat of the historical halberd (which combines elements of both spear and axe) ultimately lay as a long spear, rather than a long axe. The process of replacement of the historical halberd with pike may point to a similar replacement model in the Early Bronze Age, where in fact, the first spears start to appear at roughly the time that halberds disappear. In addition, it may be significant that similar changes were taking place around the same time in relation to daggers. These were now becoming longer and longer, changing from a stabbing weapon to a cutting and thrusting one in the form of the so-called 'rapiers' (see Molloy, this volume). It is interesting to speculate whether both the dagger and the halberd, which reflect a stabbing action, fell from fashion around the same time because of developments in combat which saw a thrusting action emerge instead, reflected by both rapier and spear.

The manner in which the Early Bronze Age halberd is likely to have been used meant that its success depended on certain norms of combat being respected. Unlike its medieval cousin, the Early Bronze Age halberd is really only suitable for single combat against a similarly or worse-armed opponent, and only in circumstances where defensive armour is not being used. A wood and leather helmet would have afforded considerable protection against a halberd-blow, as would a simple shield of wood, leather or wicker. As the halberd was probably wielded two-handed (although Cambrensis' remarks on the ability of the medieval Irish to wield their heavy battle axes one-handed should not be forgotten – O'Meara, 1951), it is difficult to see how its user could also manage a shield. Armed with a shield, a warrior equipped even with just a dagger is likely to get the better of an opponent armed with a halberd. The surprisingly early dating of the Kilmahamogue shield-former to 1950–1540 BC

(3445± 70 BP: OxA-2429. Hedges *et al.*, 1991) suggests that this form of defensive equipment could well have begun to appear in Ireland around the time that the last Irish halberds were being deposited. If that is the case, then the halberd may have disappeared because it represented outdated combat technology.

SUMMARY AND CONCLUSIONS

The evidence presented shows the Irish Early Bronze Age halberd to be extremely effective in practical trials and that the reservations expressed by previous writers are without much foundation. Ethnographic and historical parallels provide some clues as to just how it might have been used in practice and in particular have pointed to the use that could be made of the shaft.

There is no doubt that in Ireland the halberd was a popular weapon – the numbers recovered alone tell us this, exceeding as they do the population of daggers recovered for the same period. However, what we have learnt about the way it must have been used, leads us to doubt its effectiveness in the type of sporadic, small-scale raiding that is often believed to characterise warfare during this period (Harding 2000, 274). However, we also know from ethnographic and historical sources that the outcome of conflict was sometimes decided by combat between champions. The type of damage displayed by some Irish halberd blades strongly suggests that they were used in combat against an opponent armed with another edged metal weapon (O'Flaherty, 2002). This was presumably another halberd, since the daggers of the period would not have presented much of a challenge, while an axe is simply not constructed the right way to produce the type of damage observed.

In such circumstances, how then should we imagine the halberd being used? Anthropological accounts allow us to reconstruct the form which Early Bronze Age combat may have taken, with small groups of combatants facing each other, initial flights of arrows, posturing, scuffles and then the possibility of single combat between champions. It is in this context that we might imagine the halberd being brought into play, both for posturing and for actual combat. Elsewhere (O'Flaherty, forthcoming) I have argued that the halberd is a 'champion's weapon' and can only be understood when considered against the backdrop of the ritualised norms which characterise combat between champions. Here, with space to manouevre, an appreciative audience and a similarly armed opponent, the halberd would have been in its element, the weapon of choice of an Early Bronze Age champion, beautiful, costly and requiring skill and courage to wield. The limitations of the weapon, however, were such that once more effective defensive equipment was developed, such as the shield, and more effective offensive weapons such as the thrusting spear, the days of the halberd were numbered.

What's the bloody point?: Bronze Age swordsmanship in Ireland and Britain

Barry P.C. Molloy

INTRODUCTION

Weapons are tools designed to inflict bodily harm on another being, to injure or kill through force or finesse. The power of a sword to inflict harm on another, even to take a human life, can be seen as the root of its symbolic potency in ancient societies. This was a weapon possessed of qualities both highly esoteric and brutally mundane, one which was to be celebrated for over three millennia as the weapon *par excellence* of the warrior. The earliest forms of this weapon in Europe emerged sometime around 1700-1600 BC, and it quickly achieved widespread popularity in its various manifestations throughout the continent. Thus it was far back in the Middle Bronze Age that the long lineage of the sword was established.

In the centuries following this first introduction of the sword to the battlefields of Europe, the weapons panoply of the Bronze Age warrior grew ever more rich in style and variation. This near pre-occupation with martial arts, violent symbolism and the activities of combat can be seen to permeate the social world of this transformative epoch in human development. This paper will explore how these martial developments evolved in the far northwest of Europe in the islands of Ireland and Britain throughout the the Middle and Late Bronze Age.

When analysing bladed weaponry, we can speak of the process of their manufacture, their role as prestige items, as votive offerings or the importance of their typological or metallurgical affinities and the communications networks that these relate to. It is rare, however, to have a study dedicated to their use as tools of violence. This is all too frequently restricted to simple 'lip-service' mention in some articles, as Peatfield notes, because when they are referred to, '… the fearsome martial capacities of blades … are left curiously implicit' (Peatfield 1999: 67 and see Kristiansen 2002). Yet this story of violence is one which is central to their development, their very *raison d'être*, and it is one that is essential to explore as it is inextricably linked to any other roles they may have played in society.

In this paper, I will not be writing about aspects of their non-martial or socio-symbolic roles, this has been the subject of many excellent studies, and would be beyond the scope of this paper (see for example Bradley, 1990, 2005; Ramsey, 1989, 1995; Barber, 2003; Fontijn, 2005). I will write of just one story, one facet of their social role that their extant material remains gives us close insight into, one that the artefacts themselves bear physical testimony to through their scars and ruptures. That is the question of how were these weapons wielded in the hands of those ancient warriors who desired, perhaps even coveted, them so much?

The beginnings of this human story lie in the Early Bronze Age of Ireland, where we have clear evidence for the use of weapons of interpersonal combat (see O'Flaherty, this volume). It was during the Middle Bronze Age that weapons specifically designed for killing human beings began to *dominate* the material record of metalwork. Prior to this epoch, save the 'halberd', the weapons used in warfare were those which people were familiar with from hunting – weapons with which there was a more direct translation in the *act* of killing from animals to men. With weapons such as Middle Bronze Age swords, the proximity and sensual experience of killing was dramatically altered, and the social context of killing can also be seen to shift accordingly The directness of the physical and emotional experience of the act of killing is accentuated by using purpose built tools (see Molloy and Grossman, this volume).

MIDDLE BRONZE AGE SWORDS AND DAGGERS

From the tiny, simple double-edged knives of the beginning of the Bronze Age, a wide variety of forms evolved. Some of these were adapted further by the sixteenth century BC, with the lengthening of the blade beyond what could be comfortably be called a dagger (see Burgess and Gerloff 1981 and Ramsey 1989, 1995). The sword in its most archaic, even embryonic form, had arrived.

In archaeological literature spanning back well over a century, these weapons have been variously called daggers, dirks and rapiers with criteria for differentiation between these based largely on the length of any given weapon. As will be discussed below, these are light and thin weapons with a very wide variety in metric traits. They are characteristic of the Middle Bronze Age in both Ireland and Britain and have broad similarities with other continental pedigrees (Burgess and Gerloff 1981). As may be clear to some readers, the terms we use for these early weapons – dirks and rapiers in particular – are directly borrowed from later Renaissance nomenclature.

These terms are well known to prehistorians and are often acknowledged as being problematic, but it has to be stressed emphatically at this point that they confuse further an already difficult period of human history, especially for scholars of weapons from other periods. This is because they inappropriately imply very specific modes and contexts of use which are not based on a critical understanding of their forms and functions but on the recycling of antiquarian thinking of the nineteenth century – a cumulative sequence of errors that this paper will seek to redress. As difficult a path as it may be to follow for the prehistorian, it will be argued that we should abandon these borrowed robes in favour of the less functionally-loaded terms of Middle or Late Bronze Age swords and daggers, as will be discussed presently.

MECHANICAL STRUCTURE OF THESE EARLY SWORDS

It has been widely argued that these weapons were comparatively unserviceable and inadequate for interpersonal combat, most especially in the context of a multi-opponent melee. They are considered to have been used for stabbing actions alone and not to have been suitable for making attacks using the blade's edges to cut (Ramsey 1995: 59; Waddell, 2000: 185, Burgess and Gerloff 1981, Barber 2003: 147, Harding 2000: 277, Osgood 1998: 13). However, it will be argued that the design of the weapons themselves, the results of experimental test cutting with accurate replicas along with the actual damage evident on the surviving weapons all combine to give a very different picture. It will be demonstrated that they were versatile and functional weapons for use on the field of battle, and that they were most certainly not objects of purely ritual significance or limited to a single specific context of martial use.

One primary factor behind the understanding that Middle Bronze Age swords were used primarily for thrusting is the apparently weak hilting mechanism utilised (Osgood 1998: 13). The hilt plate at the base of the blade tapers from the shoulders back towards the end of the butt with a very noticeable angle (typically moving from c.5-6mm thickness at the shoulders to just 0.8-1.8mm at the end), and rivet holes were pierced through this area (usually numbering two, but there are some variations). This system of hilting the blade meant that the rivets passed through the thinnest part of the blade – a factor which has sometimes been considered to be a design flaw. While a simple thickening of this area would have made it stronger and would have been perfectly possible technologically speaking, this alteration

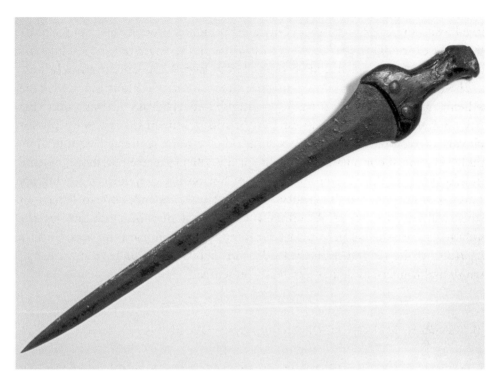

25 Middle Bronze Age sword with organic hilt from Shower, Co. Tipperary. *Courtesy of the National Museum of Ireland*

was only undertaken in the final years of the many centuries these weapons were in use. We must consider then why this taper and thin section were retained for so many centuries when they were less robust than was technologically possible.

The hilts on the vast majority of these weapons were manufactured from organic materials. These fully enclosed the butt portion of the blade – that is they covered the base (10-30mm of it), part of the two faces, and the two sides of the butt. Organic materials such as horn, antler, hardwood or bone are naturally springy and provide excellent grip when in compression. Given the wedge shape to the butt of these weapons (terminating in that very thin section noted above), we can begin to see a purpose to this design when it comes to the practicalities of establishing a firm hilting mechanism. A cut slightly narrower than the shoulder thickness of the butt of the blade would have been cut into base of the handle. This would have been wide enough that the thin base could fit in easily, thus the graduating expansion of the butt would have allowed the bronze blade to be wedged firmly into this slit in the handle. Thus a firm friction grip is formed which may have been augmented by glues or resins. This, it would appear, is the primary mechanical bond between blade and hilt, and the rivets are in fact a secondary or auxiliary element. The function of the rivets is to pinch the sides of the handle tight around the blade and to *maintain* this tightness, hence their frequently large diameter of 7mm+. They would also serve to minimise any lateral movement which would weaken the friction bond. Further supporting evidence for this might be seen in the metal hilted dagger from Belleek (Burgess and Gerloff 1981, No. 706), which clearly had an organic element wedged between the outer metal hilt and the butt of the blade contained within. There are examples where a sliver of metal survives in place after partially breaking free when being drilled (Molloy 2006), indicating that some (if not all) of these weapons had the rivet holes drilled when the hilt was already in place. We should also note that only about one in six ancient pieces displays significant damage to the hilting system, a percentage not that far removed from the swords of the Late Bronze Age in Ireland (see Eogan 1965 and Molloy 2006).

MECHANICS OF USE

These weapons tended to be slightly blade heavy, but given that the vast majority would have weighed below 500g even when hilted (see Molloy 2006), this does not create significant problems either for controlling the weapons or risking injury to the wrists. As noted above, the blades frequently have distinct cutting edges present as well as a sharp point, and edges only occur on a sword for two reasons:

- To inflict a wound on an opponent through a cutting or slicing motion using the blade's edge only.
- To assist in the penetration and removal of the point in a stabbing action as they cut as the blade enters (thus increasing the size of the wound) making this attack more effective, and they also allow easier withdrawal of the blade from the flesh.

For this latter action the area near to the point need only be sharp, although on weapons examined by the author the sharpness most frequently extended throughout the entire blade. For a sword, there are a number of basic elements common to most forms, and Amberger (1998: 94) has detailed three ways in which an edged-weapon can be used to cut flesh and/ or bone:

1 Penetration by incision and percussion
2 Penetration by incision and laceration
3 Percussion

Swords of the Middle Bronze Age are characterised by the second of these cutting process, incising and lacerating, or more colloquially 'slashing' – i.e. the edge slices the flesh as it passes along it. The blade needs to be drawn along the target in a linear action allowing the sharpness of the blade to cut; the longer the draw, the deeper the cut. While percussion is not the primary force brought to bear, the blade is 'whipped' at the target to slash-impact and in the process the blade is drawn along the target. The slicing and impact are therefore not performed as two separate actions initially, but the draw of the blade with pressure from the arm may continue briefly after the initial impact force has dissipated. This is generally referred to as a 'draw-cut' or a 'pull-cut'. More shallow cuts can be made by the edges in this manner as the blade is thrust forward or retracted on a thrust or cut. The role of thrusting with these, as with most swords (see Clements, this volume), would have been integral to their intended mode of use, and indeed some like the aforementioned 'Lissane rapier' may have been designed with this as the primary mode of intended attack. However, most weapons were not restricted to either one or the other of these modes of attack. The shorter swords and daggers in this broad class would have been less effective at cutting than the examples of around 400mm+ in length (when hilted), given that the blade would not have adequate draw length along the target. This is not to say that they were completely ineffective in this regard, because the edges could still inflict severe cuts to areas of exposed flesh when used for short, swift cutting attacks.

Many of these strikes are not likely to have been fatal immediately, the main goal would be to slice muscles, tendons or arteries seeking to debilitate rather than sever a limb clean off (see below). This is important because with the weight of the swords of the Middle Bronze Age, it would be not be possible to engage in more heavy percussive cuts for two main reasons. Firstly, these weapons are extremely fast, being capable of easily making two cuts in a single second when power is applied from the elbow (and shoulder to a limited degree). If the blade was to be drawn further back to make a blow incorporating shoulder and upper body strength, this would dramatically slow down the speed of attack, thus compromising one's own guard to too high a degree. This leads into the second reason for the use of light percussive force, and that is that these weapons were too light to actually provide a heavy force of impact. If the blade is used in a more open arc using the upper-body, the *effective* force of impact is only marginally increased as the light weight will not particularly aid in increasing power and velocity.

The relatively short length of these weapons would mean that a user would have to be relatively close to an opponent to land such a strike. Therefore, a heavy blow would not provide a significant strategic advantage, would not inflict a much more effective strike even if landed and would significantly increase risk of injury to the user. Furthermore, while the hilting device was perfectly efficient for the manner of use discussed and determined through experimentation (see below), clumsy overbearing strikes dramatically increase the risk of damage. The comparatively light force applied in the typical use of these weapons would not have represented a major risk to the structural integrity of the weapon. Of course some weapons did fail and no doubt the user suffered the consequences, but this is simply the price of warfare, a price still paid today when hi-tech weapons fail to perform or malfunction.

For these early weapons, sword-on-sword clash would not have been in the form of the grand theatrical blows of Hollywood, but would have involved far more subtle control of the weapon, and importantly of the opponent's weapon. Instead of heavy strikes and dead-blocks being made in attacks, one would rather envisage draw-cuts being made alongside lethal thrusts. Defences would have been of a more deflective nature through parries, stepping in to stifle blows or simply avoidance of strikes. Blades are redirected through manipulation rather than brute force and would more usually be slid along each other in contact situations rather than struck squarely against one another. The extent of edge damage on the Irish weapons examined by the author corroborates this – while edge damage is present on a great many pieces, it is typically quite light and infrequently distributed. When the author tested replica bronze swords against each other, even light edge-on-edge impact resulted in clear damage to the weapons on each and every strike (Molloy 2006).

TESTING MIDDLE BRONZE AGE SWORDS

Two replica Middle Bronze Age swords were used to conduct a series of tests to determine the efficacy and likely modes of use. These tests involved using the swords against straw test-cutting pieces, against replica body armours (*colour plate 12*) and the body of a recently slaughtered pig at the Ashtown Food Centre in Dublin.[2]

The pigs for test-cutting were two nine-month old females. They were suspended by the hind legs and the forelegs were held in tension by bungee cords in a horizontal position roughly at my elbow height (thus intended to represent cuts to the forearm of a human opponent). The cutting took place within half an hour of the slaughter to ensure that rigour mortis did not unduly influence the texture of the flesh and that the bones were also in suitable condition (they begin to harden soon after death).

The reason for inducing tension in the limbs was to best simulate the resistance to movement one would expect with a living subject. The cuts were thus made to the inside portion of the leg, primarily in the area of the lower leg and upper trotter. Due to the necessities of the facility being used, the pigs had been eviscerated prior to testing, and this would have had an effect on the thrusting test aspect of this project. However, the rib cage is the most difficult part to

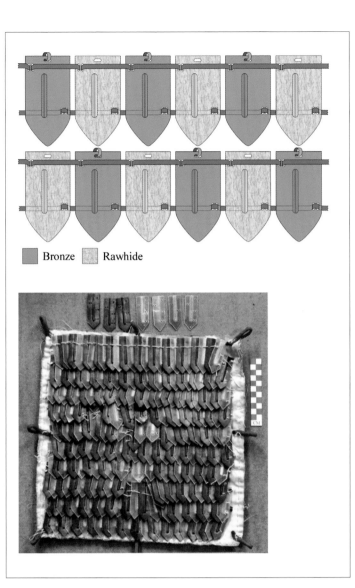

Bronze ▢ Rawhide

Left: 1 The manner of attaching scale armour to an organic backing (above) and reconstruction of this armour. *Manufactured by T. Hulit*

Below: 2 Illustration of the lacing pattern used on replica scale armour

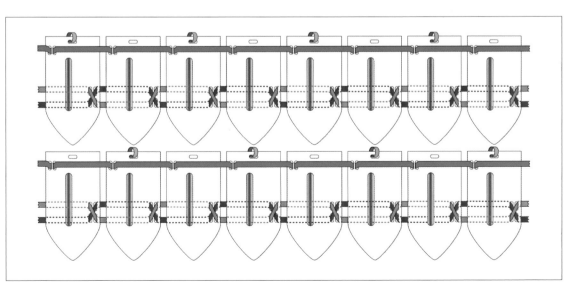

Above: 3 Replica armour made from alternating rows of rawhide and bronze scales

Left: 4 Replica armour attached to martial arts punch bag

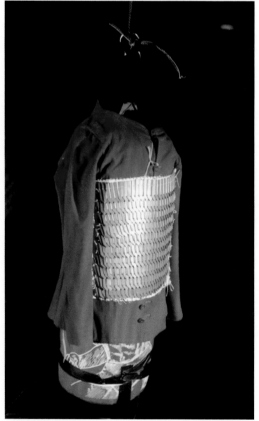

Opposite above: 5 Target set up for test shooting in Egypt with mudbrick wall behind

Opposite below: 6 Replica rawhide scale armour

7 Shooting the bow and arrow from a moving chariot

8 Downward thrust with a spear to attack the legs of an opponent

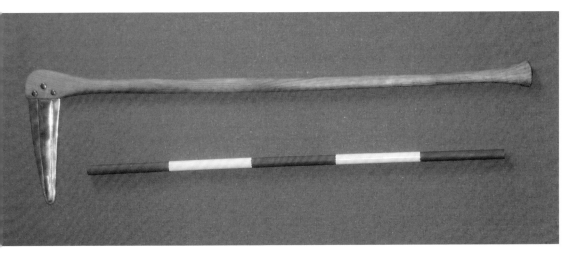

Above: 9 The replica halberd

Below left: 10 Halberd experiment: preparing for a short swift blow to a sheep's head on the ground. Carried out under strict conditions at ICM Camolin

Below right: 11 Halberd experiment: penetrating a sheep's head with the replica halberd

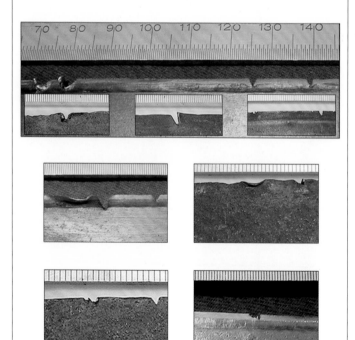

Above: 12 Straw test cutting mat, baked and waxed leather armour section and linen soaked in animal hide glue armour section

Left: 13 Comparison of damage on replica and ancient swords (the golden coloured pieces are replicas, the brown pieces are ancient swords):
Above: Burred notches and nicks from edge–on–edge impacts
Middle: Buckled edge of replica and ancient sword from impact on bone
Below: Damage to sword edge caused by impact on the edge of an unrolled copper shield edge.
All images of prehistoric sword edges reproduced courtesy of the National Museum of Ireland

Above left: 14 Persian shield made of cane and hide. On the photograph, the front side is shown. The fixing is loose so that the elasticity of the shield construction (which will take a part of an arrow's impulse when being hit) can still "work". The canes are approximately 0.7cm thick

Above right: 15 Penetration depth of arrows with bodkin-type of iron arrowheads, shot from bow no.2 of Scythian-type. The photograph shows the inner side to demonstrate the penetration depths of the arrows

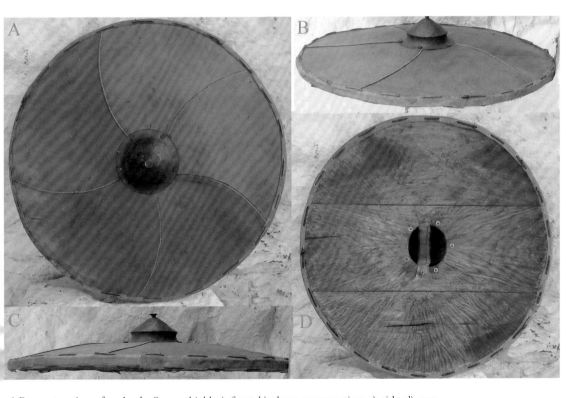

16 Reconstruction of an Anglo-Saxon shield: a). front, b). three-quarters view, c). side, d). rear

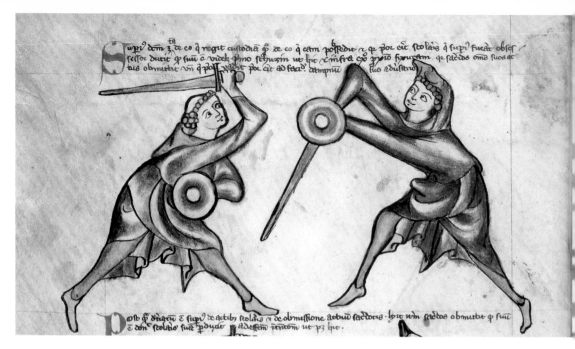

18 Dusack technique from Mair. *Österreichische Nationalbibliothek, Vienna, Cod. Vindob. 10825, fol. 101r*

penetrate with a bladed weapon and while penetration of the soft internal organs would have affected the depth of penetration by the swords, it would certainly not have increased the resistance to a degree which would influence the validity of the exercise. All test cuts were performed by the author and the proceedings were recorded by video camera and digital still cameras.

The test-cutting mats used are a traditional Japanese medium for practicing with swords, and are prepared by soaking them in water for three days, drying for a further day and then they are rolled tightly together and bound. This broadly represents the resistance of flesh to cutting with a sword, as corroborated when compared to efficacy against the pig flesh.

The armours tested against were a piece of baked and waxed leather, a piece consisting of ten layers of linen soaked in animal hide glue and a piece of 1.5mm gilding metal (a copper alloy similar to bronze sheet). These were attached to a test dummy which was fixed on top of a work bench, thus allowing a degree of movement so that the blades were not striking a completely dead target.

A replica Group IV dagger/short sword (after Burgess and Gerloff 1981) supplied by Andrew Walpole and a Group II sword provided by Neil Burridge of Bronze Age Craft were used for the testing. The former was hilted in deer antler, and when hilted measured 410mm (345mm unhilted) and weighed 250g. The edges had a thin depth before swelling out to form the central thickening or midrib, thus although sharpened, they only had a thin maximum cut-depth before cutting was impeded by the expanding angle of this central area. The latter was initially hafted using pine and subsequently with antler by the author, and was 505mm long (435mm unhilted) and weighed 355g. The edges were hardened on this latter weapon by hammering along a line from 5mm from the edge down to the edge itself, and the weapon was then sharpened (the hardening technique is discussed further below).

When using the Group IV sword for cutting against the test mats, it was only capable of cutting one or two layers, which would constitute the outer skin on living tissue. This assessment was borne out when test cutting on the pig cadavers, with the blade easily cutting the skin, but having no significant impact on the underlying muscle tissue. When the blade was used for thrusting at the chest of the animal, it easily passed through the rib cage at right angles to the ribs (hence having to cut the bone in order to pass between ribs). Likewise, when tested against armour, this weapon could easily penetrate both the hardened leather and linen pieces when thrusting, but was incapable of penetrating the copper alloy. It was clear that this short robust piece was most suited to stabbing, either by linear or arced thrusting. Cutting, while possible, would have only created superficial wounds to areas such as the face, neck and forearms.

The Group II weapon, despite being very thin in its cross-section (4mm), was considerably more versatile. Initial test-cutting on the mats resulted in the pine hilt breaking along the wood-grain, but when hafted using deer antler, there were no further problems. Indeed, neither weapon tested had any visible mechanical problems with the hilting mechanism despite being used very roughly during testing in order to push the weapons to their functional limits.

When tested against the mats, this blade was capable of cutting seven layers of mat when struck with force commensurate to its weight and drawn along the target simultaneously. Cutting on a forward thrust, it was capable of inflicting superficial damage of two or three layers. As with the above weapon, these levels of damage were born out when testing against the pig. Cuts to the middle area of the ulna, where the flesh was in the region of 30-40mm thickness, proved very effective. The blade was able to slice to the bone, cutting cleanly and easily through the flesh, and on one test cut it sliced shallowly into the bone itself. If this was compared to attack against a human target such as the forearm, the cut would serve to slice through muscle, sinew and tendons potentially disabling a limb or at the very least dramatically impeding its efficient use. This testing evidence clearly shows that these weapons were, mechanically, able to stand up to a cutting attack when correctly executed in accordance with their mechanical properties, and that such strikes could cause serious injury.

As with all of the swords tested during this program of research, the Group II sword was incapable of cutting through any of the armours set around the test dummy's chest area. For thrusting attacks, the weapon was very efficient, capable of penetrating the pig's rib cage with ease, and passed through the armour with little problem. It was noted however, that when it passed through the armour and hit the tougher material behind, the weapon sustained a slight bend, indicating that thrusting attacks could potentially also damage these weapons. This is borne out by repaired bends and surviving torsional warps on a number of ancient pieces examined in the National Museum of Ireland, Dublin.

EVIDENCE OF USE ON ANCIENT PIECES

An examination of the Middle Bronze Age swords from Ireland has proved that many weapons from all four classes (see Burgess and Gerloff 1981), have damage along their edges that were formed by force of impact with another sharp object of similar hardness and edge angle – other weapons being the most likely suspects (Molloy 2006). York's examination of a sample of swords from the Thames basin has proved that similar damage is to be found on the majority of British Middle Bronze Age swords from this area and chronological setting (York 2002: 85). For the Irish material examined by the author, it was rare to find weapons exhibiting very deep cuts or impacts to the blade edges, although there was a wide variety in the forms of damage which were found. The most frequent form of damage, found on over half of the weapons examined, was light, sharp-angled nicks caused by impact off another blade. The depth of these nicks typically indicated that the impact had not been of great force as the damage was in essence superficial. Some blades were completely cut through and broken, but the general lack of severe damage to other areas of the blade may indicate that this was either deliberate destruction of the weapon or else due to casting flaws and/or stress induced weaknesses caused during use. Significantly, there was no damage apparent to the flats of any of the blades, an area of the blade advocated for parrying and blocking in later literature (see Clements 1998 and this volume). What emerged as the general pattern, however, is that most weapons had *some* evidence of combat use, but that this evidence was rarely dramatic and was indicative of a mode of use whereby the weapons did not receive repeated forceful blade-on-blade impact.

In the case of Middle Bronze Age swords and daggers, we have weapons that have unambiguous evidence of use in combat against similar weapons, attested by the surviving damage on the weaponry. The swords had a firm and functional hilting arrangement (given their typically light weight and manner of use), two cutting edges (in many cases hardened and sharpened), a cross-section that allows the blade's edge to slice but not cleave and a point with a broad enough angle to resist breakage. The case for their effective use in combat is truly compelling.

THE USE OF MIDDLE BRONZE AGE SWORDS

We should therefore look to how these weapons *could* be used in combat, in order to see their potential effectiveness. If they were used for cutting in the manner described above we can see that hard blade-on-blade impact trauma was not to be expected, and heavy, lateral jarring of the blade-hilt bond would not be likely. Indeed, a heavy impact manner of fighting with bladed weapons had entirely no precedent in this period – the robust swords of the Later Bronze Age were still many, many generations away.

The recent dating of the Kilmahamogue shield former (Hedges *et al.*, 1991) indicates the high probability that leather shields (*26*) were used in conjunction with these weapons (as one might suspect), and consequently, defensive moves would not always require blade-on-blade contact, as this could be performed by the shields. It is certain that the warriors that used these swords in life or death contexts would have been well aware of the strengths and weaknesses of their weapons, and would have been loathe to risk using them in a manner which could leave them unarmed and at the mercy of a foe.

26 The leather shield from Clonbrin, Co. Longford. *Courtesy of the National Museum of Ireland*

Middle Bronze Age swords need not necessarily have been the primary weapon of choice on the battlefield, as there were a wide variety of spears in contemporary use, some of which are better considered as pole-arms (requiring two-handed use). While it is possible that swords were auxiliary weapons which were mainly used after the loss of a spear in combat, it is nonetheless clear that these weapons were *suitable* for use on the field of battle. The edges of the blades were capable of cutting, but in the vast majority of cases they would have been useless for cleaving – their weight and cross-section (raised central area/midribs) would severely hinder deep cutting of the edge and the repeated stress such blows would place on the hilt could prove detrimental to their integrity. The points were always sharp, typically 17-20°, and capable of penetrating flesh. If the weapon has these qualities and limitations, the manner in which it was used can be broadly interpreted as follows:

- Strikes come from the elbow and shoulder, with the wrist controlling finer movement, especially slicing cuts. The strength and reach of the blade were not sufficient for strikes involving the whole upper body and/or waist.
- Draw cuts would be the intended form of edge-attack, these are executed by slicing the blade along the target either on delivery or more likely on recovery

of a stroke (i.e. pulling as opposed to pushing the blade along the flesh). This would allow the blade to 'bite' and cut without excessively shocking the structure through force of impact.

- Thrusts would also have to take into account the mechanical properties of the weapon – attacks against hard targets such as the cranium or sternum may have been avoided. The cutting edges would facilitate the withdrawal of the blade from areas of soft tissue such as the abdomen or neck as they assist in cutting the point free on withdrawal.

It may appear quite disturbing to discuss inflicting such grievous and agonising harm on another human being, but this is what these artefacts were designed for, and how they must be understood. Lacerations to the soft tissue of the arms and legs are not merely an inconvenience to a person or the cause of nasty scarring for future memory – it is possible to cut tendons and muscles, effectively disabling a limb without physically cleaving it from the body. A stabbing attack to the chest would have to penetrate the bone, sinew and cartilage of the breast palate, and this could either break or trap a light weapon, without killing an opponent. For group combat, the most suitable stabbing attacks are to the abdomen, groin, foot, forearm, face (around the sinuses and eyes where the skull is weakest) and the neck.

A duelling stance such as that found in modern sports fencing would be unlikely when using these weapons; while fighters in lethal combat must minimise their potential target area, they still have to maximise their own striking ability. A more frontal stance is typically required to enable the use of both hands and the leading foot for offence and defence. Footwork in the Bronze Age must have been as important as it was in any other period (Wagner & Hand, 2003), as control of the distance between a fighter and his opponent is paramount in trying to control a fight to one's own advantage. The leading foot therefore should be on the same side as the leading arm, whether this is moving forward or backwards, shield or sword to the fore. With the light shields and comparatively short reach of the swords of the Middle Bronze Age, it is likely that footwork was swift and the pace of combat must have been equally quick.

Our knowledge of the demographics and regularity of Bronze Age warfare are negligible, but based on the settlement evidence, in the Middle Bronze Age we should not envisage large bodies of men numbering in the thousands regularly congregating for combat. On these grounds, one could argue that warfare was not undertaken by highly drilled infantry fighting in close formations. However, this need not be taken to imply fighting was in the form of unruly or disorganised skirmishing. We should envisage perhaps a loose system of organisation broadly analogous to Viking or Anglo-Saxon warfare.[3] While the independent prowess of the elite warrior was no doubt of significant importance on the field of battle, the cohesion of a battle line and mutual co-operation of warriors is fundamental to combat using hand-to-hand or shock weaponry. The wooden training swords (*27*) from Ireland[4] can be seen as evidence that prehistoric warriors were very much concerned with training and development of their weapon skills.

On the battlefields of the Middle Bronze Age one may have expected to find warriors wielding lighter throwing-spears, single-handed spears (probably used in conjunction with a shield), heavy two-handed spears, light swords and daggers, short-hafted large spearheads (*28*), bows and arrows and perhaps even slings. Far from representing a massively random assortment of potential weapons, this variety indicates a rich martial tradition with a wide skills base in the effective use of combat weaponry. One only has to think of the later mythological hero Cuchulainn in the epic Tain Bo Cuailgne, making use of countless different forms of spear, shield and sword as he defends Ulster against the many champions of Medb and Ailill.

THE LATE BRONZE AGE

A common belief about warfare in the Late Bronze Age is that the arrival of the leaf-shaped sword brought widespread changes in the conduct of warfare. The setting for its arrival therefore needs brief clarification before we can enter into a discussion about the impact and the changes in combat techniques that can be identified in relation to this.

A problem we face is that there has frequently been a simple belief in the literature that because the new form of sword was heavier and more robust than its predecessors, it was inherently superior. Such a pseudo-Darwinian evolution of edged-weaponry is, however, most difficult to maintain (See Clements, this volume and also Hamilakis 2002: 11). A skilled swordsman in any period, with a sword of inferior quality, is going to have a distinct strategic advantage over an unskilled swordsman wielding a superbly crafted one. It is plainly not realistic to simplify the transition from Middle to Late Bronze Age swords as a simple replacement of a poor design with a 'better' one, as will be discussed presently.

If we are to discard these unhappy base dualities of 'better' and 'worse' in the transition from one artefact form to another, then we will need to investigate how functional attributes relate to broader traditions of use (Dobres 2000, de Marrais 2004). This is especially the case when we speak of objects with such a straightforward nature as swords. The transitional period from Middle to Late Bronze Age swords is likely to have lasted decades, when we take in the entirety of the British Isles, and it would certainly have been a socially dynamic process rather than some form of 'pseudo-event' based change.

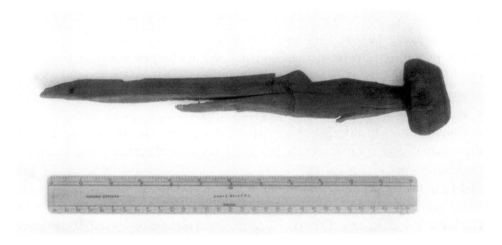

Above: 27 The Late Bronze Age wooden sword from Cappagh, Co. Kerry. *Courtesy of the National Museum of Ireland*

Right: 28 Middle Bronze Age Irish warrior with V-notch leather shield and Basal-Looped spearhead set on a short shaft. *Original illustration by Jorrit Kelder*

If we consider that blade-on-blade contact was not frequently practiced (see Molloy 2006, and below) and that shields and spears were also fundamentally important aspects of the warrior's panoply, then we need to see the changes in artefact form as part of a socio-martial as well as technological shift. The new sword's net effect on the overall conduct of warfare and related balances of power in this transitional period would be likely to have been piece-meal and lacked any immediacy. Warriors who had grown up with the martial art traditions of the older weapons need not have openly embraced the new technology and the changes it implied in modes of swordsmanship. This may have been a contributory factor to the differential pace of change in different regions of the islands. In saying this, we should also be very much aware that the existing combat traditions conversely represented a ready environment for the *reception* of the new tradition of leaf-shaped swords, when other social factors were favourable.

What is clear in any case is that there is no evidence for upheavals or broader social changes associated with the adoption of this new design.[6] While Burgess and Gerloff state boldly that the change from Middle to Late Bronze Age swords 'points inexorably in one direction: the collapse of a long established social order' (Burgess and Gerloff 1981: 113), this is clearly placing too much emphasis on the artefacts as significant agents inculcating social change. The changes which we detect in the material record may appear to have a linear inevitability moving from one form to another, but it is essential to see these changes in terms of evolving traditions of martial arts praxis and not simply the casting away of the 'old' in favour of the 'new'. This involved existing martial traditions developing responses to the new style of artefact, and modifying their combat techniques accordingly.

SO WHAT WAS SO NEW ABOUT THE LATE BRONZE AGE SWORDS?

Having set forth some of the problems associated with the nature of this transition, we can begin to analyse the character of these new weapons and discuss aspects of the changes which they represented in swordsmanship and indeed combat as a whole. A major difference with these new swords was that the tang of the weapon was integral to the handle – that is, it passed the entire way through the grip of the fist and emerged at the base of the hand. This meant that the structural integrity of the joint between blade and handle was more secure than in the previous tradition discussed above. This in turn allowed for the manufacture of heavier weapons which affected the balance and control of the weapon. This was because the full-tang not only altered the harmonics and geometry of the whole weapon but also changed the actual grip used on the hilt itself.

The most notable change, however, with these new swords was the distinct leaf-shaped blade which swelled gently out from the hilt reaching its maximum width approximately two-thirds the way from hilt to tip with a gently convex shape. There was typically a slight but notable distal taper on these weapons, with the shoulder being the thickest part and the area of the maximum width also being the thinnest area of the cross-section (save towards the point itself). The blades were typically heavier than the average Middle Bronze Age weapon, ranging roughly from 400-650g for the most part, but with occasional pieces weighing up to and over a kilogram (Eogan 1965, Molloy 2006). While many Middle Bronze Age weapons were above 400g in weight, the majority fell below this mark.

The Ballintober sword was one the earliest of the truly native forms of Late Bronze Age sword, being manufactured solely in Ireland and (primarily southern) Britain.[7] These swords were hilted in the Middle Bronze Age tradition of fitting a tang into a one-piece handle, possibly relating also to the Rosnoen swords being imported from the Continent to Southern Britain. After the initial transitional phase of introduction, the new form of weapon saw insular adaptation in the form of the Wilburton and Ewart Park (Eogan Class 4) swords. These weapons constitute an eclectic mix of sizes and weights, bound together by basic morphological, more than purely functional, traits. Within this class we find weapons ranging from 400mm long weighing in the region of 300g to weapons over 650mm long weighing three times as much. Given their long and quite heavy proportions, the replica weapons tested in my research represented functionality at the higher end of the mechanical scale, as will be discussed below.

TESTING

A replica Irish Class 4 sword from Bronze Age Foundry and a replica Ewart Park sword from Bronze Age Craft were tested in the same manner as the Middle Bronze Age swords discussed above. The former sword weighed 750g and was 550mm in length, it had a wide edge angle and was sharpened but not work hardened. The second sword weighed 845g and measured 671mm, and was work hardened with Neil Burridge of Bronze Age Craft using a specifically designed device manufactured from mild steel.[8] The reason for testing these larger blades is that they were representative of blade weights and forms found on most Classes of Late Bronze Age sword (excluding the intrusive Gundlingen sword tradition), thus being the most representative for these limited experiments.

When the Irish Class 4 sword was tested, it was capable of cutting with ease to a depth of 10 layers on the test-cutting mats. This weapon was used to cut near to the shoulder joint of the pig where there was little thickness of flesh and bone was reached almost immediately after breaking the skin. It was capable of cutting into the ulna (*c.*5mm) but not cleaving it, although the broad edge angle mitigated against this weapon cutting deep into bone as it had to separate this hard substance as it cut. When tested on the flesh of the foreleg, the weapon cut *c.*30mm of flesh (down to the bone and scoring the surface of it).

This weapon could easily stab through the organic armours tested, but was incapable of *cutting* through any of them. Its high length to weight ratio would have meant that percussive blows, although not cutting armour, would have concentrated significant force in a small area potentially damaging underlying tissue.

In test cutting with the replica Ewart Park sword from Bronze Age Craft, striking with the blade 'dead' in an axe like manner dented the test mats but did not cut them, so it may have been possible to injure bones and tissue against bare flesh if used in this manner. However, when the sword was used with the elbow leading the cut and drawing the blade along the mats it cut between 12 and 14 layers, clearly indicating the superior efficacy of this mode of use. Similarly, when tested on the pig cadaver, it cut cleanly through the flesh and into the surface of the bone in the lower foreleg section with thicker flesh and cut through many of the smaller foot bones/metacarpals.

A cut to the upper foreleg cut the flesh and severed through the ulna (*c.*25x35mm thickness) cutting further flesh and making a shallow cut to the radius. The edge of the blade which hit the bone (on initial impact) was buckled on two occasions, providing clear evidence that attacks to even an unarmoured body can result in damage to the weapon. This may have been influenced by my own inexperience at cutting flesh and bone, especially the rate of drawing the blade, as part of the cut may be altered so as to not cause this damage.

For thrusts, the steady increase in the width of the blade mitigated against its penetrative power, but it was still capable of penetrating over half-way across the pig's chest, a depth of over 180mm, just short of the maximum blade width, which would of course be fatal. When tested against the body armours, it was capable of scoring the leather and linen deeply, but with several attempts on each, it could not cut through them. In the case of the leather armour, it 'dented' on impact resulting in the transferral of energy from the weapon to a smaller area of the target, potentially injuring bones and muscle on a living opponent. It was possible to thrust through the leather and linen armours relatively easily, indicating that the point angle was well suited to penetrating both flesh and armour. As with all of the other weapons tested, this made no appreciable impact at all on the copper alloy armour. It should be noted that the body armour was simulating that of the torso, and if cuts were made to a smaller target such as the forearm, it is more likely that the swords would cut through at least partially.

When used with the elbow leading an attack, as opposed to wider arc cuts made from the shoulder, the blade strikes at a slightly acute angle to the target (i.e. not perpendicularly along its length), and is consequently drawn across the surface cutting though incision and percussion. This raises the point as to the purpose of the swelling or leaf-shape of the blade, which is a characteristic feature of the vast majority of Late Bronze Age swords in Ireland and Britain (the Carp's tongue swords of Britain being a notable exception). It has been argued that this swelling was to provide extra weight for an 'axe-like swing' (Osgood 1998: 13). However, the majority of blades are at their *minimum* thickness here, getting progressively thicker as they progress back towards the hilt, thus creating a distinct distal taper. It is highly unlikely therefore that the increase in width was simply to incur an increase in weight.

I have argued elsewhere (Molloy 2004, 2006) that it is the actual curve of the blade which was the important feature, as it allows the blade to bite deeper as it is pulled along a surface on impact, operating in much the same fashion as a curved sabre blade. This broadening of the blade also serves the function of providing better structural integrity at the centre of percussion than a straight edged blade of similar length, by reducing flexibility while retaining a thin blade cross-section. This allows a low cross-sectional profile ideal for cutting living flesh; this is a highly beneficial feature as it produces less friction through separation when cutting thus increasing the efficacy of a cut. The slight difference in edge angle between the two replicas tested had a significant impact on their efficacy, with the thinner edged (and bevelled) Ewart Park sword proving better at cutting than the Irish Class 4 sword.

EVIDENCE FOR USE

The author has conducted extensive analysis of all classes of Bronze Age weaponry from Ireland, and it is clear that the majority of weapon types in that country saw active use in combat. The edge damage on the swords is useful initially for indicating if weapons had been used in combat, but it can also be helpful in telling us the *manner* in which they were used (*colour plate 13*).

Experimental combat using the above replicas and another range of swords (further Irish examples and Aegean Bronze Age forms) was conducted to compare the damage to that on ancient pieces (Molloy 2006). The vast majority of damage on ancient swords which had not been deliberately 'killed' (see Bridgford 1997) was in the form of superficial nicking. It was immediately evident that this damage was rarely from blows struck with significant force, and indeed represented forms of damage inflicted on the replica swords when well executed parries were undertaken. Damage from dead or static blocks was extremely rare, indicating that these were actively avoided in the style of swordsmanship practiced. As with the Middle Bronze Age swords there was little or no evidence surviving for blocking or parrying using the flat of the blade as opposed to the blade edges. Some of the damage found on the ancient swords, interestingly, had correlates on the replica swords from damage inflicted when striking through the pig flesh and impacting on the bone, and also from striking the unrolled edge of a metal shield.

It is important to note that the frequently superficial nature of the damage indicates an acute awareness of the material limits of the weaponry on the part of the ancient warriors who used them in combat. Striking the edge of one sword on another rapidly deteriorates the edges and risks causing failure of the sword itself. The number of swords with broken tangs but little edge damage may further indicate that these were being struck off shields more frequently than other bladed weapons, as in this context much of the energy from the blow is transferred back (with leverage) to the area in the centre of the hand, exactly where a great many swords have failed (see Eogan 1965; Colquhoun and Burgess 1988; O'Faolain and Northover 1998).

The damage therefore tells us that many of the extant pieces saw active combat, but perhaps more importantly, that they were used in a manner which indicates a very clear knowledge of effective swordsmanship. While the term 'martial art' is often taken to indicate Asian fighting styles, in its more direct meaning as a definable system of combat passed on by masters to students, we can see that at least a loose system of martial arts was in effect in the Bronze Age of north-western Europe.

MODE OF USE

The grip used when handling these Late Bronze Age swords can either be four fingers on the handle, or else the index finger can be wrapped around the ricasso, aligning the trajectory of the blade's edge with the natural trajectory of the arm. The U-shaped depression in the hilt plates at the shoulders created a comfortable place to locate the thumb, as it fits into the curvature here and enhances control of the sword. When using this weapon, primary control and power comes from the shoulder, with the elbow slightly bent and generally 'leading' the blow with the point of the elbow moving on roughly the same trajectory as the blade edge. This allows the blade to be deployed in quite rapid tight-arced cuts, comfortably cutting as many as three times in two seconds with a sword of over 800g weight.

The wrist could also be 'broken'[9] to allow for rapid changes of direction of the blade. However, if a full handle grip was used, the shoulder, upper body and waist could all be employed in making a strike, thus increasing power and range but decreasing the rapidity of directional changes. The trade-off here clearly being an increase in combat space and force of attack (thus distance from the enemy) against control and speed of recovery (increasingly important with the proximity of an enemy's weapon).

It should be noted that while we group these weapons according to typological classes, the manner of use of weapons within each class varies dramatically in accordance with the varying weights and lengths. A 400g weapon will clearly have different combat considerations to an 800g weapon with a blade of nearly double its length. We must therefore remain cautiously aware of the role of the personal preferences of ancient warriors in the design of the various weapons we analyse today.

As with the Middle Bronze Age swords, the evidence strongly indicates that edge-on-edge contact was avoided in the style of swordsmanship practiced in the Late Bronze Age. If they were used in group combat, this indicates that shields were used in conjunction with swords as a necessary defensive weapon, as one might indeed expect given the simplicity of the concept. Unfortunately comparatively few shields survive from the Late Bronze Age in the British Isles, but the few we do have indicate a marked variety in both size and materials used. Examples of wood (Alder) have been found which were manufactured from logs split lengthways from a mature tree (i.e. not a slice across the trunk) and carved to shape. The example from Annadale in Ireland suggests that examples for practical use may have been in the region of 65-70cm diameter with a (present) weight of just over 1.8kg. There were also lighter shields of baked and waxed leather in use in the Late Bronze Age, measuring around 50cm across in the case of the shield from Clonbrin, Co. Longford.

Visually striking shields of bronze sheet would have accompanied these organic shields on the battlefield, and these ranged in size from small bucklers in the region of 30cm in diameter to larger ornate pieces of over 70cm in diameter. Early investigative experiments in the functionality of metal shields used an example which was 0.3mm thick (Coles 1962) and the swords used against this cut through it with ease. Consequently, it was argued by Coles that metal shields were purely for display rather than combat purposes, an often cited belief in archaeological literature. However, more recent experiments conducted by the author (Molloy 2006) show that many of the shields of bronze were very much functional and serviceable weapons. The replicas tested were manufactured from sheet copper (bronze sheet being unavailable) and were based on Irish examples, ranging from c.0.8 to as much as 1.5mm in thickness. In the context of this paper it must suffice to say that they withstood a variety of weapons attack, including swords, effectively (see Molloy 2006 for full discussion), and this will be the subject of a future publication.

In light of this broad range of choices in defensive weaponry, it is therefore not entirely surprising that the swords of the Late Bronze Age rarely exhibit evidence of repeated blade-on-blade contact. While re-sharpening was very common and would have removed much of the damage caused during combat on many swords, the pieces which *do* exhibit damage rarely do so to extreme levels. Far from being bouts of senseless bashing and brawling, one can see in the subtleties of design of the weaponry of the Late Bronze Age, that there was a complex martial tradition in existence with its roots firmly located in the Middle Bronze Age combat system.

CONCLUSION

It is important in artefact studies to acknowledge that each and every individual artefact came into being in the form that it is today because of conscious decisions by past people, decisions voiced to skilled craftsmen and smiths who made the vision a reality (See Kristiansen 2002: 330 - 331). In the case of weaponry, it is impossible to divorce this decision making process from the field of violent intent. Weapons fulfil many social roles – as status symbols with regard to wealth and scope of influence for example. These are, however, secondary purposes which could never have been conceived of if the artefact form never came to social prominence through other means. If a given weapon (or even a particular form of weapon) is to have a symbolic value, it must be recognised as *being* a weapon, it must represent a tool that has visibly committed violence in the past and therefore be imbued with a certain potential or embodied power. The functional analyses of weaponry which this paper has explored, reveal far more than simply the 'hows' of an artefact's use, purpose and intrinsic significance, but are also extremely beneficial in examining the 'whys' of its creation and social prestige.

Combat must be interpreted as action. It is the event(s) that take place during warfare, it is human beings utilising their physical mechanical properties, augmented by manufactured tools, to engage in activities with closely definable objectives – to kill, maim, disable or otherwise defeat other human beings by force and finesse. This world of action is partly fossilised in the forms and shapes of the tools which were used to undertake these activities, and working from the specific to the general we can begin to show how these artefacts reflect the martial systems of prehistory. While the weapons may be less informative than we might wish about the macro-environment and tactics of the battlefield, they each tell a story of experiences of life and death in the Bronze Age.

ACKNOWLEDGEMENTS

There are many people to thank for invaluable help with this research which is drawn from my PhD thesis. Firstly, I am most grateful to Alan Peatfield, my thesis supervisor, who has offered me great guidance at every stage of my work. I would also like to thank Mary Cahill and Margaret Lanin of the National Museum in Dublin and Richard Warner and Sinead MacCartan of the Ulster Museum for access and much assistance in examining the material covered in this paper. Thanks are also due to Tony Kenny of the Ashtown food centre for invaluable assistance with the program of testing, and to Ciaran Flanagan for help with the testing process. Thanks to Charles Molloy for comments on early drafts of this chapter and to Kristian Kristiansen, Joanna Bruck, Philip De Souza and George Eogan for advice on various aspects of this work (all errors and mistakes, as they say, are my very own!). I am also very grateful to Neil Burridge of www.bronze-age-craft.com for his constant advice and enthusiasm for this work, including the provision of several replica weapons. Thanks also to all on the Ancient Weapons forum of www.swordforum.com for frequent, informed and lively discussion on this topic. This research was carried out under funding from the Irish Research Council for Humanities and Social Sciences.

The reconstruction of
Scythian bows

Erhard Godehardt, Jerzy Jaworski, Peter Pieper and Hans Michael
Schellenberg

INTRODUCTION

For ancient Mediterranean or Asiatic bows, we mostly have only paintings
and carvings or some fragments from the handles or tips. From the tomb of
Tutankhamun, a series of wooden self-bows and composite bows have been
found. Additionally, only two relics of Scythian bows are known today. One is
from a burial site from the Black Sea, and the other one from a Kurgan burial
in Aržan (Tuva, Siberia). We reconstructed bows closely approximating the
Scythian type, the shape of which is known from Greek vase paintings and
engravings on Scythian bowls (see Lissarrague 1990 for a catalogue of archers
on Attic vase paintings). Since we wanted to make these bows with moderate
draw weights, below 25kp at a draw length of 60cm, we decided to make
sinew-backed bows as well as composite bows of wood, horn and sinew. We
then conducted some experiments, shooting arrows with different types of tips
into different types of shields, thus checking the penetrative power of these
bows with low draw weights. Some of the results of these experiments will be
presented below.

Ancient bows can be classified into several groups according to the materials
used. We have bows completely made of wood (with the exception of the
bowstring, of course). Here we have the so-called self-bows, made of one piece
of wood like the famous English longbow or laminated bows, consisting of
several stripes of wood. Then there are bows of wood which are strengthened
by several layers of sinew or plant fibres glued onto their back.[1] Because of its
elasticity, which is superior to that of plant fibres, sinew has been used more often
than plant fibres like hemp or linen. Some peoples used horn or antler instead of

wood, especially in regions where the wood was of inferior quality. We therefore call them sinew-backed bows. Then there is the third (and most elaborate) type – the composite bow. These are usually composed of a wooden core, several layers of sinew glued onto its back and stripes of horn glued to its belly. The idea for this combination of materials is that sinew has a higher resistance against tension than wood, and horn is more resistant against pressure.

Another classification is according to the shape of the bows. We have the straight stave (when unstrung) like the English or the Alamannian longbow or the flatbow, which can be traced back to 2000BC (the Maere Heath bow). When stringed (or braced) then they look like the capital letter D. Then we have the large group of bows whose ends are recurved.[2] The tips can be round as pictures of Scythian and Hellenistic bows show, and they can also be straight and stiff like those on old Persian, Hungarian or Turkish bows. The limbs[3] and handle (or riser) of such a bow can be straight, or the limbs can be straight and the handle reflexed away from the archer, or the whole bow can be in C-shaped (showing away from the archer like a Turkish composite bow) when unstrung. The limbs – with the exception of the recurved tips –can also be deflexed on a reflexed handle. To this group belong the already mentioned Turkish bows, as well as the Scythian, Greek and Persian bows, and the horn-bows of American Plains Indians. The next group consists of the so-called angular bows. Examples of these have been found in the burial site of Tutankhamun (see Blyth 1980, Healy 1991, Hickman 1959, McLeod 1970, McLeod 1982, Wise 1981). They also have been very commonly used by the Assyrians, as pictures show (Wise 1981, Healy 1992). When unstrung, these bows look like two sickles (or letters C), lashed together at their ends so that the handle forms an angle with the tip, with this angle pointing away from the archer. The two C-shaped limbs become nearly straight when the bow is stringed. There are bows of other shapes, which have been used in ancient times, like the bow from the famous Naramsin stele dating to c.2300 BC (see the respective figure in Humble 1980: 20). However, there are no findings of such bows or parts of them. So we can only guess that they were commonly used in those old days.

These two ways of classifying bows are not independent of one another. Self-bows or flat-bows are usually longer than sinew-backed or composite bows (at least the bending parts are longer). This construction is necessary to prevent the 'wooden stick' from breaking during the drawing process. The backing of sinew or plant fibres makes the bow stronger and protects the wooden part so that it can be bent further before breaking, thus allowing for the bow to be made shorter. While an unstrung 'all-wooden' bow's silhouette is usually straight or shows recurved tips, the shape of sinew-backed or composite bows is more sophisticated, as discussed above. During the drying process of the glue in the sinew-backing, the limbs of such a bow are increasingly bent in the direction away from the inner-side (the belly). In this way, the bowyers get the C-shaped silhouette of a Turkish composite bow. This means that after stringing such a bow it has a higher pre-load than a wooden bow. This often will result in a faster arrow cast (if we compare a sinew-backed bow with a wooden bow of the same draw weight at a given draw length).[4]

The admissible draw length of a good Turkish composite bow, which measures 110cm over the back of the bow from tip to tip (not the length of the bowstring), can be as high as 90cm or more and thus is the same as that of an English longbow with a stave length of approximately 200cm. Such a composite bow looks fairly overdrawn but will not break! The same holds for sinew-backed horn-bows (horn strips and sinew only). Sinew-backed wooden bows or bows with antler instead of wood generally cannot be drawn to such an extreme length; their range for the draw length is between that of composite bows and wooden self-bows. They 'stack' earlier (which means that the archer feels that the string should not be drawn further). So why not use only composite bows given their apparent superiority? They are more time-consuming to manufacture than sinew-backed bows with a 'spine' or kernel of only wood or antler or horn. The whole fabrication process can take up to two years or more (see the chapter on composite bows written by Charles Grayson in the second volume of *The Traditional Archer's Bible*, Allely *et al.* 1992, and the chapter on Korean bows written by Jeff Schmidt in the third volume of this series). Most of the time required in manufacturing these bows is the drying process of the hide glue. Such a bow should not be used before the glue has thoroughly set. The characteristics (that is, the physical parameters) of such a bow will change over the whole drying period, and after that time, there will still be different characteristics depending on the air humidity and temperature. This dependence which results in different arrow speeds can also be seen in wooden bows and sinew-backed wooden bows, but it is stronger for composite bows and even stronger in sinew-backed horn-bows. This means that an all-wooden longbow is not only been easier and faster to make but is also usually more forgiving than a horn-bow which is much shorter and lighter and thus more 'springy' in the archer's hand. So why shall an archer use other bows than a longbow or a flat-bow? In a forest, a shorter bow has several advantages as one can imagine. Horse archers like the American Plains Indians, the Scythians, the Parthians or the Avars would have preferred shorter bows because they can aim and shoot to the front, to each side and even backwards (the famous Parthian shot) with short bows.

THE RECONSTRUCTION OF THE 'SCYTHIAN' BOW

Archaeological background

Composite bows have been made and used since ancient times. The Naramsin stele, which dates to c.2300 BC, shows a bow which cannot be made of wood alone. The shape of this bow indicates that it is at least a sinew-backed bow, maybe even a true composite bow with horn and sinew glued onto a wooden kernel. Unfortunately, due to the fact that the materials used in bow making do not survive well, we cannot rely directly on archaeological findings of such bows, but only on pictorial evidence. Only under very good conditions can these materials survive; thus, composite bows have been found at Tutankhamun's burial site (see Blyth 1980, Healy 1991, Hickman 1959, McLeod 1970, McLeod 1982, Wise 1981 for pictures). Many bas-reliefs of Assyrian bows are known, proving that this type of composite bow was very popular among other nations between 1300 BC and 600 BC. This tradition of the use of composite bows was continued by the Persian kingdom and its successors.

At least from the sixth century BC onward, Greek vase paintings usually show archers with short reflexed (or recurved) bows of the Scythian type. Thus it seems that the Scythian bow was the favourite type in use during the classic era. Hunting scenes showing Artemis on an archaic Boiotian kantharos (Buchholz et al. 1973: J54) and two Greek men hunting deer from a hydria from Caere (Buchholz et al. 1973: J74, Tölle-Kastenbein 1980:84-85), prove that the short reflexed bow was not reserved to horse warriors of the Ukraine or Siberia.

Only two examples of Scythian bows have been found; one is from Kurgan 2 of the Three Brothers Kurgans in the south of Kerč on the Crimean peninsula (see Eckhardt 1991: 144), and another in October 2001, during an excavation organized by the Deutsches Archäologisches Institut, under H. Parzinger and A. Nagler together with K. Čugunov from St. Petersburg in Aržan in Tuva, Siberia (29 shows this bow in situ and a reconstruction as suggested by the archaeologists of the Hermitage in St Petersburg, see also Čugunov et al. 2003).

From both bows only the wooden parts remained. Both bows were most probably gifts made for the burials which did not work at all. So perhaps, for this purpose they have been made of wood only with a richly decorated covering of bark or fabric. The bow found in Aržan, especially, is much too clumsy in its proportions. It is approximately 100cm long; the limbs are composed of three layers of wooden strips and are approximately 3cm thick; two additional wooden strips were added to the riser so that the bow is about 5cm thick at this part. According to the reconstruction by the archaeologists in St Petersburg, the bow has a reflexed riser and deflexed limbs without recurved tips. It is very similar to the 'double-curved' bows used by some tribes of the American Plains Indians.

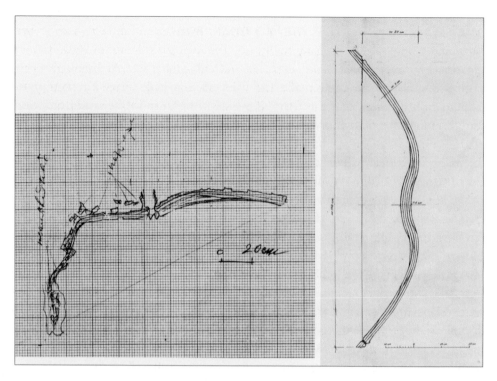

29 Scythian bow found in October 2001 during an excavation organized by the German Archaeological Institute under H. Parzinger together with M.P. Grjaznov from St Petersburg in Aržan in Tuva, Siberia (on the left side, this bow is shown in situ, and on the right side a reconstruction as suggested by the archaeologists of the Hermitage in St Petersburg). *All drawings by kind permission of H. Parzinger, the president of the German Archaeological Institute (Deutsches Archäologisches Institut, DAI) in Berlin*

However, this reconstruction is very different from the type shown in all the Greek vase paintings or Scythian works of art (cf. the Scythians shown on the famous electron bowl or on the gold decorative plaque, both from the Kul Oba burial). Our conclusion therefore is that until now the best information about the Scythian and Greek bows can be drawn from vase paintings and bas-reliefs and some finds of bow risers and tips, both usually made of bone or antler.

THE RECONSTRUCTION OF SCYTHIAN BOWS

From literature we are told that ancient and medieval war bows had very high draw weights. Such hypotheses most often rely only on the fact that the English longbows had draw weights of 40-80kp at a draw length of 76cm, sometimes even more (see Hardy 1992, Rees 1993, Strickland *et al.* 2005). This idea of high draw weights is also based on some bas-reliefs, such as a famous Assyrian one showing two archers stringing a bow, shown in many books (see the respective figures in Bulanda 1913: 26, Marcotty 1997: 50, Eckhardt 1991: 144 and Yadin 1963: 295). Archaeologists have found English longbows from the late fifteenth and early sixteenth century, for example on the wreck of the Mary Rose ship of Henry VIII (see Stirland 2001, Strickland *et al.* 2005). From these findings, high draw weights have been estimated.

The method of either backing a bow stave with sinew to prevent it from breaking or adding sinew at the back and horn at the belly is typical for the elaborate bows of the Asiatic archers and archers from India, Egypt, the Eastern Mediterranean region and the Arabian Peninsula. It allows the bows to be produced in much shorter lengths than pure wooden bows without the danger of breaking. Additionally, when the bow is unstrung the limbs or at least their outer parts are usually recurved. This gives a higher pre-load of energy, as discussed earlier, when such a bow is stringed as compared to an all-wooden longbow which is usually a straight stave when it is not braced. Taking all of this into account, the short Scythian or Greek bows should be more efficient than a longbow of the English type or a wooden flatbow, since less limb masses have to be accelerated in the short bows when loosing the arrow (this means that at the same draw weight, arrows shot from a Scythian bow should be faster).

Assuming that in ancient and medieval times the medical service for those persons hit by arrows was not optimal, we can imagine that often a slight wound was enough to cause a serious infection and death (this knowledge may have caused panic in troops seeing horse archers riding against them). Thus, there was no need for the archers to use bows with very high draw weights in those times where the body armour was either absent or not as effective as the medieval plate armour. The arguments for low bow weights (just enough for the respective archer to deliver a deadly shot without difficulty when aiming, and also to loose the arrow softly without big movements) hold even more if we consider the horse archers of the steppe (see also the Experiment by Junkelmann 1992: 149-173, and Figs. 137-9 and 151-3 made with a Sasanian composit bow built by Edward McEwen with a draw weight of 28kp). Adam Karpowicz, who made several Turkish composite flight bows of draw weights up to 41kp, proved that for bow weights higher than 32kp, no significant increase in the cast width or speed of arrows can be reported. A reason for this may be that a bow with greater draw weight has also more inert mass, slowing down the speed of the limbs. He therefore suggests an optimum of about 27-30kp for the draw weight at a draw length of approximately 75cm, enabling an archer to aim smoothly and giving enough speed to the arrow[5] (see also Asbell 2000 for a discussion on draw weights, Bergman *et al.* 1982, Hickman 1937, Kooi 1993, McEwen *et al.* 1991 and Miller *et al.* 1986 on early bow construction, and Becker *et al.* 2002 or Klimpel *et al.* 2006 on the quality of ancient body armour).

Greek vase paintings and Scythian engravings and small figurines did not seem to be a sound basis for the reconstruction of such bow. We also knew that we could not rely on the two bows found in burial sites. Then we saw pictures of a bow found in Subeixi (or Subeshi) in Xinjiang, China. These pictures have been published in the Letter of November 2002 of the Asiatic Traditional Archery Network (www.atarn.org), and a report on them is given in Dwyer 2003. This bow looks very similar to most of those bows shown on the Greek vase paintings, especially the painting of the deer hunting scene mentioned above. The reflex in the riser and the recurves of the Subeixi bow are not as sharp as on the Scythian pieces of art. But these representations seem to be a little exaggerated. This bow is wrapped with thread (possibly silk thread) and lacquered over the whole length. So we do not know whether it is an all-wooden bow, a bow backed with sinew or a bow of the composite type. The overall length is about 120cm. Because of the high conformity between this bow and the paintings, we decided to use only this information as the basis for our reconstructions.

The Subeixi bow proves our opinion about the shape of an unstrung bow commonly used by the Scythians or Greek of the sixth to second centuries BC. Since we could not decide whether the bow from Subeixi was a true composite bow or not, we (that is Michael Bittl of RedHawk, Wolfgang Schwerk and the first author, Erhard Godehardt) agreed to build several bows of each type. It is harder to draw a short sinew-backed bow which has a draw weight of 21kp at a draw length of 60cm, than to draw a composite bow with a characteristic of 25kp at 75cm, and the force-draw-curve of the sinew-backed bow is steeper than that of the other one. To be able to draw the bows which we wanted to be made, we decided that their draw weights should be in a range which we hoped to manage safely after some short training. The draw weights for each pair of bows (one composite bow and one of the sinew-backed type) should be similar. The maximum draw weight should not exceed 250N (approximately 25.5kp) at a draw length of 62cm.

For draw weights below 30kp at draw lengths up to 65cm, sinew-backed bows are as safe as composite bows in that they will not break when treated properly. For higher draw weights, the horn layers are necessary to prevent the danger of breaks. Since the process of making composite bows is much more complicated and time-consuming than that of making sinew-backed wooden bows, those composite bows are much more expensive than bows of the other type. We do not believe that bows with draw weights over 30kp were commonly used by horse archers, since the additional power does not result in significantly higher cast, as discussed earlier. Thus, it is probable that the common warriors may have used sinew-backed bows, while the richer noblemen could afford the more expensive composite bows which are safer than the sinew-backed versions and which give higher speed to an arrow at the same draw weight. Within the American Plains Indian tribes, sinew-backed horn bows as short as 1m in length, with draw lengths not exceeding 55-60cm and draw weights of not more than 30kp have been used (for a detailed discussion see Hamilton 1982). These bow hunters were capable of killing buffaloes, as is historically testified. So the pictures showing rather short bows used by Greek or Scythian archers, in our opinion, do not exaggerate the shortness of the bows. Also, when paintings or plaques show a bow at full draw, then rarely the archer's hand which draws the bow, is shown resting on the breast or chin, the draw length is shorter (see the respective plates in Tölle-Kastenbein 1980).

Michael Bittl made three composite bows and Wolfgang Schwerk made three sinew-backed bows (one of the sinew-backed bows is shown in *30*). The wood used for the sinew-backed bows was Osage orange (Maclura pomifera or Toxylon pomiferum). For the wooden kernel of the composite bows, Osage orange or mulberry was taken. The sinew fibres were from the legs of pronghorns or of buffalos. The overall lengths of all six bows are close to 115cm (measurements taken along the back of the bows following the curvature). The three sinew-backed bows were made so that their shape came close to the Subeixi bow; the three composite bows had more sharply bent recurves and risers, and they came close to the bows shown on the painting with Artemis as huntress, also mentioned above. For the unbraced sinew-backed bows, the line connecting the two nocks is about 10cm in front of the deepest point of the riser. This gives a good portion of pre-load (energy) to the bows when braced. For the composite bows, this distance is about 7cm.

OUR PRELIMINARY WORK

The arrows have to fit the draw weight of a bow; they should neither be too heavy nor too light. In the first case the arrow speed would be low and the cast only short; in the second case, the arrow could not take enough energy from the bow. This results in a considerable hand shock since the energy left has to be adsorbed in other ways. Another reason that bows with higher draw weight need arrows which are thicker than those used on weaker bows is the fact that an arrow shaft bends around a bow when it is driven forward by the string. A very small shaft then could even break during this early casting phase. Also, such a shaft tends to go too much to the right side. A shaft which is too thick tends to pass the target on the left side (this effect, which holds for a right-handed archer, is called the archer's paradox, more information can be found in Allely *et al.* 1992 and in many other books on archery). In our experiments on the penetrative power of ancient bows with low draw weights, the arrow masses range between 22-51g. This gives arrow speeds, for example, for the sinew-backed Scythian bow with the lowest force-draw curve, of between 32-42m/s. The types of arrowheads included in this experiment are shown in figure *31*.

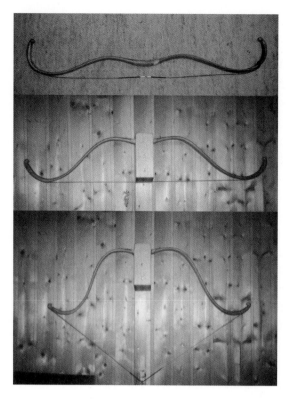

30 Our reconstruction of a Scythian bow made of sinew-backed wood (without horn). Total length over back 117cm, brace height 15.2cm. The photographs show the bow not braced on the top, the braced bow in the middle; and the same bow at full draw on the bottom. This bow is that with the median force-draw curve (220N at 60cm draw length). *Bow made by Wolfgang Schwerk*

Detailed tables of our results, together with tables for the efficiencies of all bows and arrow types used for the speed tests will be presented in another paper. Some preliminary results have been presented and are published further in Godehardt *et al.* 2006.

Here we show two photographs of our preliminary experiments when shooting at a Roman scutum. For this part of the experiment, only two bows had been used, the Scythian bow no.1, with a mass of 0.304kg, and a sinew-backed bow with a slight reflex in the handle and recurved tips of the type used over centuries by the Bashkirs, with a mass of 0.367kg. This bow was borrowed from Wolfgang Schwerk. At that time we still had to perform the experiments on the arrow speeds and efficiencies. Additionally, only the arrows with the five types of iron tips shown (on the right part of figure *31*) and with the lightest bronze tips (shown on the very left side of figure *31*) were ready for use. Since we did not believe that these light bronze tips would survive the hits on the scutum, we used only arrows with iron tips for this preliminary experiment. We shot several rounds of five arrows (one arrow of each type of head per round) at the scutum. After every round, the arrows were drawn off the shield. Figure *32* shows the result of the third round of five arrows. The bow which has been used for this round is

31 Arrow heads of bronze and iron included in this trial and for future experiments

the Bashkir bow. The force-draw-curve of this bow is a little bit steeper than that of the lightest Scythian bow (bow no.1), but it is always below that of bow no.2. The draw length in this experiment was always approximately 62.5cm, taken from the outer side of the riser, or close to 60cm if measured from the inner side of the riser to the string (at the points where the arrows rested, the thickness of the riser of the Bashkir bow is 3.4cm, and that of the Scythian bow no.1 is 2.8cm). To get approximately the same draw lengths for every arrow, the shafts were marked at a distance of 62.5cm from the bottom of the arrow nocks, and the archer not shooting in the respective round gave the command to the active archer to loose the arrow when this mark reached the front of the bow's handle.

The scutum is composed of four layers of wood (1.2cm) and covered with hide on both sides. In our experiment, which had been performed in June 2004 on two dry and sunny warm days, the distance between the two archers (E. Godehardt and J. Jaworski) and the scutum was 12m. All arrows penetrated the shield from the first round on. While during the first rounds, the arrows did not penetrate the shield for more than 5cm, after some rounds, the structure of the scutum was broken. Then the shield could hardly prevent an arrow from causing severe wounds to the shield bearer, as figure *34* demonstrates.

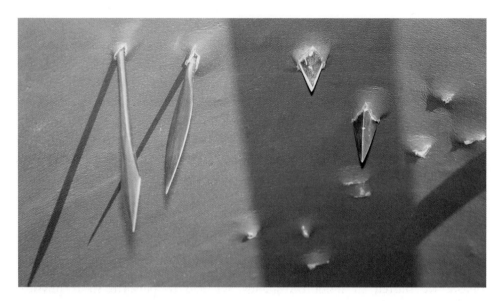

32 Penetration depth of arrows shot in several rounds of five arrows per round from a bow of Scythian-type and a bow as used over centuries by the Bashkirs of southern Siberia on a Roman scutum of the Dura Europos type. The Scythian bow used for this trial is the lightest of the series of three bows made by Wolfgang Schwerk (205 N at a draw length of 60 cm). The Bashkir bow is a little bit stronger

As a first result, we can take the conclusion that with an average efficiency of roughly 50% for light arrows and 55-58% for heavier arrows (see figure *38* for the efficiencies of the sinew-backed Scythian bows), both bows, the Bashkir and the Scythian bow no.1, are capable of casting arrows which penetrate even a Roman scutum. They should have a bigger effect on lighter shields or plain wooden shields, as a comparison with the work of H. Riesch implies. The penetration depth of an individual arrow depends – amongst other factors – on the type of arrowhead and the number of volleys already delivered to a shield. The small kite-shaped iron arrowheads with long iron foreshaft gave the best results. Arrows with these shafts penetrated for the whole length of the foreshaft on the first hit, the same hold for the leaf-shaped tips (*32*). Arrows with the bodkin-type head showed the following behaviour: the head stuck in the shield before the maximum width of the point got in, or when this part could enter the shield completely then a good part of the wooden shaft could also penetrate before it was stopped. For all these trials, we drew the two bows approximately 60cm (measured from the inner side of the riser to the point of the string where the arrow was nocked).

It is probable that the strategy of archers and skirmishers in ancient battles was to deliver several volleys of arrows to the scuta (or shields of similar type) of the advancing enemies. Our results show that especially under these conditions, arrows shot from light bows also, would penetrate shields to a considerable depth and were able to cause severe wounds to the shield bearers, if their shields had become weaker and their structure broken after some rounds of arrow hits. Since bows with low draw weights already showed good results on scuta, and since the draw lengths were rather short in our trial, we can conclude that this type of bow could be used very successfully by horse archers like the Scythians or Parthians. As experienced and skilful archers, they could rely on bows of low to medium draw weights (220-250N were enough as we have seen). Under these conditions, they could deliver a large series of arrows to an enemy before becoming tired.

BOW PHYSICS AND PENETRATIVE POWER OF THE SINEW–BACKED SCYTHIAN BOWS

Before we started to shoot on shields, we had to perform some physical experiments to describe the influence of the draw weight, bow size and mass, and the weights and shapes of the arrowheads upon the arrow flight (especially upon the starting speed). For all the bows we derived the:

1 individual draw length–force curves and the stored energies;
2 starting speeds of the arrows for the bows and the different types (and masses) of arrows and arrowheads, and the kinetic energies and impulses of these arrows for the different bows;
3 efficiencies as ratios of the kinetic energies of the arrows, and the stored energies of the bows.

From these results, we hope to get an answer to the question for a good combination of bow type and arrow type (for example, whether heavy arrows shall be used with heavier or stronger bows only). If necessary, then in further experiments, we will determine not only the starting speeds of the arrows, but will derive distance–speed diagrams and curves.

Theory and concepts of the physics of bows and arrows can be found in the papers cited at the beginning of section 3 above. For the more practically oriented reader, the basics are given in Eckhardt 1996, and in Karger *et al.*1998, Marcotty 1997, Marlow 1981, Reindl 1996a and 1996b. There is one weak point in most of the theoretical approaches however: when the authors present results, based on physical experiments, then most often they use shooting machines where the bows are fixed and a mechanism is used to release the arrow. This is done to exclude effects, as slightly different draw lengths between the different shots are given when archers shoot. But this gives an arrow speed and flight which is different from that when a human uses a bow. The archer's paradox is one reason for this effect; other reasons are the way an archer releases an arrow and slightly different draw lengths for each shot. There are devices, as in FITA archery, to force an archer to have always the same draw length, however, we do not use such mechanic devices to get the draw-force-curves and the speed tables for the arrows since ancient archers probably did not do so.

Until now, we have performed the experiments on bow physics with four modern versions of bows of types used by Huns, Avars, Magyars and Turks, together with a modern so-called horse bow of Korean style. Additionally, the physical characteristics of the sinew-backed Bashkir bow, three sinew-backed Scythian bows and two composite bows of 'Scythian shape' have been derived. A third Scythian composite bow is in preparation at the time of writing this article. We also found that the force-draw-curves of the other two composite bows changed a lot over the first half-year after they had been finished. A reason for this may be that the drying process is rather long, much longer than for sinew-backed bows. For the sinew-backed bows, we did not find changes in the respective curves during the last three months. So within this paper, we present only results for the three sinew-backed bows of Scythian type. The draw-force-diagrams of these three bows are given in figure 33.

From the force draw curves in figure 33, the stored energy for the bows can be derived as the areas under the curves. For the lightest bow (no.1) we get 46.51J, the second bow stored 48.26J, and the third one stored 51.22J, all computed for a draw length of 60cm (from the inner side of the riser to the point of the string where the arrow was nocked). As can be seen from the diagram, the bows can be drawn further. However, this is a very comfortable draw length for Erhard Godehardt and Jerzy Jaworski, the archers in this study (this holds for the short sinew-backed or composite bows for which the shooting style is different to the style when using longer bows or bows made of modern materials).

The weights (masses) of the six types of arrowheads used in our experiments until now range at an average of only 4g for the Scythian bronze arrowheads, and between 8-19g for the other bronze points and the iron points with the highest weights for the three-bladed and the leaf-shaped iron arrowheads. The wooden shafts were all about 72cm long; those used with the Scythian arrowheads were barrelled and thus were a little bit lighter than the other shafts. For fletching, we used 12.5cm long feathers on all arrows. The total arrow weights ranged around 23g for the arrows with Scythian bronze tips, between 34-43g for the other arrows with bronze tips, and from 42-54g for those with iron tips. We determined the starting speed which each bow delivers to arrows together with the stored energies of the bows and the kinetic energies and impulses given to the arrows (at a draw length of 60cm for all bows). Five arrows of each of the ten arrowhead-types have been included in this step to be able to get some representative results with valid averages and standard deviations.

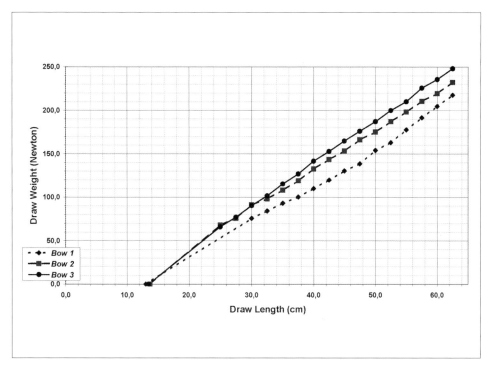

33 Force-draw-curves of the three Scythian bows (all three bows made of sinew-backed wood)

The sinew backed bow of Bashkir type gave average arrow speed. The Scythian bow no.1 with the lowest draw weight had poor speed results. The Scythian bows nos.2 and 3 were much better as the diagram of figure *34* shows. The computation of the efficiencies of the different bows gave a slightly different result. For the heavier arrows with the iron points, the average efficiency of the Bashkir bow is at 59%, that of the lightest Scythian bow at 56%, and those of the other Scythian bows at 59% and 60% respectively. With the lightest arrows (Scythian bronze points), we got efficiencies of 51% for the Bashkir bow, and 43%, 45% or 47% for the Scythian sinew-backed bows respectively. All the parameters of these bows are computed at a draw length of 60cm (measured from the inner side of the handle; this corresponds quite well to the data given in Godehardt *et al.* 2006, where the draw length was taken from the outer side of the riser to the bow string and was given as 62.5cm). Similar to the results presented in Karger *et al.* 1998, we did not take the arrow velocities when the arrows left the bows but 1m behind. Thus we underestimated the starting speeds and the efficiencies since during the first meter of travelling, the arrows already lose some speed. This bias in our estimates is bigger than that in Riesch 1999, since he put the speedometer 50cm in front of the bow.

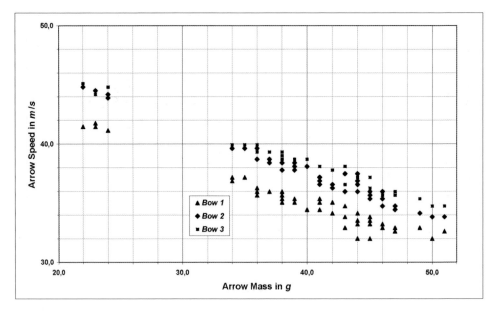

34 Scatter gram of arrow masses against arrow speeds for the three sinew-backed bows and five arrows of each of the ten different arrow heads (a total of 50 arrows). The speed values have been taken by a speedometer at a distance of 1 m in front of the bows (thus it is not the starting speed v0 at point zero, but a little bit below)

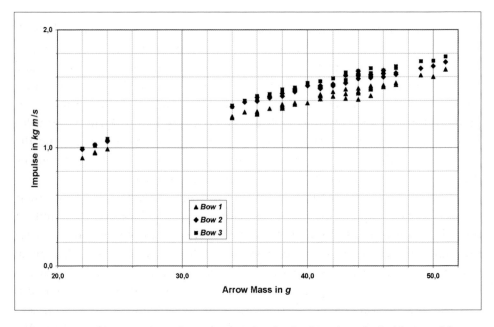

35 Scatter gram of arrow masses against arrow impulses for the three sinew-backed bows and five arrows of each of the ten different arrow heads (a total of 50 arrows). The impulse values have been calculated for a distance of 1m in front of the bows

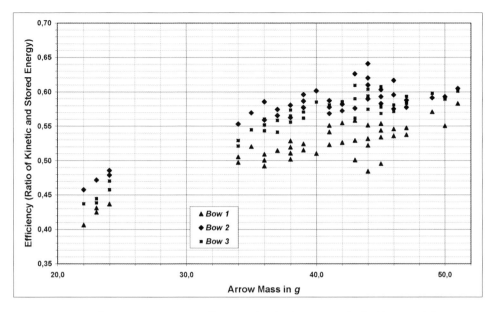

36 Scatter gram of arrow masses against efficiencies for the three sinew-backed bows and five arrows of each of the ten different arrow heads (a total of 50 arrows). Since the speed values have been taken at a distance of 1m in front of the bows, the efficiencies are not those of the starting speed v0 at point zero, but a little bit below

The impulses given in figure *35* are valid also only for 1m of arrow flight. It would have been of greater value to calculate these impulses (and the arrow speeds) at the distance between the bows – or the archer's bow hand – and the scutum, to get the 'hitting impulse'. However, the speedometer had only a comparatively small window for the arrows to pass through (and it was not our property but lent to us for the trials by the company Dutch Archery Specialist from Roggel (The Netherlands) and we did not trust our abilities to send the arrows always through this window. Therefore we gave up getting the arrow speeds and impulses at the distance between bow and shield.

As shown in Riesch 1999, the penetration depth depends – amongst others things – on the shape of the arrowhead and its weight. Therefore, as we did for the calculation of the parameters for the bow physics, we will use arrows with the same different types of heads together with each bow. For each type of arrowhead, several arrows will be used to be able to make a statistical comparison of bow type and arrow type, concerning the penetration depth. Within this experiment, we will not check the penetration capabilities of our bows and arrows on armour, blocks of gelatine or ballistic soaps, or on animal corpses. We refer to the results given in Karger *et al.* 1998 and Sudhues 2004; a discussion on arrow wounds is given in Hain 1989.

At the moment, we have 10 straight wooden shields, covered with hide or fabric, another 10 cane shields of the Persian or Scythian type, and five Roman scuta. After the preliminary test from June 2004, which has been described above, Erhard Godehardt performed in January 2006 a second trial during a cold but sunny day, this time using the light cane shields as targets. These shields have been made of cane (approximately 0.7cm thick), woven vertically and parallel to each other into rawhide, into which had been cut a pattern of holes where the rods could be pushed through. The cane rods were woven onto the hide while it was still supple and uncured. When the hide was dry and hard, the combined virtues of the materials resulted in a shield of great lightness, yet of great resilience and rigidity. The cane shields for our experiment were approximately 65cm wide and 110cm high and were all made by M. Bittl. Photographs of such a shield, which have been found together with similar ones during the excavations in Dura Europos in the year 1933 are shown in Sekunda 1992: 16 and 21. This shield is dated to have been used during the Sassanian period around AD 250. Shields of the same construction already have been used by the Scythians as a photograph in Karasulas 2004: 59 shows. The shield shown is from a barrow at Pazyryk and is dated to the fifth century BC. It is rectangular in shape and not as large as the shields from Dura Europos. The famous comb from the fourth century BC Solokha royal burial mound shows how such a shield of cane or osiers (in the shape of a Thrakian pelte) was used by a Scythian foot soldier (see Cernenko *et al.* 1983: 14–16). *Colour plate 14* shows a cane shield made by M. Bittl and used in our January trial. The two leather strips as handles are conjectural.

For this actual shooting experiment, the archer decided not to shoot all the arrows as in the trial from June 2004. He restricted his choice to those arrows with the three-bladed heads, bodkin-type heads and kite-shaped heads with long foreshafts (all forged of iron, see *31*, fifth to seventh arrows from the left). We wanted to check whether the good results of the bodkin-type tips and the kite-type ones shown on the scutum could also repeated on the cane shields. Additionally, we were interested whether the three-bladed iron arrowheads with broad blades had also little penetrative power. To check the quality of the bronze tips, the three-bladed socketed tips of Scythian type had been included in this trial. The blades of this type of tips were rather small, and the bases of the sockets had diameters of approximately 0.6cm. They were smaller than the arrow shafts which had to be carved to fit into the sockets (see the arrow at the left side of *31*). These tips were the lightest ones in the experiment. All shafts used in this trial had a binding of linen thread, covering the shafts on a length of 2.5cm from its front end for the tips with thongs (or thorns), the shafts with the socketed tips had bindings of only 1.5 cm length. The whole binding area was covered by birch tar to smoothen it and to prevent the thread from getting cut when gliding through the shield parts. The binding also should prevent the shafts from breaking behind the tips.

For this experiment, the bow was not drawn to a draw length of 60cm, but slightly less. The draw lengths were between 58-9cm this time (but not shorter). The reason for this was that it was a sunny but cold January day with a temperature around 0° centigrade when the shooting was performed. Also, it was the first archery day after a break of more than two months which means that the archer was in a 'sub-optimal condition'. The results of this experiment are shown in figures 37-39. Five arrows of each type of tips were shot onto a cane shield, the measurements and photographs were taken, and then a new shield was used for the next round of five arrows.

Taking into account the short draw lengths and thus the lower draw weight, the penetration depths were amazingly good for two types of arrowheads, the kite-shaped tips and the bodkin-like tips. The cane shields showed virtually no protective mechanism against these arrows. The three-bladed iron tips, however, did not penetrate the shield deep enough to hurt its bearer. One of these arrowheads could only cut into the surface of the shield, and the arrow fell down when the next one hit the shield. The three-bladed bronze tips with rather small blades performed a little bit better. They penetrated the shield until the beginning of the wooden shafts reached the cane or the space between two canes. The shafts – or the bindings round them – were broader than the sockets of the shafts, thus the arrows were stopped by growing friction. One of these arrows could not enter the shield; the shaft broke directly behind the socket, and both parts bounced back from the shield. Table 1 gives the numerical results.

Since this type of very light cane shield has been found in a fortress, and since it does not prevent arrows with certain types of tips to enter the body but prevents arrows at least from passing it, our opinion is that this type of shield was not worn by soldiers during combat. It seems more probable to us that this type of shield was used on the walls of fortified places. Such shields should be fixed onto stands to protect people passing at least 50cm behind them. Under such conditions, the light cane shield could guarantee good protection against arrows. Additionally, due to their lightness and simple construction, damaged shields could easily be replaced. This type of shield also could have been used as a kind of 'mobile wall' by the light infantry. Fixed onto stands at some distance in front of the troops, these men could wait and let the first volleys from the opposite archers pass before advancing further. These cane shields could also protect archers like the medieval *pavese*, as has been discussed by Sekunda 1992. The protective value of these cane shields must have been good enough, since otherwise, they would not have been used for a time period of at least 700 years.

Left: 37 Penetration depth of arrows with three-bladed iron arrow heads (broad blades), shot from bow no.2 of Scythian-type. The photograph shows the front side of the Persian cane shield. Only four arrow heads penetrated the canes slightly

Below: 38 Penetration depth of arrows with kite-shaped iron arrow heads, shot from bow no.2 of Scythian-type. The photograph shows the inner side to demonstrate the penetration depths of the arrows. The first arrow from top shows a severely bent tip. The tip at the right side of this photograph was slightly bent

39 Penetration depth of arrows with three-bladed bronze arrow heads of Scythian type, shot from the Scythian bow no.2. The photograph shows the inner side of the Persian cane shield. One arrow bounced back directly after hitting the shield (the shaft of this arrow broke directly behind the socket of the bronze tip). Only four arrow heads penetrated the canes slightly (two on the top of the off-white leather grip, one at the right hand of the grip, through the raw hide, and the fourth at the upper right part of the photograph)

CONCLUSION

We found that the efficiency of a bow depends on the weight of the arrow used. This fact, however, is well known. Lighter arrows tend to take less from the energy stored in the bow. What was surprising for us was the fact that for the lighter arrows with bronze tips there was nearly no difference in efficiencies of the different bows (at the two different draw lengths) as the respective diagram shows. Meanwhile, we checked that the lightest Scythian bow can be drawn to about 65cm before it starts to stack. It also has been used in two so called '3D-tournaments' where archers have to hit three-dimensional animal figures made of foam at different distances. The bow did not show any sign of weakness over the whole day, even in humid weather.

We could prove that also with light bows and heavy arrows (42-54g), a good effect on shields can be reached. Heavy arrows can be used with good results from bows with low-draw weights. Lighter arrows like those with the bodkin-type heads could also be used with good results. As another result from our first experiment, we can take the conclusion that with an average efficiency of roughly 50% for light arrows and 55–58% for heavier arrows, both the Bashkir and the Scythian bow are able to cast arrows which penetrate even a Roman scutum. They should have a bigger effect on lighter shields or plain wooden shields, as a comparison with the work of H. Riesch (Riesch 1999, 2001a, 2001b, 2002) implies. The penetration depth of an individual arrow depends – among other factors – on the type of arrowhead and the number of volleys already delivered to a shield. The small kite-shaped iron tips with long foreshaft gave the best results. Arrows with these shafts penetrated the scutum for the whole length of the foreshaft front from the first round onward; similar results hold for the leaf-shaped tips (32). Arrows with bodkin-type heads showed the following behaviour: either the head stuck in the shield before the maximum width of the point entered, or when this part could penetrate the shield then a good part of the shaft would also penetrate it, before the arrow was stopped. Both types of iron arrow-head consisting of three broad blades gave no good results concerning their penetration depth (on this preliminary trial we did not take measurements of the penetration depths of all the different arrows, though we took many photographs).

The results of the January trial are similar to that of the experiment using the scutum. Again, the kite-shaped arrowheads performed best (even if one of them was bent severely). The bodkin-type arrowheads could penetrate the shield completely directly from the first shot on, so they gave better results than on the scutum, where the plywood-like construction prevented penetration at the first round. The small diameters of the sockets of the Scythian bronze arrowheads led us to believe that these had not been fixed to the wooden shaft directly; probably they had been glued to foreshafts of hardwood with a diameter of less than 0.5cm, which were inserted into the proper shafts. This would probably allow an arrow to penetrate into the shield or other body protection for the whole length of the foreshaft (in the same way as the arrows with the iron foreshafts did). This construction is even more probable for the bronze arrowheads with smaller sockets, of diameters less than 0.4cm, which also have been found during excavations in the Scythian main lands.

For all these trials until now, the draw lengths of the two wooden bows have been approximately 60cm or slightly less. After testing these bows, now also at draw lengths of 65cm (for the Scythian bow no.1) and 63cm (for the bows no.2 and 3), we are convinced that the penetrative power against shields will be much better if the bows are used at 'full draw'.

The fact that it was possible to rely on the Greek vase paintings and the Scythian pieces of art (together with one single bow from Subeixi) for the reconstruction of bows which really work, however, was the most important consequence of this part of our project on ancient archery. This encourages us to continue our work with other types of ancient bows as discussed in the previous paragraph.

APPENDIX

Traditionally, in archery the old English units are used. However, in physics we use a unit system based on the decimal system. Draw weights therefore are given here either in kiloponds (kp) or in Newtons (N). We have 1kp = 9.81N, and thus 1lb = 0.454 kp = 4.45N. Draw lengths and other distances are measured in metres or centimetres; and we have 1in = 2.54cm, 1ft = 30.48cm, and 1 yard = 0.914m. The physical unit for inert or heavy mass is 1kg where a body with a mass of 1kg has the weight of 1kp. The masses (weights) of arrows or arrowheads traditionally are given in grains; here they are given in grams (g), and 1 grain = 0.0648g. The energy is measured in Joules (J), where 1J = 1Nm. The kinetic energy of an arrow at a given distance in front of the bow is the product of the squared speed at that distance multiplied by the arrow mass and divided by two. The stored energy of the bow is given by the area under the force-draw-curve of that bow, starting at the brace height and ending at the respective draw length of the archer. The efficiency of a bow is the ratio of the kinetic energy of an arrow when leaving the bow (at distance 0) and the stored energy of the bow.

ACKNOWLEDGEMENTS

This work was supported by the *Deutsche Forschungsgemeinschaft* (DFG grant no. Go 490/11-1). The reconstruction of the Scythian bows has been also supported by the *Deutsche Forschungsgemeinschaft* (DFG grant no. 436 RUS 18/9/03). Our thanks go also to H. Parzinger and A. Nagler from the 'Deutsches Archäologisches Institut' who provided us with the drawings of the bow found during their excavations in Aržan, and to N. Sekunda who provided us with several photographs of different cane shields of the Dura-Europos-type to help us understand their construction.

The Early Anglo-Saxon shield: reconstruction as an aid to interpretation

Richard Underwood

INTRODUCTION

The shield wall is one of the most striking poetic images of the Anglo-Saxon world. In battle, the lime-wood 'fortress of shields' provided the only defence for most warriors from the iron 'point and edge' of their enemies' weapons. While at face value a shield may appear to be a very simple object, in practice the design of the shield requires a difficult balance between size and weight, strength and manoeuvrability. The shield must be light enough to allow the warrior to dodge and parry without tiring, yet must withstand repeated blows by weapons designed to cleave both wood and flesh. Only now are we beginning to understand how this was achieved.

The shield was a very personal possession; frequently taken to the grave to serve again in the afterlife. It marked the owner as a warrior – a man permitted to bear arms, responsible for the defence of the land, willing to fight for kith and kin. Like the warrior himself, its sacrifice was celebrated:

I am an exile, iron-wounded,
blade-battered, battle-sated,
sword-weary. War I see often,
fight foes. I fear no comfort
or help comes for me in cruel strife
before I am wrecked among warriors,
but hammered blades hack me,
hard-edged hate-sharp handiwork of smiths
strikes me in strongholds; I must stay for

a crueller clash. No cure was ever
found by folk in their fields
which could heal my wounds with herbs,
but day and night through deadly blows
the swords' wounds widen in my flesh.

Exeter Book Riddle 5; translation: Porter 1995

Much can be told about this important class of arteface from archaeological and written sources, but, as will be demonstrated, the subtleties of design and structure are brought out more fully through experimental reconstruction. This chapter will investigate the role of the shield in the Early Anglo-Saxon world.

ANGLO–SAXON SHIELDS — EVIDENCE AND ISSUES

The main source of evidence for Early Anglo-Saxon shields comes from excavations of the iron fittings of the shield in furnished graves. Unfortunately, the perishable nature of the shield board leaves a number of gaps in our knowledge. Grave evidence from England is supplemented by a limited number of continental finds of complete shields and by representations in manuscript illustrations, sculpture and on metalwork, albeit generally later in date.

Nearly a quarter of male burials from England contain evidence for a shield, whereas other items of defensive weaponry are far more sparsely represented in the archaeological record. A mere handful of helmets and pieces of ring-mail survive, and these are the province of wealthy burials.

Shields were manufactured from boards of wood bound together to form a disk (see below on construction). An iron boss or *umbo* was affixed to the centre of the shield to protect the hand of the user, the wooden boards being cut away at this point to allow the attachment of a separate handle. The shield was often then covered by leather and decorated with fittings of iron or bronze.

In the extant poetry from the Anglo-Saxon world, shields are said to be constructed from lime, but in reality a variety of other species of tree were used in their manufacture. The most common of these are alder, willow and poplar, but examples are also known to have been manufactured from maple, birch, ash and oak. The former three are particularly suitable, being tough yet comparatively light, with alder known to have been used in shield manufacture as far back as the Bronze Age (Molloy, this volume).

STRUCTURE

Unfortunately, the wooden boards of these shields rarely survive in the ground. Archaeologists often have to reconstruct the dimensions of the shield from the impressions/differences in soil colour left in the earth of a burial, the position of surviving fittings and the dimensions of the grave itself. Consequently, estimates of the size of shields vary; the most recent comprehensive survey (Dickinson and Härke 1992) suggested most shields were in the region of 0.45-0.66m in diameter, but they could be as little as 0.34m and as large as 0.92m. Estimates of the thickness of the shields range from 5-13mm, but most would have been about 6-8mm thick. The shields when fully fitted with handle and boss would have ranged in weight from 3-5kg. There is a tendency for the larger shields to be later in date, perhaps indicating a gradual change in certain aspects of the fighting environment. The shields were constructed from planks of wood, as described below in detail, and would have ranged from 3 to 9 planks depending on the design and size of the shield.

The shields were often covered in leather on the front (and sometimes the back also), serving to strengthen the weapon by holding the planks tightly together and thus reducing damage through splitting along the grain (see Godehardt *et al.*, this volume). The rim of the shield may have been bound separately with leather or hide, and pictorial representations sometimes show a raised rim suggestive of this edging.

The shields may also have been painted; evidence for this comes from literary sources and continental finds. The epic *Beowulf* has references to 'bright' and 'yellow' shields and there are Danish finds with traces of red paint, while the Viking shields from the Gokstad ship were painted black and yellow. The leather covering may also have been coloured, either dyed or of different natural colours.

The decoration of the shields could have been variable and individualistic, functioning to identify individuals in battle. On three separate occasions in the poem *The Battle of Maldon* there are references to warriors lifting their shield aloft before making a speech. Such a visual action may have functioned as an element of giving a command on a battlefield and, through the individual elements of the shield's decoration, to have allowed warriors to identify the commander.

The boss
An iron boss was attached to the centre of the shield board to protect the hand from enemy weapons. The shapes of the bosses were complex, generally conical, with a number of different designs that were at least in part chronologically dependent (see Dickinson and Härke 1992), strongly contrasting with the round domed bosses of the later Anglo-Viking period. It was attached to the wooden

board with iron, or occasionally bronze, rivets. The heads of these rivets are generally broader than required functionally and some examples were coated in silver or tin.

The grip

The shield was held by a central iron grip that spanned the hole cut in the planks beneath the boss. These were typically a simple short strap of iron, 0.10–0.16m in length. The iron grip was built up to form a comfortable grip using leather, cloth, wood or a combination of such organic materials.

Construction

Areas of debate about the construction of Anglo-Saxon shields include: how large were shields? How were they constructed? Were they flat, curved in one dimension only or convex (lentoid) and how were the planks that make up the shield-board held together?

The most recent publications on Anglo-Saxon shields are Dickinson and Härke (1992) and Stephenson (2002). Dickinson and Härke consider convex shield boards to be present, though unusual, in the Early Anglo-Saxon period and suggest they may have been shaped by softening the wood with steam or hot oil. Stephenson argues against convex boards, but proposes curvature in one plane as a by-product of gluing the planks together. Both consider at length the method by which the planks were held together, in the absence of evidence of metal nails or clips. Options discussed include dowels, rebating or cross-pieces/batons. None of these, however, appear satisfactory, being either at odds with the available evidence or impractical as a robust method of construction.

Academic interest has naturally focused on the iron boss and other fittings that survive, so that developments in the form of the boss have been seen as more significant than they would have been if complete shields had survived. Thus, Dickinson and Härke infer a transition from individual combat to fighting in formation in the sixth century on the basis of changes in the shape of the boss and the thickness and shape of the board. Reconstruction demonstrates that the size of the board is the most significant factor in determining for what style of combat it was developed, rather than boss shape, larger shields being more suited to fighting in formation and against archery. Great care, however, should be taken in developing any theories regarding the nature of warfare on the basis of studies of weapons. Rather, greater significance should be placed on understanding the social and economic context, since factors such as the aims of the combatants and the size of forces employed are likely to have a greater influence on the nature of ancient warfare than modest changes in weapon technology. For a discussion of the nature of Anglo-Saxon warfare see Underwood (2001).

THE RECONSTRUCTION

The reconstruction shield (*colour plate 16*) is made of poplar, which, along with alder and willow, is one of the most common species identified from finds of shields. All three woods have a good balance of toughness to weight and a close grain that makes them resistant to splitting. It is made of three equal width planks with a total diameter of 0.72m. The planks were glued together before the wood was shaped; the edges were simply butted together and joined using animal-bone glue. Planks 50mm thick were used and a convex board formed by hollowing out the centre and thinning the edges. The resulting board varies in thickness across the diameter between approximately 10-15mm, being thickest at the rim and thinnest near the centre. The entire thickness of the planks was used; hence, the front surface curves by 35mm over the radius. This is a relatively shallow curve, though still noticeable to the eye and sufficient to change the physical properties of the board. The shaping of the wood was undertaken using chisels and took approximately 40 hours; however, the time taken would probably reduce significantly with experience.

The curvature of the board increases its strength without any increase in weight. In addition, the convex board formed is robust with the planks simply glued together and does not require the planks to be joined with dowels or rebates or to be reinforced with batons. This is because the glued joint curves along its length so that any torque applied to the joint is balanced by the compression of the wood at either end of the joint. If the planks were flat even modest torque would cause the glue to fracture.

This form of manufacture is consistent with timber processing methods in the Anglo-Saxon period, which was undertaken without significant use of saws. Planks would be formed by splitting a tree either once into half-rounds or several times radially to form segments and then reducing the excess to form planks using axes (Goodburn, 2001). In either case, thin planks could only be formed by reducing thicker planks. Forming curved planks is therefore little more effort than making flat planks if the planks have to be thin.

The board is covered with leather. The curvature of the board requires the leather to be cut into panels. Five panels were used, each a curved sided triangle. They were laid on the board so that they overlapped, marked up, cut to size and then stitched together using linen thread. The resulting cover fitted the board easily and was attached using animal glue. The edge of the cover was secured, and the rim of the shield strengthened with rawhide. The rawhide was soaked to make it flexible and secured by stitching to the board through pre-drilled holes using leather thong.

This use of leather panels to form a cover is consistent with the predominant type of decoration of shields in representations from the period in England and

40 Tenth- or eleventh-century manuscript illustration of swordsmen engaged in single combat showing the spiral pattern on shield board (MS Cotton Cleopatra C VIII). *Courtesy of M. Daniels*

on the continent, i.e. a number of lines curving out from the boss in a broad spiral; this is strong and convincing evidence for the existence of convex shields. Examples include a tenth- or eleventh-century manuscript illustration of two swordsmen engaged in single combat (MS Cotton Cleopatra C VIII) (*40*), the eighth- or ninth-century Trier Apokalypse (Cod. 31, f.63, Stadtbibliothek, Trier), the early eleventh-century illustration of the 'Vision of Habukuk' in the Bible de St Vaast (MS 435, Bibliothèque Municipale, Arras) and carvings of horsemen on the Gotland picture stones and the seventh-century stone slab from Hornhausen (*41*). That the pattern derives from the leather covering of a convex board is most clearly illustrated in a detail from the ninth-century Stuttgart Psalter (*42*). Indeed, the ubiquity of this pattern in examples from across Europe and spanning over 500 years would be surprising were it not related to the method of construction.

Shields are frequently depicted with rims in illustrations and carvings; however, finds are rare suggesting perishable materials may have been used. The copper alloy shield rim from Sutton Hoo is pierced, suggesting it was sewn to the board and surviving shield boards from both Viking and Roman contexts have holes around the edge suggesting a perishable rim sewn to the board.

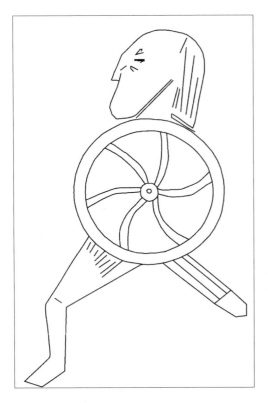

Left: 41 Detail from a seventh-century carved stone slab from Hornhausen showing the spiral pattern on shield board. *Drawn by R. Underwood*

Below: 42 Detail from the ninth-century Stuttgart Psalter showing a shield with a stitched leather covering. *Drawn by K. Dixon*

The shield was finished by attaching a short iron flanged grip enclosing a wooden handle and an iron carinated boss. The complete shield weighs 4kg, in line with Dickinson and Härke's estimates.

THE USE OF SHIELDS IN ANGLO-SAXON WARFARE

For most warriors on the Anglo-Saxon battlefield, the shield was their only effective item of personal defence. This weapon was one of the principle possessions to characterise a man as a warrior – while all free men would have possessed a spear, this was a tool of warfare that also had a dual function in hunting. As with the fabled Spartan saying of 'return with your shield or on it', Tacitus remarks on contemporary Germanic warriors for whom the ultimate disgrace was to return from battle without their shield, since this would indicate that it had been cast away fleeing from the enemy.

The variation in the sizes of the shields is important and clearly not random, as the differences in size indicate differences in modes of use. This in turn may reflect differentiation of roles within the warband, regional styles or personal preferences. It is also possible that shields used in the resolution of 'private' disputes through formal duels or small skirmishes differed from those designed for use in larger-scale conflicts. Overlying these differences, changes in the proportions of smaller and larger shields over time may indicate variations in the nature of warfare, reflecting changes in Anglo-Saxon society.

A small shield is by virtue of its size going to be lighter and more manoeuvrable. It is well suited to single combat or smaller-scale skirmishes as a result of these factors. Its manoeuvrability means that it can be actively used in combat, with the central iron boss used to parry blows (as opposed to the wooden boards) and can also be used to strike the enemy, as can the rim of these smaller shields. In this regard, it is a more active element in the fighting system as it is used not merely to impede an opponent's weapon, but to seek to control both it and the combat space of an adversary. The complex shape of many Anglo-Saxon shield bosses, with the button at the tip and carinated structure, can assist by 'capturing' an opponent's sword. In a world where social violence and/or raiding were at times endemic, the smaller shields also have the mundane advantage of being suitable to carry around on a daily basis.

Larger shields, on the other hand, are more useful in battles between large formed groups, particularly as missile weapons would have been in use. In single combat, the large board gives greater 'static' protection by virtue of its body coverage, although at the penalty of being less manoeuvrable and also limiting the field of vision of the warrior, thus masking an opponent's movements. In full-scale battles, however, larger shields can be brought together to form a 'shield wall' formation. These larger proportions are essential in this context as each warrior in the line is not only vulnerable to attack from a single warrior in front of him, but also from men either side of this opponent; this is countered by the protection afforded by the shields of the warriors standing to either side.

There is significant debate about how close together men stood within the shield wall. Was it a solid mass of overlapping shields, a static barrier, or a looser line with the warriors actively using their shields to deflect blows aimed both at themselves and their comrades? The debate makes the assumption that there was a single 'ideal' shield wall. Analysis of the nature of battles, however, suggests that the density of the shield wall would have been entirely dependent on the tactical situation, in particular the nature of the ground and the size of the forces. Essential to effective defence was to secure the flanks of the shield wall against envelopment. This was generally done using terrain features such as rivers, dense woods or bogs. The two forces would then deploy as fully as possible in the available space rather than deploying to a prescribed spacing. By selecting a battlefield with a limited frontage a smaller force could largely negate the numerical advantage of their opponents. Fords in rivers would give such a limited frontage and many battles appear, from place name evidence, to have taken place at fords. Gaining the most advantageous ground on which to fight would have been, and remains, one of the most important skills of a general.

This argument is consistent with the observed trend for the size of shields to increase through the Early Anglo-Saxon period (Dickinson and Härke, 1992), at a time when the size of armies can be assumed to have been increasing, as the many independent kingdoms of the earliest period coalesced. Identifying defensive positions with secure flanks is more problematic with smaller forces; therefore, the trend towards larger forces could also be seen as a trend towards battles between armies using the shield wall formation and away from skirmishes. This is not to suggest that the shield wall formation was not used in the earliest period, rather, that the frequency of encounters in which it was tactically appropriate increased over time.

While shields were the primary line of defence for most Anglo-Saxon warriors, they could and did fail in combat and the warriors wielding them died as a result. That was the nature of warfare. Repeated sword blows, spear thrusts or even archery (see Godehardt et al., this volume) could result in shivering of the planks and disintegration of the shields. Such damage could be mitigated by tilting the shields and using them actively to deflect or parry blows rather than block them in a 'dead' fashion. The boss could also be used, on occasion, to receive a blow as it was typically more durable than the wooden aspect of the shields. Convex shields, as discussed above, also have the advantage that weapons' attacks tend to deflect from the surface more naturally (see Pittman, this volume).

CONCLUSIONS — THE VALUE OF RECONSTRUCTION

Reconstruction of an archaeological find can be a valuable method of gaining understanding of its form, manufacture and use. Practical constraints cannot be glossed over, and the significance of evidence that may have been ignored can be recognised. Above all, reconstruction consolidates academic knowledge into practical understanding.

The value is significantly enhanced if the reconstruction is undertaken using the tools available in the period, either copies or modern versions with similar properties, and by starting with base materials and undertaking all stages of the manufacture.

A reconstruction of an Anglo-Saxon shield demonstrates the value of this approach as an aid to understanding:

- The shape of the complete shield
- The method of construction of the board
- The predominant form of decoration of the shield

This in turn enhances the way we can investigate the role of this important class of artefact in Anglo-Saxon society. These weapons of the rank-and-file warrior can be seen as intelligently crafted tools of war, with subtleties of design beyond what has previously been suggested for their construction. Its value in society and to the individual warrior can therefore be seen to be commensurate with its skilled craftsmanship.

Warriors of the Mycenaean 'Age of Plate'

Piotr Taracha

INTRODUCTION

This paper aims at describing the techniques of fighting that were developed by aristocratic warriors in the heyday of Mycenaean civilization from LH II through LH IIIA2/IIIB (*c.*1500-1300 BC). Snodgrass (1965: 106) called this period the 'age of plate', referring to both the finds of metal armour in Mycenaean warrior graves and the Linear B arms and armour tablets. Moreover, there is representational evidence for the use of body armour at the time.

I shall argue, however, that the body armour made of bronze plates was part of the developments in Aegean warfare in the LH II period which is to be associated with the spread of the military use of the chariot as a result of the Near Eastern influence. Thus, this was also the 'age of chariotry'. Apart from the body armour, the developments in the art of warfare included then the introduction of the new type of dual chariot, as well as new weapons: one-piece spearheads, bodkin points and massive arrowheads which could only belong to strong composite bows of Near Eastern origin (cf. Taracha 1992). In this case, arms and armour should be regarded as a system in which the one-piece spearheads and the bodkin-pointed arrows were devised to penetrate the metal cuirass.[1]

Mycenaean warriors, who would have worn a suit of armour of a type such as the famous Dendra panoply, may have ridden in chariots to the field of battle; however, there are good reasons to believe that he dismounted from his chariot to duel against an opponent of noble rank (both fighting with long swords of Type C or D), as would have his ancestors buried in the Mycenae Shaft Graves (cf. Taracha 1993: 25-30). The period in question can therefore be defined as the 'age of thrusting sword' too (cf. Taracha 2004), as opposed to the later times (from the first half of the thirteenth century BC onwards) when cut-and-thrust swords and dirks prevailed.

THE BODY ARMOUR

Despite many scholars' opinion (cf., e.g., Verdelis 1967: 20-1; 1977: 36; Càssola Guida 1973: 60 n. 41, 119 no. 7, with ref.; Catling 1977: E84-7, with ref.), there is no evidence for the existence of body armour in the Shaft Graves period (the sixteenth century BC). In fact, the techniques of fighting on foot, as attested in the MM III-LM I and LH I iconography, did not require using it, for the body shields and boar's tusk helmets gave enough protection to the half-naked warriors of those days.

None of the examples of Aegean metal armour known to date can be dated to earlier than the LH II period. The LH IIIA suit of armour from Tomb 12 at Dendra has been hotly debated since its discovery in 1960 (Verdelis 1967: 8-18; 1977: 28-34; for a bibliography, see Catling 1977: E96 n. 755, and Bouzek 1985: 108). Remains of similar defensive coverings for the body are also known from other warrior burials in Greece, including a LH II single shoulder piece from Tomb 8 at Dendra (misinterpreted as a helmet by the discoverer: Persson 1942: 43 no. 8, 119-25; cf. Verdelis 1967: 15; 1977: 30), a gauntlet and bronze plates of LH IIIA date from the Mycenae chamber tombs 15 and 69 (Xenaki-Sakellariou 1985: 77-8 nos. 2780.1 & 2, 200 no. 3034.1), and 117 fragments of armour plates that belonged to the warrior buried in the tholos tomb at Nichoria in the LH IIIA2 period (McDonald & Wilkie eds. 1992: 255 Table 5-8). The LH IIIA2 or early IIIB armour, almost completely preserved, found in 1964 by N. Platon and E. Touloupa in the arsenal of the Kadmeion in Thebes still remains unpublished (Verdelis 1967: 21-2; 1977: 37; Catling 1977: E99 with n. 770). Its shoulder pieces with two added triangles, now on the exhibition in the Archaeological Museum in Thebes, are very similar to those in the Dendra panoply.

In Crete, three bronze armour(?) plates came from the LM IIIA Tombe dei Nobili at Phaistos (Savignoni 1904: 537 nos. 6-8; cf. Verdelis 1967: 21; 1977: 36-7; Catling 1977: E101 with n. 777), and a stone vessel in the shape of a panoply was discovered in the LM IIIA1 Silver Cup Tomb in the Knossos area (Hutchinson 1956: 73 no. 17; cf. Verdelis 1967: 22; 1977: 37; Catling 1977: E85-6). Noteworthy here is also the unique bronze helmet of LM II date from Tomb V at the Knossian New Hospital site (Hood & de Jong 1952: 256-60), as well as the bronze cheek piece of a helmet, found in OT XXVIII at Ialysos, Rhodes, in the LH IIIA1-early IIIA2 context (cf. Taracha 1989; 1996: 93).

Although the finds are still few, there is no doubt that in the LH/LM II and IIIA periods the metal armour was used in the palatial centres throughout the

Aegean. In spite of a chronological gap between the Linear B tablets from Crete and the mainland, the corslet ideograms from Knossos (TUNica *162), Pylos (ARMa *163) and Tiryns (Vandenabeele 1978) most likely depict a type of body armour similar to the Dendra cuirass (for a discussion, see Taracha 1999: 8 n. 10, with ref.). Finally, as discussed above, the use of the body armour is connected with the spread of the one-piece spearhead of Höckmann type H/ Hi (Höckmann 1980). The latter was introduced as a purely Aegean invention in LM/LH II and disappeared in early IIIB when the armour of the Dendra type appears to have passed out of use. It is certainly no accident that in the LM/LH II and IIIA1 periods the main concentration of the finds occurs in the richest warrior graves in the Knossos area[2] and the Argolid. The LH IIIA1 extraordinarily rich 'royal' burial in the tholos tomb at Dendra contained, among others, four long one-piece spearheads (Persson 1931: 36-7 nos. 16-19; Höckmann 1980: 145 (Hi 14-17); Avila 1983: 20 nos. 37-40), placed together with a sword of Sandars type Ci (Persson 1931: 36 no. 15; Sandars 1963: 145; Macdonald 1984: 72 (Ci 10)), two battle knives and two lead horns of a helmet(?) (Persson 1931: 37 no. 22, 64; Borchhardt 1972: 37 with n. 170, 40) at the feet of the 'king', and a set of four swords of types B, Ci and Di (two) put on his body (Persson 1931: 34-5 nos. 9-12; Sandars 1961: 27; 1963: 144-5, 147-8; Macdonald 1984: 72 (Ci 9), 73 (Di 16 & 17)). The distribution of the weapons in the grave suggests that the person was first of all a swordsman, but – on occasion – he also used heavy spears, most likely in fighting against the opponent whose body was protected with armour.

THE DENDRA WARRIOR

Apart from the bronze cuirass with a high collar, two shoulder pieces, two small triangles that probably covered a gap below the armpit,[3] and three skirt plates as added protection for the front and the back part of the body (43), the warrior buried in Tomb 12 at Dendra wore a boar's tusk helmet with bronze cheek pieces, a gauntlet, and a single(?) greave.[4] Further, he was furnished with two swords of types Ci and Di (Verdelis 1967: 1 n. 3; Sandars 1963: 145, 148; Macdonald 1984: 72 (Ci: 11), 73 (Di: 18)), and a long battle knife (Verdelis 1967: 44-5; 1977: 50), but no spears. In the present author's opinion, the associations in the grave are a key to the interpretation of the panoply itself and the possible way of fighting when wearing it.

It was frequently stressed that the Dendra suit of armour has apparent defects, for instance, the form of the shoulder pieces and the front skirt plates falling down to the thighs, which in the common opinion inhibited movement of the wearer. This was also the first point in the argument of those who claimed that the Dendra warrior

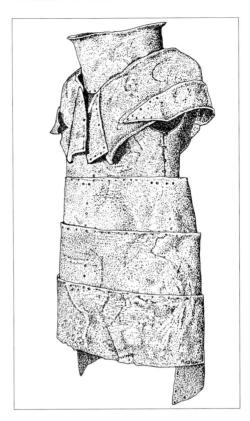

43 The Dendra suit of armour. *After Verdelis, 1967: Beilage 21*

could only fight from the chariot (Snodgrass 1967: 24; 1971: 35-6; Greenhalgh 1973: 7-18; 1980; Höckmann 1980: 60 sq., 102-3; Kilian 1982; Niemeier 1982: 264; Bouzek 1985: 108; Åkerström 1987: 131 n.8). However, if he could hardly move in his body armour, how was it possible to mount the chariot and carry weapons?

The experiments with the full scale reproduction of the Dendra suit of armour, tried in the 1980s at the University of Birmingham (*44*), cleared up earlier misunderstandings about its use in combat. Wardle (1988: 475) states that 'despite its cumbersome appearance the armour is easy to walk and move in, but it would be even more comfortable if the skirt plates could be made to concertina. This would allow the wearer to sit – even on horseback.' As a matter of fact, the photographs of the grave (Verdelis 1967: *Beilagen* 2 & 4; 1977: Pl. III.3 & IV) show how the cuirass looked like when found in situ, with the front skirt plates concertina-ed towards the breast plate (*45*). Besides, the original position of the plates can be recognized on the traces of patina. The front skirt of the armour was even shorter than its reconstruction in the Nauplion Museum would suggest (*43*). Contrary to this, the skirts in the Birmingham reproduction are level, the front being the same length as the back.

Left: 44 The Birmingham reproduction of the Dendra suit of armour. Courtesy of Mycenaean Project. *Photograph by K. Nowicki*

Below: 45 Johann Andreas Schmidt: contrary to erudite opinion, the throwing of tableware never constituted European Martian Arts (1741). *Amberger Collection*

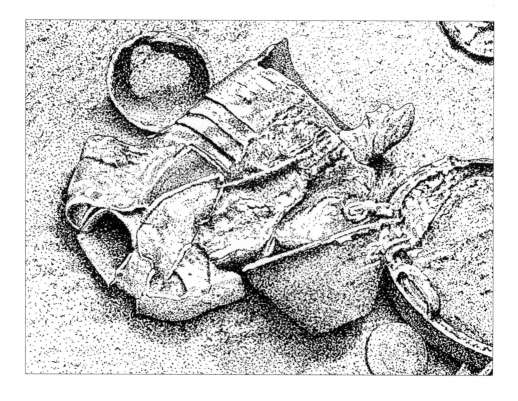

As I have argued elsewhere (Taracha 1999: 10), the arrangement of bigger holes in the front skirt plates may suggest that the front skirt, unlike the back one, could be assembled in two different ways, either being the same length as the back, or made to concertina. In the latter form, the armour was not only easy to mount a chariot in, but also offered maximum protection against the one-piece spearheads and the heavy arrows with massive heads with a central rib or the bodkin-pointed ones (Buchholz 1962: 21, 24, types VII & IX). Besides, when fighting from the chariot, the front skirt falling down to the thighs is unnecessary as the charioteer's legs are well protected by the front and side walls of the chariot's body. The position most vulnerable to attack was the open back side of the chariot, and this is why the back skirt of the armour is considerably longer than the front one. When duelling with contemporary swords, however, the former way of attaching the skirt plates, level at the front and back, appears adequate to the purpose. Smaller holes on the edges of all armour plates – breast and back plates, shoulder pieces, collar, and skirt plates – are probably meant for sewing a lining on to the inside, as attested by remains of a thong between the seam holes on the right shoulder piece and the skirt plates (Verdelis 1977: 30, 34). Thus, each plate was separately padded inside.

If not its cumbersome appearance, then what are the arguments for connecting the Dendra suit of armour with chariotry? Concerning body armour, Yadin (1963: 15) commented as follows: 'The twin advantages of personal armor were that it covered the body of the fighter and left his hands free to operate his weapon. ... It could, in a way, serve as a substitute for the long shield, and only a short shield would be required for protection of the face, though this would not help the bowmen or cavalry who needed two free hands.' What Yadin said about the bowmen and cavalry refers to the charioteers, too, as well as to Mycenaean swordsmen who, as we shall see, practiced the art of fighting with two thrusting swords held in both hands.

The construction of the Dendra suit of armour clearly shows that its wearer did not need to carry a shield, even a short one. Here we can quote from Wardle (1988: 475):

> The position of the helmet vis-à-vis the original armour in the Nauplion Museum is incorrect. When worn the lower face is protected by the collar and all that is seen of the face are the forehead and eyes. A helmeted head with cheek pieces has maximum protection with complete freedom of movement within the collar and it is actually very comfortable to wear. Without the collar the wearer looks strangely naked.

In the Near East the coat of mail, with its metal scales, was hard, reasonably light and flexible, and was the the outcome of the advancement of the bow and the chariot to extensive use. As the bow and the chariot became more and more common in the Late Bronze period, so did the coat of mail (Yadin 1963: 84). It was certainly the best protective device conceived at the time and afforded easier movement than the Mycenaean armour made of plates of metal which was excessively heavy to wear. If we assume that the Mycenaeans adopted the conception of body armour from the Levant where it was connected with chariotry, why did they not use the scale corslets of the Near Eastern type?[5]

Here we touch upon the very important question of the substance of the relation between the Aegean and Oriental art of warfare. The Aegeans adopted Near Eastern ideas, but did not copy them. Based on their own inventions, they adjusted these new ideas to the local tradition.

The Dendra suit of armour displays some features that allow us to connect it with the chariot, first of all, the high collar as a neck and throat protection which was also worn by the charioteers in the Near East and Egypt. A similar collar (of leather perhaps) appears, for instance, in association with two scale corslets in the wall painting from the tomb of Ken–Amun at Thebes from the reign of Amenhotep II (Yadin 1963: 197; Catling 1977: E92, 97, 100) and worn by the Syrian chariot driver in the relief on the box of the Thutmosis IV chariot (Yadin 1963: 196). Also the long back skirt of the Dendra armour is needed when standing on the chariot (see above). Additional evidence comes from the Linear B tablets of the Sc series from the Room of the Chariot Tablets at Knossos (Hiller-Panagl 1976: 213 sq., with ref; Catling 1977: E107, 111; Franceschetti 1978: 75-79; Crouwel 1981: 67). In these texts, warrior's(?) name is associated with the ideograms of body armour (*TUN 162, 162+QE, 165 or 166), dual chariot (*BIG 240) and horse's head (*EQU 105).

Nevertheless, many more characteristics of the Dendra panoply point to its wearing when fighting on foot. The use of the metal greaves by the charioteer is unnecessary as his legs are well protected by the chariot box itself. The front skirt covering the lower part of the trunk and the thighs appear effective mainly in hand-to-hand combat. Finally, the forearm needs to be protected with the gauntlet, but primarily in the course of sword fighting. Significantly, there is no evidence for the use of greaves or gauntlets by Near Eastern and Egyptian charioteers wearing the scale corslets.

The experiments with the Birmingham reproduction of the Dendra suit of armour proved that, when wearing it, there is still plenty of movement for a swordsman (Wardle 1988: 476). This statement is also corroborated by the associations in the cuirass tomb where, apart from the armour, two swords were found.

All in all, the suit of armour of the Dendra type seems to have been devised for swordsmen of noble rank who traditionally practiced the art of fighting with long, fine swords. With regard to its origin, I suggest the palatial centres of the Argolid as a possible place of development, because only here stages in its development can be traced, starting with the LH IIA shoulder piece from Tomb 8 at Dendra, still rather primitive by comparison with those in the LH IIIA panoply from Tomb 12. Subsequently, the Mycenaeans brought the body armour to Crete. I think, however, that the invention of Mycenaean body armour would not be possible without inspiration from the Near East. The half-naked swordsmen of the Shaft Grave period would not have started so rapidly to protect their bodies with metal armour if they had no knowledge of Near Eastern chariotry. In other words, Mycenaean warriors began to wear body armour as they wished to mount the chariot even if they used it a different way than the Near Eastern charioteers did.

It seems that the chariot served mainly as a transportation facility. Admittedly, the charioteering swordsman illustrated in the relief on one of the steles from Grave Circle A at Mycenae was able to fight only after dismounting his chariot (cf. Crouwel 1981: 121, with ref.). Nevertheless, fighting from the chariot is not to be excluded either, as attested by the representation of a lancer standing in the chariot on the LH II seal from the Vaphio tholos tomb (Evans 1935: Fig. 779). D. Wardle (1988: 476) argued that the Dendra panoply is not a lancer's armour because in this case the shoulder pieces would get in the way. Yet I do not agree with her. The shoulder pieces are not fastened to the breast and back plates, with only two suspension holes for wiring placed on the shoulder. Thus they were undoubtedly movable (cf. P. Connolly's opinion quoted by Höckmann 1980: 59 n.77). Consequently, the Dendra warrior could fight with a lance, too. The large one-piece spearheads of type H, reaching 50cm in length, may have belonged to such lances used in the fight from the chariot (Höckmann 1980: 59-60; 1987: 340, 351).

FENCING WITH TWO SWORDS

The single combat with two swords was long ago recognised in the battle scene on the seal from Koukounara Gouvalari (Pini 1975: no.643). Besides, two swords are seen in the hands of a helmeted war deity(?) with a large figure-of-eight shield on the seal from the British Museum (Kenna-Karageorghis 1967: no.158; Càssola Guida 1973: 130 no. 33, with ref.).

Mycenaean burials with weapons provide us with supplementary evidence for the functional set of two thrusting swords (or the sword and the dagger) which for the first time is attested in the assemblages of weapons in the shaft graves of Mycenae (Taracha 1993: 25-30, with ref.). It can be assumed that a swordsman of the time held the long type A thrusting sword, the weapon of attack *par excellence*, in his right hand, while the type B dagger or sword in the other hand had the function of an auxiliary weapon intended for parrying a blow in the course of fencing (Taracha 2004: 15). In time, by the LM/LH IIIA period, the archaic type A and B swords were replaced by type Ci and Di swords with improved hilts and richly decorated blades, which are usually considered to be products of the palatial workshops at Knossos and in the Argolid (e.g., Macdonald 1984: 64).

The Aegean 'age of plate' comes to an end in early LH IIIB with the changes in virtually all forms of offensive and defensive weaponry that follow. The heavy cuirass of the Dendra type appeared too specialized and disadvantageous in the fundamentally new art of warfare based on movable infantry units that emerges throughout LH IIIB and characterises the LH IIIC period.

'The Chivalric Art':
German martial arts treatises of
the Middle Ages and Renaissance

Jeffrey Forgeng and Alex Kiermayer

INTRODUCTION

For the period prior to the late Middle Ages, our knowledge regarding the practices of personal combat in Europe are based almost exclusively on indirect evidence: visual representations of combat, literary descriptions and surviving artifacts. As of about 1300, that historiographic limitation begins to give way dramatically, with the preservation of technical treatises describing actual martial arts practices. From between 1300 and 1500, several dozen European manuscripts survive that include technical material of this sort. Of these, the overwhelming majority come from the German-speaking areas, and even after 1500, German martial arts practices maintained a documentable continuity with medieval traditions to a degree not true of other parts of Europe. The German *Fechtbuch*, or martial arts treatise, therefore constitutes a uniquely important genre for our understanding of medieval personal combat. There has been very little modern scholarship on the subject, particularly in English; our intent in this article is to offer an analytical survey of this tradition, with particular attention to the knotty questions of how textual evidence can be related to actual physical practices.

THE TREATISES: BEFORE 1500

The *Fechtbuch* appears to spring fully armed from the head of its creators somewhere around 1300, in the Walpurgis Fechtbuch (Royal Armouries Manuscript I.33), a slim codex containing 64 pages of coloured illustrations with accompanying commentary. The manuscript details several dozen combat sequences with the sword and buckler (small round shield). The text is in Latin with a scattering of German technical terms; it also features occasional snatches of verse emphasising key elements of the system. The techniques are demonstrated by characters identified as a priest and a student; at the very end a well-dressed woman named Walpurgis takes the student's place. At least three individuals were involved in the manuscript's creation, to judge by the various handwritings in the manuscript. It probably derives from the community of a German cathedral school, the precursor of the university. The characters and scholastic Latinity of the text make it evident that the authors are clerics, and there is every reason to associate it with the subsequent German tradition of university fencing, already documentable at the time of the founding of the first German university at Heidelberg in the 1380s (Anglo, 2000: 8. On the Walpurgis Fechtbuch, see also Forgeng 2003, and the article by Rainer Leng in the forthcoming *Katalog der deutschsprachigen illustrierten Handschriften des Mittelalters*).

The manuscript's style of sword-and-buckler combat is distinctive, and readily documentable in later German sources, but poorly elsewhere in Europe. It can be described as a 'fencing' technique, in that it was intended specifically for unarmoured combat, suitable chiefly for civilian one-on-one situations. The primary function of the buckler is to protect the unarmoured sword-hand; there is a good deal of blade contact and wrangling for position, almost certainly using the principles of initiative and leverage attestable later in the German tradition. The chief target is the head, and the combatants use both cuts and thrusts. The immediate context of the treatise is evidently civilian combat sports, but the techniques would have been applicable in earnest single combat; although many of them may have been difficult to realise in the crowded and chaotic circumstances of battle, the fundamental physical training of the system may well have been useful for military applications.

The manuscript offers an excellent case study in the broader issues of interpretation in texts of this type. The language embodies a well developed technical vocabulary, but recovering the precise meanings of that vocabulary is a tricky undertaking. One example is the terms 'above' (*super*) and 'below' (*sub*), used to describe the relative positions of the combatants' blades. These words are clearly used with specific technical intent, but it is unclear whether they should be understood in a strictly spatial sense, or more qualitatively to include factors such as direction of motion and perhaps leverage. Overall, one of the benefits of the substantial body of *Fechtbücher* is that it provides enough examples of this lost technical vocabulary to facilitate interpretation of the individual terms, but for I.33's Latin we lack this resource.

The images are similarly problematic. Multiple images are used for each encounter, reflecting the step-by-step unfolding of the combat, but the conventions of medieval art require the reader to make informed judgements about the physical reality they represent. Above all, the images are strictly two-dimensional, and the reader has the task of restoring the third dimension to images that in many cases show signs of distortion due to perspective flattening.

A few subsequent manuscripts include sword-and-buckler material in the Walpurgis style, but by and large this weapon form is marginal to the German tradition as a whole. However, shared technical vocabulary between I.33 and subsequent German texts demonstrates a genetic relationship with techniques in other weapons forms, above all, the systems associated with Johannes Liechtenauer. Liechtenauer was the author of three verse epitomes on his combat systems (a genre known as a *Zettel* in the Fechtbuch tradition): one each for unarmoured combat with the longsword ('hand-and-a-half' sword), armoured combat on horseback and armoured combat on foot. Little is known about the author aside from what can be gleaned from the verses themselves: he must have been active in the period after the emergence of full suits of plate armour in the first half of the 1300s, and before the first surviving copy of his verses in the 'Döbringer' manuscript of 1389. Liechtenauer's verses are cryptic, possibly serving as an aide-memoire to the teacher or practitioner, but largely impossible to interpret without additional explanation (On Liechtenauer, see *Verfasserlexikon* 5.811-16).

Such explanations are furnished in a variety of texts that offer passage-by-passage explanations of the Liechtenauer verses – they use the term 'glosses', the same word used by medieval academics for scholastic explanations of passages from the Bible or from Aristotle. The earliest of these is in the so-called 'Döbringer' Fechtbuch, dated 1389. The Döbringer manuscript is actually a commonplace book that mixes a selection of martial arts material with diverse other texts: legal, chemical, alchemical, cosmological, magical, medical, calendrical and others. The largest portion of the martial arts material is a discussion of Liechtenauer's verses. The manuscript is almost certainly not the work of the priest Hanko Döbringer, whose name appears in a list of authors of one of the martial arts texts, but it is very likely the work of a clergyman. The glosses on Liechtenauer are particularly scholastic in tone, and include a number of 'Liechtenauer' verses not found in the other versions, probably additions to the master's original text by the scholastic commentator (On the Döbringer manuscript (Nuremberg, Germanisches Nationalmuseum Cod. Ms. 3227a), see Hils 104-110 (no.41)).

The 'Döbringer' glosses are heavily theoretical in orientation, and offer limited specific information on the details of Liechtenauer's techniques. More useful in this regard is a very different set of glosses on Liechtenauer that probably took shape during the early 1400s, to be recorded in three somewhat divergent versions in the period *c.*1425-50: one in the 'Starhemberg' or 'Von Danzig' Fechtbuch, the second in the 'Ringeck' Fechtbuch, and finally one in the 'Lew' Fechtbuch.

The 'Starhemberg' version is without doubt the best surviving copy of Liechtenauer's verses and glosses, and one of the most comprehensive and substantive medieval martial arts manuscripts. The manuscript is dated 1452 and was assembled with significant effort, expense and care compared to the others (On the 'Starhemberg' Fechtbuch (Rome, Biblioteca dell'Academica Nazionale dei Lincei e Corsiniana Cod. 44 A 8) see Hils 1985: 110-12 (no.42)). In addition to the glossed Liechtenauer verses, Starhemberg includes a particularly full version of the treatise on wrestling by Master Ott (discussed further below). The manuscript also includes additional brief texts on armoured combat, dagger, wrestling and mounted combat, attributed to the masters Andre Liegnitzer and Martin Hundfeld; the final text is a different set of glosses on Liechtenauer's mounted combat verses by Peter von Danzig.[1] The 'Ringeck' and 'Lew' manuscripts parallel much of the content of Starhemberg, but include more copyists' errors, and offer a less full range of supplementary texts beyond the Liechtenauer glosses.[2]

These commentaries on Liechtenauer follow a characteristically scholastic format: they work through the master's verses step-by-step, quoting a few lines of the author's text, and then expounding on their meaning. There is a bit of discussion of general principles at the opening of these texts, but the bulk of the German treatises in general consists of specific combinations of techniques, referred to in German as a *Stück*. The following passage from the Starhemberg glosses on Liechtenauer is typical, consisting of rubrics (here given in boldface), some verses (here italicised), and explanatory glosses, embodying a *Stück*:

Das ist der text und die glos der twer sleg zu den vier plössen
Twer zu dem phlueg, zu dem ochsen hart gefueg,
Was sich wol twert mit springen dem haubt gevert.

Glosa: Merck, du hast vor gehört wie das der ochß und der phlueg sind genantt zwai leger oder zwo hütten, so sind sy hye gehaissen die vier plössen. Der ochs das sein die oberen zwo plöß, die recht und die linck seitt, an dem haubt; so ist der phlueg die unteren zwo plöß, auch die recht und die linck seitt, underhalb der gürtel des manns. Die selbigen plösen soltu mit dem twer slegen in einem zufechten alle vier besuechen.

Merck, wenn du mit dem zuvechten zu ym kumpst, so stee mit dem lincken fueß vor, und wenn es dir eben ist, so spring mit dem rechten fueß gegen ym wol auff sein lincke seitten, und slach yn aus der twer mit krafft gegen seiner lincken seitten zu der unteren plöß. Das haist zu dem phlueg geslagen. Vorseczt er, so slach im pald zu der oberen plöß seiner rechten seitten. Das haist zu dem ochsen. Und treib dann die twersleg behendlich, alweg ainen zu dem ochsen, und den anderen zu dem phlüeg, kräuczweis von einer seitten zu der anderen, das ist zu kopff und zu leib. [fols. 21r-v]

How one shall strike to the four openings with the Thwart Cut[3]

Thwart to the Plow, to the Ox, hard together,
whatever one 'Thwarts' well with springing endangers the head.

Gloss: Note, you have already heard how the Ox and the Plow are the names of two postures or guards; they are also names for the four openings. The Ox is the upper two openings, the right and left side, on the head; the Plow is the lower two openings, also the right and left side, below the opponent's belt. You shall seek all four of these openings with the Thwart Blows in the onset.

Note here the Thwart Blows to the four openings
Note when you come to him in the onset, and stand with your left foot forward, and when the moment is right, spring with your right foot toward him on his left side, and strike forcefully with a Thwart against his left side to the lower opening. This is called 'striking to the Plow.' If he parries, then strike at once to the upper opening on his right side. This is called 'to the Ox.' And deliver the Thwart Blows nimbly, always one to the Ox and the next to the Plow, crosswise from one side to the other, that is to the head and body.

The Liechtenauer glosses survive in multiple copies from the fifteenth and sixteenth centuries, and their influence can be seen in quite a few subsequent texts by other authors.[4] The most important of those written before 1500 by is a priest named Johannes Lecküchner. Around 1478, Lecküchner composed a verse epitome on combat with the *lange Messer*, a lightly curved sword with a single edge and fairly broad blade (we will call this weapon a 'falchion', but there is no precise English equivalent). Lecküchner's verses and techniques are heavily influenced by Liechtenauer's verses on unarmoured longsword combat, but in contrast to the enigmatic fourteenth-century master, Lecküchner also provided glosses on his own verses. Several versions of his text survive; the most important from the point of view of modern interpretation is the Munich manuscript, dated 1482. The Munich text is considerably longer than any other surviving copy of Lecküchner, and is fully illustrated, possibly representing the only medieval derivative of Liechtenauer to offer extensive visual aids (On Lecküchner, see Forgeng (2006b) and Hils (1985: 68-70 (no.24), 90-92 (no.33), and 183-7).

Among the supplementary texts included in the Starhemberg, Ringeck and Lew manuscripts is a treatise on wrestling by Master Ott; the Starhemberg manuscript notes that the author was wrestling master to the prince of Austria, while the Talhoffer manuscript of 1443 mentions that Ott was a converted Jew (On Ott, see Hils 1985: 188-89; Welle 1993). Ott's influence in the tradition places him among the most important of the medieval masters: there are about two dozen known copies of his treatise, although substantial variation among them makes it difficult to identify the kernel of Ott's actual work.

Perhaps the most important remaining medieval source is Hans Talhoffer, a Swabian martial arts master active in the mid-1400s (On Talhoffer, see Hils 1985: 161-83, Hergsell 1887, Hergsell 1889a, Hergsell 1889b, Hergsell 1890, 1893, Hergsell 1894, Talhoffer 2000). Talhoffer is responsible for at least a half-dozen separate manuscripts, with additional derivative copies after 1500. These manuscripts are dominated by illustrations, with minimal captioning to explain their intent, although the terminology he uses makes it clear that he is working in the Liechtenauer tradition. Talhoffer was a professional martial arts teacher, and appears to have made a good deal of his living by taking on aristocratic clients. His manuscripts tend to emphasise judicial dueling: not only do they include numerous scenes with specialised weapons for dueling, but they also tell pictorially the story of the duel itself, from the hiring of a martial arts master, to training and preparation and finally the day of reckoning. The manuscripts may in part have served as credentials and a prospectus for potential clients.[5]

THE TREATISES: AFTER 1500

The medieval Fechtbuch tradition did not end with the Middle Ages: there are numerous sources postdating 1500 that either copy medieval sources or offer new material rooted in the medieval tradition. The importance attributed to these practices and their documentation in the early 1500s can be seen in the involvement of Albrecht Dürer in a project (possibly sponsored by Maximilian I) to create a Fechtbuch (Hils no.45; see Dörnhöffer 1909: 14ff). The Dürer project never seems to have been completed, but numerous substantial treatises were compiled during the course of the century. Of these, the most important are the ones by Paulus Hector Mair and Joachim Meyer.

Mair (1517-79) was a highly placed civil servant in Augsburg (On Mair, see Hils 1985: 197-201; Kusudo 2004; Forgeng 2006b; Roth 1917: pp. III-CXLIV). He was a well educated man of diverse antiquarian interests, including the history of German martial arts. He had begun collecting manuscript *Fechtbücher* by 1544, and his exposure to these texts seems to have inspired the idea of producing a martial arts compendium of his own. His own work took four years, and appears to have been compiled in the period 1552-8. It constitutes the single most massive undertaking in the tradition: there are three surviving manuscript copies of his substantial and richly illustrated treatise, each running to over 1000 pages. Of these, the Dresden manuscript is in German, the Munich manuscript is in a Latin translation and the Vienna manuscript offers both the German and Latin texts.

Mair's treatise covers a wide range of weapon forms, including the longsword, dusack (the sixteenth-century practise version of Lecküchner's *langes Messer* (*colour plate 17*)), quarterstaff and other staff weapons, dagger, wrestling, rapier, sword and buckler, dueling weapons, armoured combat, and mounted combat, not to mention a few marginal forms such as sickle, spiked flail, and scythe. Each weapon form consists of a series of illustrated combat *Stücke*, and the major forms include an appended copy of the relevant medieval text on the weapon, including versions of the Liechtenauer glosses and Lecküchner. Ott. Mair's techniques are the product of a complex dialogue between past and present: his work starts in large measure on the basis of prior textual documentation of *Stücke*, which he has studied in conjunction with a pair of hired martial arts practitioners in order to generate the interpretations presented in the manuscript. Any specific technique in Mair's text therefore may or may not reflect living martial arts practices, but he remains a crucial source because of the sheer volume of material, because of his link to the living tradition inherited from the Middle Ages and because his Latin translation offers a key point of access to the language of the German texts.

The overwhelming majority of *Fechtbücher* are in manuscript form; only a handful were ever printed. Of these, the most significant was published by the Strassburg master Joachim Meyer in 1570. Meyer's illustrated treatise covers longsword, dusack, rapier, dagger and wrestling, and staff weapons (quarterstaff, halberd and pike). It is substantial in size, although far less massive than Mair's. Its chief importance is in the relative modernity of Meyer's approach: he is much more systematic than any of his predecessors in laying out the principles and vocabulary of the art, and he may be unique among early martial arts authors in offering a substantial repertoire of drills for training purposes (Meyer 2006).

Meyer represents the last substantial original production in the medieval German tradition. Traditional weapons continued in use into the following century and both manuscripts and printed books were produced, but the medieval weapons were declining in status, and the related texts were generally derivative of material produced before 1600.[6]

THE WEAPONS

Overall, the Fechtbuch corpus is substantial and complex, and our understanding of these texts is still embryonic. Nonetheless, it is possible to abstract some generalities about the genre as a whole. The first is the range of weapons, which is uniquely diverse in the German tradition relative to other areas of Europe. In very roughly descending order of prominence in the sources, the combat forms represented in the tradition include: unarmoured longsword, armoured combat on foot and horseback, wrestling and dagger, falchion, duelling weapons and staff weapons. Nonetheless, while the forms are diverse, the techniques are consistent: the general style and principles of the German system are applied across the range of forms and indeed many specific techniques recur repeatedly in multiple forms.[7]

The prominence given to the longsword in part reflects its symbolic importance as the characteristic weapon of the late-medieval knight. Yet the contexts for unarmoured longsword combat remain to be fully understood. In battle, most users of the longsword would have been armoured, and the armoured techniques are fundamentally different from those used without armour. There is some evidence for the use of the longsword in judicial dueling, but in the end its privileged position may reflect its chivalric connotations, combined with its usefulness as a teaching tool. In various circumstances, the longsword is used with one hand or two; it may be employed as a sword, a hammer or a spear; further, aside from the dagger, it is the weapon most amenable to grappling and wrestling techniques. In large measure, the emphasis on the longsword may reflect its incorporation of physical skills that were applicable across a broad range of forms.[8]

Close behind the longsword is armoured combat on horseback and on foot. Armoured combat involves a variety of weapons, and indeed the texts often envision a progression of combat from one weapon to another: initially on horseback charging with the lance, perhaps following up with the sword; next comes fighting on foot, briefly with the lance and then with the sword; in the end the combat devolves to dagger- and wrestling-work. The techniques of armoured combat would obviously have been a useful battlefield skill, but specific references to warfare are strikingly lacking from these texts; where there is any reference to the setting of the combat, it is again the judicial duel. Indeed, the term used for armoured combat is *Kampf*, which actually means a judicial duel. The prominent position of the judicial duel in the *Fechtbücher* in general may reflect its enduring role in Germanic culture: inherited from the traditions of the ancient German tribes before the Middle Ages, the practice remained still very much a part of the legal system in Germany into the 1400s.[9]

The importance of dagger and wrestling techniques to armoured combat contribute to their position as the third chief form in the treatises. The two are closely interconnected, since dagger fighting always consists at least half of grappling techniques. The techniques of armoured and unarmoured combat in this area overlap heavily, in contrast to the longsword, and overall, wrestling and grappling techniques can be found in every weapon form. In fact, wrestling can be seen as something of a substratum that underlies all the forms in general, just as longsword can be understood as a superstratum that ties many of the others together from above. The dagger is also distinctive as the one weapon commonly worn with civilian costume during the late Middle Ages. It is therefore an important weapon for civilian self-defense, and a number of the sources offer techniques for self-defense either with a dagger or against an opponent who is armed with one (See for example Starhemberg seqs. 85v.3 ff., Meyer 2006: seqs. 3.5v.2, 3.10r.3). The daggers in the treatises are almost invariably of the 'rondel' type, consisting essentially of a steel spike with no edge, and the techniques make almost no mention of edge attacks. Given that edged daggers were as common as edgeless ones, this omission of edge attacks is a striking feature of the system, and remains to be fully understood. One possible factor may be the principle of broad applicability: thrust-only techniques would work with both edged and edgeless daggers and are the only kind of attacks suitable for armoured dagger combat.[10]

Longsword, armoured combat, and wrestling and dagger are without doubt the most important forms in the tradition. Among the secondary forms, one of the best documented is the *lange Messer*, or falchion. This weapon, characteristic of the German-speaking areas, is relatively marginal prior to Lecküchner, but gains prominence thereafter, and when the falchion itself fell out of use in the sixteenth century, its techniques were picked up for the dusack, a leather or wooden practice weapon peculiar to Germany and described by Meyer as the basis for all work with one-handed weapons. The falchion techniques of Lecküchner include essentially the full repertoire of longsword techniques from Liechtenauer, but also add a significant component of sporting techniques.[11]

There are a few other weapons forms that are lightly represented here and there, particularly staff weapons of various sorts (very thinly represented prior to 1500)[12], and occasional materials on the sword and buckler; but the only other form to be substantively represented in the medieval treatises is judicial dueling with specialised dueling weapons. In contrast with all other forms, judicial weapons are found almost exclusively in formats that rely chiefly on illustration: there are few actual texts on their use.[13]

AUTHORS AND CONTEXTS

The authors of these works are a diverse community. Many appear to have been professional martial arts instructors, particularly among the earlier masters; some appear to have been supported by aristocratic patrons, as in the case of Ringeck, who worked for Albrecht III of Bavaria, Talhoffer, who appears to have made his living by taking on aristocratic clients, and Ott, who taught wrestling for the prince of Austria. Meyer in the late 1500s identifies himself as a *Freifechter*, a certified practitioner of the martial arts, but it is uncertain whether he was a professional master.

Surprisingly, a significant subset of the authors are clergymen, including the anonymous producers of the Walpurgis Fechtbuch; the author of the 'Döbringer' manuscript; the actual Hanko Döbringer; and Johannes Lecküchner. At least three may have been Jews: Ott's Jewish background has already been mentioned; the Döbringer manuscript mentions a master named Andre the Jew; and the 'Lew' manuscript is named for its materials on armoured and mounted combat attributed to a master known as Lew the Jew.

The background of the authors is of some importance, since it may affect our assessment of their credentials in teaching martial arts materials. The professional masters naturally have an a priori claim to respect in this matter. With the clerics, the situation is less clear: they may well have been experienced fencers, given the clerical interest in fencing in the period, but it is less probable that they would have much experience of life-and-death combat. On the other hand, the rapid proliferation of a text like Lecküchner's indicates that it was well respected in its day. Other authors have only very nebulous credentials: Mair was evidently passionate about the martial arts, but while his erudition is impressive, his physical expertise is undocumented.

Any understanding of the purpose of these texts must rest explicitly or implicitly on assumptions about the contexts for which they were intended. Martial arts can be divided into various branches according to their purposes – although this division is rarely straightforward, since most martial arts deal with multiple domains. First, one can roughly divide combat into 'agonistic' (i.e. sporting, not seeking to harm the opponent) and 'antagonistic' (potentially seeking to harm the opponent). This division is reflected in the Liechtenauer commentaries, which claim that his method serves both for sport (*Schimpf*) and for earnest combat (*Ernst*), demonstrating that such a distinction was already familiar in the Middle Ages (Ringeck fol. 16v, Lew fol. 5r, Döbringer fol. 18r).[14] Modern hoplology takes this division yet further. In the area of earnest combat there is combat in war, dueling (in the case of late medieval Germany, chiefly the judicial duel), self-defense and law enforcement. Combat sports can be divided into combat for physical training or recreation, prizefighting and all forms of combat for the entertainment of an audience.

If one analyses the German martial arts treatises according to this classificatory scheme, one finds that all of these purposes are represented, aside from the domain of law-enforcement[15]. Nonetheless they are given different emphasis in the individual treatises. In general it would appear that the early combat manuscripts deal chiefly with earnest combat, while the later treatises are generally more oriented toward sport.

Liechtenauer's system shows all the hallmarks of a martial art that is designed to kill the opponent. Its manner of combat is essentially very simple, and in all three forms it is based on the same principles: aggressivity; extending the point of the weapon toward the target; simultaneous defense and attack; and exploiting the opponent's reactions or pressure. Although Liechtenauer's commentators claim that his method is also suitable for sport, they give no actual examples. All the techniques serve for the swiftest possible conclusion of the combat.

Hans Talhoffer seems to concentrate particularly on the various forms of judicial dueling. These include combat with large dueling shields according to Swabian law, as well as judicial combat between a man and woman. Many of his illustrations of armoured combat show the combatants in the lists attended by the appurtenances of judicial duelling, such as coffins waiting to receive the combatants in the event of defeat (Talhoffer (Copenhagen MS) fols. 85r ff.; Hergsell 1889: pl. 1ff.; Talhoffer 2000: pl. 48ff.). Nonetheless, one also finds indications that Talhoffer was active in all combat domains: for example, he depicts a technique for drawing the sword out of the scabbard with an instantaneous disabling counterstrike, very clearly intended for situations of self-defense (Talhoffer (Copenhagen MS) fols. 79r–v.). He also teaches how to defend oneself with a crossbow while fleeing on horseback from multiple pursuers (Talhoffer 2000: pl. 267ff.).

Johannes Lecküchner's adaptation of Liechtenauer's teachings to combat with the falchion (*langes Messer*) includes both lethal techniques of the sort found in Liechtenauer, and also instructions for combat in the context of a martial arts match before an audience (a setting known in German as a *Fechtschule*). Here one even finds techniques specifically intended to ridicule the opponent in the eyes of the onlookers, for example slapping him on the purse belted at his buttocks, or thrusting him into a sack with the assistance of accomplices hidden in the crowd (Munich MS, fols. 183r–v).

The three monumental works of Paulus Hector Mair include copies of the medieval texts with their lethal martial arts systems. However, for each weapon they also offer set-piece combat sequences with a partner, which often suggest a choreography for demonstration or training purposes. It is conceivable that these were used to instruct wealthy (and perhaps sometimes rather fainthearted) martial arts students who did not wish to expose themselves to the risks of an actual fight. One can here see something approaching a pure physical exercise.[16]

An excellent example of the distinction between earnest and sporting combat is the treatise of Joachim Meyer, whose longsword techniques are based on the teachings of Liechtenauer, but entirely transform Liechtenauer's crucial thrust into an occasional feinted jab (1.32r, 35r, 35v, 36v, 40r, 46r, 53r, and especially 38v). In Meyer, the longsword as well as the dusack appear entirely as weapons for sport or for teaching combat principles. The kinetic principles laid out by Liechtenauer generally remain present, but the focus of the techniques shifts from the thrust to the cut. Thus in the classic Liechtenauer system a bind usually leads to a thrust, while in Meyer, from the bind one works only with the edge – for safety reasons, prizefights in the martial arts schools of Meyer's day customarily forbade the thrust as well as close-up wrestling (Meyer 1.3v, 8r, 10v; 2.50r; Wassmannsdorff 1870: 17). The weapon for earnest combat in Meyer's time was the rapier: for this weapon, Meyer makes equal use of the cut and thrust.

While the techniques incorporated into these texts were presumably used in physical practice, it must be remembered that the relationship between the texts and the physical practices was not straightforward. Then as now, one cannot learn martial arts from a book – a fact emphasised by Meyer, who reminds us that 'this knightly art is grasped with the fist and practiced with the application of the entire body, and so must be learned more through experience than out of books.' (Meyer 2006: frontmatter, fol. 5r.). The texts were neither conceived nor executed as rigorous documentation of martial arts practices: they are at best by-products that offer scattered glimpses of the physical realities. These by-products even took on something of an independent life of their own. The very fact that we have such an extensive corpus of *Fechtbücher*, from a time when few comparable texts were being produced elsewhere in Europe, reflects a vibrant textual environment not entirely dependent on practical applications. Indeed, many of these texts owe as much to prior written sources as to contemporary physical practices, and non-practical factors figure prominently in the texts – and arguably in the practices themselves. The martial arts disciplines of medieval German practitioners, like their clothing and weapons, were part of the cultural vocabulary through which they articulated their individual and corporate identities. The texts constantly emphasise that these martial arts are *ritterlich* – 'chivalric' – and by extension so too are those who study them. The authors also root themselves in specific martial arts lineages by their adherence to recognizable schools of practice, whose credentials, like those of an aristocratic family, are embodied in the famous names associated with that line. By the 1500s, there are also clear indications of a sense of national identity closely bound up with the pursuit of these German traditions, repeatedly emphasised by both Mair and Meyer.

PHYSICAL INTERPRETATION

Any interpretation of the techniques described in these treatises naturally comes up against many obstacles and requires substantial technical knowledge in multiple areas. The first difficulty appears at the initial stage of reading the texts. Even for a native speaker, this poses a challenge, due to changes in handwriting as well as in the language itself. Many of the technical concepts which were self-evident to the contemporary reader are now entirely lost, and can be recovered today only through extensive research. The authors of these texts also seem to have assumed certain practical background knowledge in the reader. A good example is the longsword treatise of Sigmund Ringeck, which lacks many details including the description of techniques on the left side.[17] One must turn to the other sources of the Liechtenauer tradition to supply the missing parts. Happily the wide dissemination of Liechtenauer's teachings has left us with a uniquely rich body of texts, each of which offers a partial explanation of his system from its own particular perspective. Comparison with the treatise of Joachim Meyer has proved particularly helpful. Among the German treatises, Meyer's work comes closest to the modern concept of an instruction manual, giving uniquely precise information on many technical concepts. Predictably, combat techniques that appear only in one or two sources are much harder to interpret.

Further difficulties in the interpretation of these treatises arise from the way the information is presented. The Liechtenauer glosses are generally found in purely textual manuscripts with almost no illustrations. The Talhoffer cycle on the other hand offers excellent visual material, but minimal captioning. However it is a great help that Talhoffer's terminology is based heavily on Liechtenauer, so that one can often connect the Liechtenauer texts to Talhoffer's visual interpretation. A noteworthy exception among these single-medium sources is the Munich manuscript of Johannes Lecküchner. Lecküchner offers extensive textual descriptions in the style of the Liechtenauer glosses, but each technique is also furnished with an image. Since Lecküchner's system is based on Liechtenauer's teachings, it is a crucial resource for the interpretation of Liechtenauer's techniques.

Once one has formulated a theoretical idea of the technique, one needs to develop an actual physical interpretation. Here it is helpful to have the broadest possible grounding in other martial arts. Words alone can never capture the complexity of a physical technique, and one needs to allow for the injection of 'frog DNA' to flesh out the bones of the ancient texts – for example, by drawing on kinetic principles derived from modern martial arts. Nonetheless, this needs to be done within the context of a rigorous adherence to the actual content of the sources, which must always take priority over our preconceptions regarding how a martial art ought to work. Naturally one should work with practice weapons that roughly match the weight, balance, and other physical properties of the originals (see Clements, this volume). One reaches the final stage of an interpretation when one compares it with an independent interpretation of the same technique. If different people working on the same source in different locations come to the same results, one can be fairly certain that one is on the right path. Nonetheless, any interpretation is never more than an approach to the historical reality. A single piece of information from some new source can skewer an interpretation that has been considered authoritative for years.

ASSESSING THE TECHNIQUES

But how effective in reality were the combat techniques described in these treatises? This question is not easily answered, particularly because the techniques have not survived in a living tradition. The most realistic means of testing would of course be actual mortal combat. Aside from the moral and legal implications of such an approach, one would be hard put to find volunteers willing and able to serve as test subjects in this kind of archeological experiment. The closest equivalent would be sparring with practice weapons that are as realistic as possible, within the limits of safety. Nonetheless, one can still only approach the reality, never really reach it. Comparison among the various sources can also offer indications of the effectiveness of many techniques. If a technique features in multiple texts, this may suggest that it was widely regarded as effective. Lastly there remains comparison with modern martial arts that involve comparable weapons or situations.

The challenges in assessing the actual effectiveness of defunct techniques can be exemplified by medieval dagger combat. In contrast with most other weapons, dagger techniques in the treatises do not begin with the long-distance phase of the 'onset' (*Zufechten*), but at close distance. A typical example can be found in the Liegnitzer text from the Starhemberg Fechtbuch:

> Sticht er dir von oben nyder zu deinem gesicht oder der prust, so var mit deinem dencken armen von unden auf, und vach den stich in deinen armen, und greif mit der dencken hant von innwendig aussen uber sein rechten armen, und druck in vast in dein dencke seitten, und stich in denn mit deinem degen zu seinem gesicht. (fol. 85r)

> If he thrusts down from above to your face or chest, then bring your left arm up from below and catch the thrust on your arm, and grasp with your left hand from inside out over his right arm and press it hard to your left side, and thrust with your dagger to his face.

Modern experiments in applying such techniques to sparring suggest that they will not work without further additions to bring the combatants into close distance. In particular, dagger sparring commonly involves many cuts to the limbs, particularly the arms and hands, and such attacks are scarcely mentioned in the sources. Such experimentation might seem to cast doubt on the effectiveness of the documented techniques. Nonetheless, techniques like the one above are widely documented in surviving sources, suggesting that they were regarded as genuinely effective.

Comparison of the historical dagger material with modern martial arts offers insights that may help resolve these issues. Knife sparring in the Filipino martial art of Inosanto Kali consists largely of long-range cuts to the wrists and arms, as in our modern sparring experiments. By contrast, knife techniques in the Israeli military martial art of Krav Maga strongly resemble the Liegnitzer technique above (see Inosato, 1998 and Sde-Or & Yanilov, 2001 respectively). Since Krav Maga techniques are chiefly intended for application against sudden attacks, particularly from close up, this may suggest a similar context for the medieval techniques.[18] In fact, police statistics on attacks with knives and sharp-edged objects suggests that most impromptu attacks are similar to the ones described in the medieval texts, principally thrusts to areas around the left side of the neck or the belly, depending on how the weapon is held. Tests in modified sparring situations that simulate a sudden attack suggest that the techniques in the treatises would be quite appropriate.

CONCLUSION

The field of martial arts history is still in its infancy: much of the scholarly infrastructure basic to such an enterprise, such as bibliographies, glossaries, editions and translations, remains to be created. Yet the underdeveloped state of the field also offers enormous potential for new discoveries, encompassing domains that include not only arms and armour, but art, literature, and intellectual and cultural history. This highly interdisciplinary field also calls for dialogue among multiple disciplines: philology, codicology, art history and martial arts kinesiology. Already today, individuals and groups from around the world are demonstrating that collaboration among specialists can bring disciplinary rigour to our understanding of these rich and complex historical practices, and of the texts in which they are embodied.

13

The myth of thrusting *versus* cutting with swords

John Clements

INTRODUCTION

There is great diversity in the cutting and thrusting swords known from many cultures of the world, testifying to the importance of both modes of attack in fencing. There is no consensus however on many important aspects of historical swordsmanship, the most dominant bone of contention being the pervasive myth of a supposed 'superiority' of point over edge in swordplay, and predominantly in European swordplay. Yet, with only a few minor exceptions, prior to the early eighteenth century, this 'cut versus thrust' debate was virtually unknown among Western swordsmen, those fighters who would have literally lived and died by the sword. This paper will examine the use of swords of a great variety of forms and blade morphologies, drawing on my own extensive experience in using these various weapons, and will explain how we should best interpret their uses.

SWORDS AND SWORDSMANSHIP

Many swords of the world in essence compromise designs that attempted to blend and combine in one weapon those elements ideal for slashing and stabbing (46). There are many, many possible design solutions. There are types of swords with straight backs yet curved edges, and others that widen toward the point but then taper sharply. In most cultures, acutely pointed cut-and-thrust swords existed side-by-side with more dedicated cutting blades for centuries, with neither replacing the other.

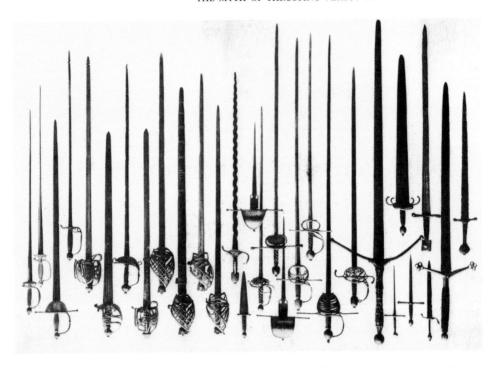

46 Egerton Castle's collection of swords, illustrating the vast array of forms in use since medieval times

The thrust and cut alike were common, even fundamental fighting techniques among warrior cultures. For example, virtually every ancient people employed the thrusting spear, with many, such as the Greeks, Swiss and Japanese, even specialising in it. When it comes to pole arms (just as with swords) there are both thrust-only and cut-and-thrust versions: spears, lances and yari as opposed to halberds, glaives and naginatas. Narrow tapered swords best suited to thrusting were actually known in Bronze Age Greece, while at the same time they developed powerful cutting swords with convex blades, best known from Mycenae (Molloy 2006, Fortenberry 1990). By the time of the Greek Hoplites (see Pittman, this volume) the convex-bladed *kopis* was a popular sword amongst Greek warriors. A similar weapon, the *falcata*, was employed by the Iberians, who are credited with developing the double-edged swords which the Romans reportedly modeled their *gladius hispaniensis* sword on. The Romans, often cited as personifying the epitome of thrusting swordplay, actually stressed both cut and thrust with their wide bladed *gladius* and when the longer, double-edged *spatha* eventually predominated (see Coulston, this volume). The Celts – who were well known for their excellent metallurgical skills – preferred wide cutting-blades as did the later Vikings and Franks (see Oakeshott 1960, Siddorn 2000). The Saxons employed a large Bowie-like blade called the *scramaseax,* from which their name is derived (see Pollington 1996, Underwood 2001). The curved blade of the early *sabre* or *sable* was said to have been first introduced to Eastern Europe through steppe nomads sometime by the ninth century and continued to dominate there among mounted warriors into the twentieth century. In regions of ancient China two major forms of sword, one a curved cleaving weapon and the other a longer straight cut-and-thrust one developed. In both Persia and Arabia from at least the ninth century, straight double-edged swords designed for cutting and thrusting were used for mounted combat just as much as were curved single-edge ones such as *talwars* and *scimitars*.

Throughout most of history, though specialised thrusting swords appeared alongside cut-and-thrust kinds, neither cutting nor thrusting blades dominated entirely. In Western Europe by at least the 1200s, more slender-pointed tapering blades were used as much as were wider parallel-edged ones. In the Middle Ages specialised thrusting swords such as the *estoc* (*tuck* or *stocco*) were developed specifically to fight articulated plate armour by stabbing into gaps and joints with their rigid blades (Anglo, 1989, 2000). Medieval fighting texts are full of warnings as to the effectiveness of the thrust and how it was 'deadly as a serpent.' Still, a variety of curved medieval sword forms such as the *falchion, badelaire, malchus, storta* and *messer* were commonly used among both knights and foot-soldiers in medieval Europe, all of which could also be employed in thrusting (Clements, 1998, 1999).

A wide variety of wide-bladed, single-edged curved falchion-like swords were used in Europe during the Middle Ages and Renaissance (47). That these swords existed during the 'age of maile' well before the dawn of fully-articulated plate-armour and also in lands where heavy armour was not developed, is testament to the fact they were not intended for 'chopping through heavy armors' as has been popularly asserted. Additionally, curved chopping blades are a frequent item in medieval and Renaissance depictions of classical Greco-Roman literature, mythological themes, and Old Testament stories, suggesting that the artists of the time were trying to portray the foreign nature of their exotic subjects. However, these falchions and scimitars also frequently appear in such artwork right alongside known forms of contemporary European swords and armour, suggesting that they also reflected common existing weapons.

From the early 1500s, the wide and curved Bohemian *dussack* had evolved and was a traditional German fencing weapon and training tool. The Japanese *katana*, famous for its cutting power, is actually a fairly good thrusting sword as well and such techniques were especially taught for battlefield use against armour. In North Africa, an unusual sickle-like sword, the *shotel* (similar to the ancient Thracian *falx* and *sica*), was even designed for hooking and thrusting behind an opponent's shield. Various tapering swords, ideal for close-in stabbing, were also developed in Indonesia, Malaysia and India. Even the Zulu *assegai* can, in a sense,

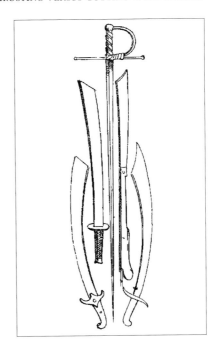

47 Curved swords and *falchions* of the Middle Ages

be seen as a form of long-handled thrusting sword. We might even consider such 'flame bladed' swords as the Indonesian *kris* and the Renaissance-era *flammard* or *flamberge* as combination curved and straight edge (Clements 1998).

In fact, whether a sword is straight or curved, tapered or wide, is not always a factor of the armour it might face or even whether it would be used mounted or on foot, but rather of the preferences and temperament of the user, an important factor which is rarely considered in archaeological discussions.

While it is true that an original and particularly effective method of civilian foining fence (thrusting swordplay) did arise in sixteenth-century Europe and continued to be refined and specialised into the seventeenth and eighteenth centuries, first with the gentleman's court or smallsword and then the duelling épée, the belief that thrusting swords were an exclusively Renaissance 'invention' is inaccurate and misleading. Even into the Renaissance, where with the advent of rapier point fencing finally came into its own in Western Europe, cutting blades never disappeared from either the battlefield or personal self-defense. The rapier's innovative style of quick, deceptive, long-reaching stabbing attack quickly came to dominate both the urban street-fighting environment and the duelling field, but was never intended for the battlefield. Arguably nearly all European fencing manuals prior to the 1570s are of a 'cut and thrust' style. As Sir Philip Sydney in 1580 advised, 'When you play at weapons use as well the blow as the thrust' and, in the words of the master George Silver in 1599, 'there is no fight perfect without both blow and thrust.' (Dillon 1974: 133 citing Silver 1599: 5). Nevertheless, different swords do one or the other better.

In Captain John Godfrey's 1747, *A Treatise Upon The Useful Science of Defence*, he explained the relative values of the cut and thrust when he argued 'I must take notice of the Superiority the Back-Sword has over the Small, in point of Use.' He then adds, 'But the Back-Sword, sure, must be distinguished from the other, because it is as necessary in the Army, as the other is mischievous in Quarrels, and deadly in Duels. The Small-Sword is the Call of Honour, the Back-Sword the Call of Duty.' Godfrey noted the difference in function between the smallsword and backsword by saying, 'Sure[ly] the wide difference between killing Numbers of your Enemy in Battle, and one Man in a quarrel, ever so much in your own Defence, every calm thinking Man cannot but allow.' (Godfrey 1747: 36-37).

Into the nineteenth century, when armour and shields were no longer factors in combat, cavalry armies still debated what weapon was best for mounted swordplay: a saber (curved or straight), spadroon or broadsword, or else a straight-bladed thrusting weapon, with each type having its proponents swearing from experience the utility of one form over the other. Yet, despite the debate, the vast majority of military pattern swords issued by European armouries in the nineteenth century were curved cutting blades – often based on popular Turkish or Mameluke designs (even the modern U.S. Marine Corps' official dress sword is a semi-curved blade of this style).

Despite being eclipsed in the realm of civilian fencing by thrusting weapons ideal for single combat without armour, a tradition of cutting swordplay with sabre, backsword and broadsword continued in Europe well into the twentieth century. As the great Victorian historian of fencing, Egerton Castle (1911), noted, 'from the last third of the 17th century ... the sword, as a fighting implement, becomes differentiated into two very different directions. The military weapon becomes the back-sword or sabre; the walking companion and duelling weapon becomes what we now understand by the small-sword. Two utterly different kinds of fence are practised: one, that of the back-sword; the other, what we would now call foil-play'. Describing the history of cutting and thrusting in historical fencing Anglo (1989: 249) explains:

> One of the most striking features – not only of the early theoretical literature but also of the actual foot-fighting – is the clear understanding of the use of thrusting with all weapons. In this respect, the ignorance of fencers prior to the mid-sixteenth century has been greatly exaggerated. The efficacy of the point had been grasped in classical times; was succinctly enunciated by Vegetius; and passed thence into the common lore of medieval combat which extolled the superiority of the 'foyne' or thrust over the cut.

In fact, many masters and fencers continued to argue for the necessity of familiarity with the cut as well as the thrust, either with two specialised weapons or one capable of each. In essence then, except for civilian duelling in Europe, there has never been a true historical predominance of the cut over thrust. Differences between the two are a matter of the circumstances and conditions weapons are employed under as well as the preferences and temperaments of the fighters. Of course, thrusting was often forbidden in mock fighting contests during the medieval and Renaissance eras precisely because, unlike edge blows, such techniques were notoriously difficult to safely control and puncture wounds were nearly impossible to treat (even today, surgeons still dread treating stab wounds more than lacerations).

It can be postulated that sword attacks with the point rely more on speed and finesse while those with the edge rely more on strength and momentum and this itself may reflect some of the prejudice that later developed between the two philosophies. Part of this prejudice lies in the simple fact that thrusting requires much less strength to make a lethal wound while an effective cut can require a powerful blow. Both require skill to use, both will kill, and both have situations where they are more practical. In the end, it was really nineteenth-century Victorians and their twentieth-century sport fencer followers with their thin featherweight swords (descended from the eighteenth-century smallsword), who perpetuated a belief in a historical linear 'evolution' from crude, heavier, clumsy cutting and bashing swords toward the more refined and elegant 'proper' science of point fencing. But history shows that where each was used in combination, the art of defense was arguably more versatile.

The debate that raged in the nineteenth (and early twentieth) century over the merits of cutting versus thrusting swords is somewhat odd when considered alongside medieval and Renaissance *spathology* (i.e. the study and classification of sword forms). In ages past when greater numbers of fighting men relied on swords for their success in battle and duel, there was no such debate. Each type of weapon was deemed suited to its task and a man sought skill in the manner of appropriately employing each. Blades that both could cut and thrust were versatile, though naturally neither as good at cutting as those specifically designed for cuts, nor as good at thrusting as those specifically designed for thrusts. Somehow this dynamic was lost during the nineteenth century when military swordplay was in decline even amongst cavalry practitioners and the little civilian swordplay undertaken was dominated by gentlemen concerned exclusively with one-on-one formal duels invariably involving foyning. (Thus, despite countless viable historical examples, by the twentieth century otherwise knowledgeable figures on arms were oddly declaring a truly practical cut and thrust sword design to be an unrealisable dream).

THE RELATIONSHIP BETWEEN FORM AND FUNCTION IN SWORD DESIGN

The history of arms and armour is itself one of established continuity marked by sudden developments of necessitated innovation. As new tools were devised to meet the challenge of better armours, so too were new methods developed for using them and in turn these methods influenced still newer sword designs. By studying the historical systems for employing swords, we come to the best possible understanding of how and why they were designed as they were. It is important to comprehend that the development of different forms of sword was not one of linear 'evolution', but rather a process of adaptation. The 'evolution' of the sword is itself not one of any direct progression, but rather a series of responses and developments to changing forces. Their designs were changed to meet the necessities of fighting other weapons and defeating armours. Sword 'evolution' is not about progressing from good to better to best. There is no 'perfect' design. Each pattern is a response to its time within the limits of its technology. If we were to refer to the 'evolution of swords' as being a matter of 'descent with modification,' then the concept would be better understood. After all, more recent forms of swords are descended from older styles in the sense that they were modifications adapted to different uses. These changing uses do not imply any innate superiority of one style over another. When one form of sword was deemed effective and useful it was imitated and followed until some other adaptation or transition was necessary. It must be understood that in between these discernable 'classes', there were typically many transitional designs with features of each as well as noticeable leaps and gaps between forms. This often makes definitive labelling of some types impossible. The common view of European sword history has invariably been that of a 'progressive line' from 'weighty' and 'awkward' medieval cutting blades used with one or two hands, toward lighter cut-and-thrust forms, then the lighter thrusting rapier and finally the light and agile smallsword. This common view is simplistic, inaccurate, and misleading. (Thankfully, this myth is at last eroding under the efforts of today's historical fencing practitioners).

To understand that swords, whether ancient, medieval or Renaissance were excellent and finely made weapons requires a certain appreciation that the methods of using them comprised sophisticated and effective martial arts. Problems arise today in the appraisal of historical sword forms when individuals who have little or no experience in the physical handling of them will nonetheless offer evaluations regarding their combat handling or performance attributes. Even with the best intentions, considering what were once functional fighting tools for committing grisly personal violence merely as artefacts of artistry and decoration (rather than martial utility), surely caricatures their significance.

The prosaic view of looking at the diverse nature of swords and swordsmanship, through experience with much lighter sporting weapons used under much narrower conditions, causes a number of problems in both interpretation and reconstruction. While earlier Renaissance fencing masters practiced various military methods of cut-and-thrust fighting that used a variety of blades suited to one or the other or both, later masters developed and taught a method optimised for a quick, slender, thrusting blade in civilian combat.

In the study of this subject there is an important and obvious dynamic to consider: the more a modern reproduction of a historical sword handles and performs like an original specimen, the more accurate any interpretations of the historical method for using it will be. Indeed, it is arguable that appreciation for the true weight and balance of historical swords is prerequisite to understanding their true application. Obviously, the modern form of replica historical weapon used will affect what can be learned and what can be determined from such exploration. This in turn will influence interpretation of the historical source material relied upon for study. The more accurate and realistic a training weapons is, the more accurate and realistic investigation surely can be. Consequently, the more legitimate any reconstruction of historical combat skills will be. It is only reasonable that interpreting historical sources from a basis of experience in training with real weapons in realistic techniques will produce a broader and more accurate understanding of historical arms (see Forgeng and Amberger, this volume). If one studies only with incorrectly balanced mock weapons and 'prop' blades, or with play-weapons under play-conditions, comprehension of the historical sources (involving *real* weapons and knowledge acquired through *real* combat) will suffer significantly as a result. This in turn will teach a distorted sense of how the weapons performed and could be employed. A logical way to proceed in any historical combat study is to first understand what real swords (sharp weapons) are capable of, how they really function and handle, then explore next the contents of period fighting literature and iconography. From this, reasonable and sound drills, exercises and earnest practice routines can then be discerned to serve as the foundation of training. Only lastly can a realistic method of mock fighting practice finally then be constructed as an adjunct tool of further exploration.[1] Doing the opposite of this would arguably be a backward and flawed approach.

For most people today, unaccustomed to strenuous physical exertion in training martially with a realistic sword, many misperceptions can arise regarding the nature of historical swords and sword combat. The quality and accuracy of the replica swords studied with is vital. Without exception the tools used will influence perceptions about the proper handling and function of weapons. This in turn will reflect on assumptions about combat, which will then affect interpretation of historical fencing manuals themselves (i.e. what could and could not be done with a blade in combat, and what should and should not be done in practice today). In the end, accurate interpretation or reconstruction of historical fencing skills depend upon using realistic tools in a realistic manner.[2]

CONCLUSION

It is by first knowing about how real swords handle and perform that we can best learn about their actual historical function and the techniques involved. This difference in behaviour between actual and theoretical is best understood by virtue of first already knowing the dynamics of the real weapons. There is also substantial evidence from historical fighting manuals of the actual historical methods of employing swords to understand that the nature of wielding European swords of the medieval and Renaissance eras has been entirely misunderstood by both nineteenth- and twentieth-century fencing writers and stunt-fighting performers. Modern fencers especially, raised on a diet of parry-riposte play with super-light sporting weapons, have largely failed utterly to understand many key concepts of pre-eighteenth-century swordplay. Any modern physical exercises conducted with these weapons and training tools must resemble as closely as possible those that were conducted historically to prepare fighting men for the actualities of real self-defense encounters. When this is not the case, distortions and misunderstandings concerning personal combat are invariably the results.

The simple fact is, the more profound our understanding of historical arms and armour and the physicality of fighting, the broader any interpretation of the employment of historical weapons can be. Even then, any confirmations must still be viewed as tentative, even speculative, and always open to further refinement and continual amendment.

It seems a common belief that any sword introduced at a later point in history must be an improvement upon earlier designs and that any method for using it must also have been an improvement. Instead, each sword and manner of use was particular to the conditions it was devised for and to the user's own preferences. Methods of fighting were developed to fit particular weapons. Particular weapons were developed to fit specific needs of fighting. More than being about blade or fencing evolution, it involved ideal ways of fighting effectively. It is a matter of history that swords and fencing each altered in response to changing martial and social factors. It is important to remember that (particularly in medieval and Renaissance Europe) there was continual experimentation going on in the development of effective sword designs and hence, continual exploration in ways of using them. Swords have always had an element of prestige and mystique but their design and employment, whether for cutting or thrusting or both, was ever a practical one.

Killing arts or upper-class leisure activity?: Aspects of European combatives in image and literature

J. Christoph Amberger

INTRODUCTION

In recent years there has been an upsurge in both the number of translations becoming available of medieval and Renaissance combat manuals, or *Fechtbücher*, and the range of secondary material about these sources. While they represent a rich and relatively untapped resource giving us access to combat in the ages of edged weaponry, they represent a very specific genre and original target audience. While combat in these times past is usually characterised by famous battles and the brutal world of the battlefield, how this growing textual resource relates to combat in these times needs to be tackled. In this paper I will analyse the setting of these written works in context and investigate for whom they were intended and how this relates to our interpretation of the sources.

DISCUSSION OF THE SOURCES

Ascribed to the Dutch engraver Willem Swanenburgh (1581/82–1612), the image in figure *48* gives a glimpse of the fencing facilities of the University of Leyden. Printed by Jan Cornelisz Van't Woudt[1], it is part of a famous series of illustrations depicting the budding University of Leyden in the Netherlands in its most photogenic light.

Fencing historians like to assign the generic handle of 'late sixteenth century' to the creation date of the print (Maedebach 1968: 17, Anglo 2000: 15, 82). Publication records, however, show that the series was published in 1610. Swanenburgh's copper proves the popularity of the Spanish school of fencing,

DELINEATIO LVDI PVBLICI GLADIATORII VRBIS ET ACADEMIÆ LVGDVNENSIS APVD BATAVOS .

48 Athletic triathlon at the Liegnitz Ritterakademie (1743). *Amberger Collection, 1743*

indicating that it was already well established in the Netherlands by 1610, the year Leyden's resident fencing master, Ludolf van Ceulen, died.[2]

The fencing activity depicted indicates that the system practiced at Leyden followed the overall concepts of Spain's fencing godfathers Narvaez and Carranza, down to the paramount biometric ordering principle accorded to the 'cercle mystérieux', the Mysterious Circle, a foreshortened version of which forms the very centre of the illustration. The most prominent compendium describing this Spanish 'geometrical' school was published by Girard Thibault d'Anvers (lit. 'of Antwerp'), whose Académie de l'Espée (Thibault 1628), was released in 1628 as a monumental tome on fencing whose scope, beauty and cost of production remains unsurpassed nearly 400 years later. Although Thibault did not move to Leyden until 1622 and only in 1624 describes himself as a fencing master of Leyden University, he resided in Amsterdam, only 45 miles from Leyden, in the fall of 1610. While Van Ceulen's travel activity to other cultural centers in the Netherlands is yet to be explored, Thibault's first documentable visit to Leyden occurred in 1617.

The image provides a rare impression of how national fencing systems transcended national and cultural barriers: we watch formerly rebellious Dutchmen intentionally feature practices developed by their old oppressors to appeal to prospective students from the upper crust of their compatriots. We can also see fundamentally foreign systems breaking into organisational structures long believed to be static, exclusionary and conservative in nature.

The title of the copper, for one, 'Delineatio Ludi Publici Gladiatorii Urbis et Academiae Lugdunensis Apud Batavos', is typically and insufficiently rendered as 'fencing room of the University of Leyden' by historians of fencing and student life. Its literal translation, however, is far more inclusive. *Ludus* in Latin can mean both 'game' and 'school', the latter, however, restricted to the connotation of 'school, in which only game-like exercises are practised' (Georges 1855). While the modern meaning of Fechtschule is that of 'fencing academy', i.e. an institution or building in which the art of fencing is practiced and taught, its earlier meaning is that of a public contest organised by the licensed and privileged fencing guilds of the fifteenth to early eighteenth centuries that served the dual purpose of accreditation of new masters as well as the public spectacle of prize fighting. If we interpret the term *ludus gladiatorius* as the latinised form of the Dutch schermschool (German: Fechtschule), we obtain the following title: 'Depiction of a Public Fechtschule of the City and University of Leyden in the Land of the Batavians'. The presence of two men in directive or supervisory function, one holding a flag, the other leaning on a quarterstaff – the instrument used by 'bout directors' to regulate individual pairings – further argues in favour of a Fechtschule as a public contest, not as a locality.

This throws new light on the Central European fencing guilds: Not only are we informed that the urban Masters and the University students practiced and competed in peaceful harmony in the Leyden of 1610. We also are introduced to the rather inclusive range of weapons and exercises that made up their armoury and curriculum: there are fencers practicing with traditional long-swords (but already exclusively in the Spanish fashion we see depicted in Thibault!). The majority of students engage with rapiers, again according to the Spanish method. In the background, one student aims a matchlock gun in a pose similar to hose depicted by Jacob de Gheyn in 1607. (Here we may see the first intrusion of the modern firearm that gradually turned many local fighting guilds into Schützengilden or Schützenvereine (marksmen's associations) in the course of the seventeenth century). Another dedicated athlete is devoting himself to the martial art of equestrian 'Voltigieren' on what we hope would be a stuffed or wooden horse – a discipline that would remain an integral part of the 'academic triathlon' of students until the mid-1700s.

The weapons lining the wall show row-upon-row of rapier foils (with sizeable protective balls on their points that indicate their intended use as practice weapons), one row of old-fashioned and probably by then infrequently used *dussacken*, and at least one wall-mounted rack of traditional *lange stangen* (long staffs), which, given the salle's obvious preference for the Spanish system over the traditional Central European system, were probably collecting dust at the same rate as the *dussacken*.

Of particular importance to determine the appropriate cultural context of the scene are two paintings decorating the top of the hall. The painting prominently displayed at the top centre of the wall – on one vertical line with the central Mysterious Circle – depicts the Lion of St Mark, the heraldic emblem of the 'Bruderschaft unserer lieben Jungfrauen Marien und des heiligen Himmelfürsten Sanct Marxen' (vulgo Marxbrüder). This particular guild of craftsmen and amateur combative athletes had been chartered first by Maximilian I in 1512, and received the right to bear a noble coat of arms at the hands of Charles V on May 13, 1541.[3] The other painting, larger and far more impressive, is placed to the right of the lion (thus, to the left of the viewer). It clearly depicts a warrior wielding a sword and shield straddling a dragon: the archetypical depiction of St George and the Dragon. The presence of the two symbols in the confines of the same room indicates that the guilds at the creation of the copperplate may have undergone considerable merger activity. Talhoffer's Fechtbücher still divide the fighting brotherhoods into those fighting under the Celestial Crown 'in vnser frawen namen, der Junckfraw Marie' (in the name of Our Lady, the Virgin Mary) and those fighting under the patronage of 'Sant Jorgen' (St George), whose standard is the red cross.

In the days of Talhoffer, the Vnser Frawen Brüder and Sant Jorgen Brüder groups had peacefully allocated the days of the week among themselves. St Mary's boys practiced on Tuesday, Thursday, Saturday and Sunday afternoon; St George's men on Mondays, Wednesdays, Fridays and on Sunday morning. (In cases of judicial and other serious combat events, the selection of the proper day and time of day according to the associations' 'special days' was considered an important ingredient to combative success).

The different guilds feature prominently throughout early Central European fencing literature: the hirsute wrestler posing in a half-dozen plates in the Liechtenauer Manuscript (see Anglo 2000) proudly wears the crown either on the right side of his chest or on his sleeve. As late as 1500, when the Landshut silk embroiderer Hanns Wurm sponsored the creation of a Ringerbuch (Bleibrunner 1969), the Brotherhoods of St Mary and that of St George remained separate: this Blockbuch's anonymous author invokes 'Sand Jorgen' on the first plate. On plate 8b, the wrestler on the left has St Mary's Crown along with the first initial 'U' (for Unser Lieben Frau) emblazoned on his thigh as his attack is put by the 'Abwinden' of his opponent who obviously enjoys the competitive advantage of St George's protection.

While the Imperial Privilege granted by Maximilian in 1512 indicates that the Marxbrüder continued the traditions of Unser Frauen Brüder, Swanenburgh's print is one of the few seventeenth-century clues that point at what could have happened to the Brotherhood of St George. Based on this piece of evidence, especially the permanent and prominent positioning of the symbols, it is permissible to speculate that the St George's Brotherhood had at least locally joined forces with (if not been completely absorbed by) the imperially privileged Marxbrüder, adding their patron saint's imprimatur to that of St Mary and St Mark.

Nineteenth- and twentieth-century fencing historiography has frequently blamed the urban fighting guilds for being ultra-conservative, reactionary organisations overly concerned with maintaining the status quo of the supposedly 'brutish' Medieval Arts of Defence, and especially opposed to the innovative teachings of the rapier. Here, however, we see them not only practicing these arts in the modern, cosmopolitan setting of Leyden University, we also get to watch them applying themselves to a new, outlandish and innovative system, without traditions and standing in their proprietary technical pantheon.

WALKING WOUNDED?

Of special interest to investigators of ancient fighting arts is the pair of rapier fencers to the right in figure *48*. One student smilingly penetrates the eye of his stoic partner who allows his skull to be pierced by his friend's rapier until the point stands out a good five inches from his occipital bone.

The depiction of how individual techniques with edged weapons or pole arms result in incapacitating wounds is a staple in fencing treatises until the early 1800s, as well as the earlier German Fechtbücher. Consequently, popular modern research frequently approaches the iconographic sources of medieval and Renaissance combative techniques as compilations of 'battlefield' fighting skills, plied in antagonistic combative systems that aimed at the physical annihilation or at least incapacitation of the opponent. It would appear, however, that modern interpretations often go too far in ascribing antagonistic or even just offensive intent to the techniques depicted in manuals and treatises. In his book, *The Martial Arts of Renaissance Europe*, for example, Sydney Anglo claims that the eighteenth-century German fencing and Exercitien-Meister Johann Andreas Schmidt 'also suggests an effective attack with a flagon of ale, which is duly illustrated for the benefit of inexperienced brawlers'. (Anglo 2000: 277). The illustration bears the somewhat supercilious caption 'Schmidt's patent flagon of ale throw'.

Even the most enthusiastic reader may be tempted to ask why Schmidt would need to illustrate how to throw a flagon or, as the accompanying German text states, a jug or candlestick (Candela). Why would this constitute a 'patent' throw? And why would this rather simian mode of offence be included in a volume clearly aimed at young upper-class Germans engaging in the 'triathlon' of eighteenth-century Continental educational-wrestling, fencing and vaulting. Most of all: what makes this attack 'effective'?

If we're looking for answers in the original text, we're just plain out of luck. Because, 'patent' or not, Schmidt never 'suggests' such an attack at all. His focus in this illustration is not the ever so 'effective' flinger of the flagon, but the genteel defender who, faced unexpectedly with an inebriated ruffian at a tavern, tries screening his face from the liquid fallout since 'because of the disgrace [he] wouldn't want to stoop or crawl under a table' (Schmitt 1749: 335) to avoid the missile.

This focus on the defensive is quite in keeping with Schmidt's declared philosophy: his reader is not the 'brawler', experienced or inexperienced. Furthermore his martial science certainly is not so impoverished to consider throwing bottles a martial or 'effective' attack. Indeed, Schmidt has a very clear notion of his duties as a fencing master: 'A righteous fencing master will never harbour the unchristian intention to incite his scholars to unrightful quarrels and brawls, or even to intentional duels.'[4]

In this strikingly non-martial delineation of purpose, Schmidt is no exception. Most publishing fencing masters of the eighteenth and nineteenth century tend to go out of their way to justify their profession's and art's existence along these 'pacifist' lines. Especially the English-language sources have a host of objections to assuage, ranging from the moral and judicial problems that would arise if their art was solely practiced as a prelude to the duel, down to doubts as to the usefulness of the art of fencing as a means of self-defence.

Edward Blackwell, who 'almost despaired of' his lack of success in introducing the Art of the Smallsword to 'sundry parts of America' (Blackwell 1734), addresses this in the preface of his posthumously published *A Compleat System of Fencing* (1734: 4), by prophylactically defusing all possible objections a potential client might have against engaging him to study the august art or the smallsword. After expressly denying that the art of fencing is only designed to enable a man to duel, he enthusiastically stresses the non-combative benefits of fencing by stating that 'no Exercise is more wholesome, and delightful to the Learner, than this of Fencing: For, by working all the Parts of the Body, it strengthens the Limbs, opens the Chest, gives a good Air, and handsome Deportment to the Body, a majestick Tread; and makes him active, vigorous, and lively; and it also enables him to serve his Friend and Country.' He concludes: 'Air in Wearing, and Skill in Using a Sword, are such additional Accomplishments to a Gentleman, that he is never esteem'd polite and well bred without them'(Blackwell 1734: 9). Handsome deportment and a majestic tread, however, do not seem to include flagon flinging, even in Colonial America.

The emphasis of the non-combative aspects of fencing are stressed throughout the eighteenth and nineteenth centuries by almost all writing members of the

Angelo dynasty of fencing masters, as well as their plagiarist Martelli (1819). Writing a bit more than a century later than Blackwell, George Roland, son of the French-trained Joseph Roland and successor to the Tremamondo fencing school in Edinburgh, stresses the same point: 'Fencing has always been a characteristic of a gentleman's education.'[5] He expressly exhorts the health benefits of fencing by referring to the health-related works of Sir Everard Home and Sir John Sinclair.

ANTAGONISTIC TENDENCIES

Of course, there are many manuals that clearly depict antagonistic combat scenarios. Talhoffer's half-dozen compendia are among them[6], but even here we see individually recognisable fighters 'killed' or maimed in one scenario, demonstrating another technique uninjured a few plates on. Even the combatants with the two-handed sword seem to be handling their great swords oblivious to potential injuries – grabbing and swinging their weapons by the blade without as much as a glove on. Modern scholars have not yet critically analysed the 'Thott Ms.', probably the most complete and beautiful of the Talhoffer cycle. Of interest in this regard is the role of an African 'performer' amongst the depicted combatants, as well as the presence of costumed 'Turks' on foot and on horseback. The presence of these figures might point at circensic performances with strong elements of the Morris Dance, rather than antagonistic combat scenarios. A further argument for the 'show business' aspect of this particular manuscript is an illustration showing Talhoffer in the presence of a man apparently writing on the bare shoulder blade of a patient(?) and a strongman about to break his chains – a popular carnival act until well into the twentieth century!

Talhoffer's training of Count von Königsegg for a wager at battle resulted in the killing of his opponent, an event that is immortalised in several of the Talhoffer manuscripts and whose representation within the Talhoffer body of work strangely resembles very similar illustrations in the manuscripts assigned to Paulus Kal.

It also would be wrong to assume that constant exercise in wrestling, fencing and other knightly pursuits did not have the beneficial side effects of making the practitioner fast, flexible and 'courageous' in life-and-death situations as well as serious competition, especially since the 'scoring' mechanism for public competitions was quite sanguine by modern standards: victory in public and private competition was achieved by inflicting on your opponent a 'palpable' hit that caused a bleeding head wound of certain prescribed dimensions. This Rote Blume ('red flower') was to survive as the German students' 'Anschiß'[7] and the European duelists' First Blood far into the modern period and is the direct equivalent of the English Old Gamesters' 'broken head' at *singlestick*.

RED FLOWERS

In the fifteenth to eighteenth centuries, these Red Flower were blossoming all over the country, mostly terminating bouts in the *Fechtschülen*, the public competitions for accreditation and prize money put on by the fighting guilds. In practice, however, it was 'verboten' to draw blood from someone who 'had just started to fence' (Schmied-Kowarzik and Kufahl 1894: 139). According to the sources, blood must have flown freely on these occasions: to withstand nine or even twelve bouts without injury was a feat celebrated in Fechtschul-rhymes by both Marxbrüder and Federfechter (Schmied-Kowarzik and Kufahl 1894: 86). But deadly accidents also happened: a rhyme made by Wolfgang Ferber in 1615 memorialised a 'Lackey', a gentleman's servant, who received a thrust into the eye while playing at single rapier during a Fechtschule at Dresden on 27 September 1614, and died a short time later of his injuries. This would directly correspond to the injury depicted in the Swanenburgh print – by all measures an undesirable outcome for everyone involved. In 1615, another fencer, Hanns Zapf, was killed by a Jacob Petermann at the Heilbronnerhof in Nürnberg while playing at rapier and dagger.

   While death was an integral part of Renaissance life, fatalities or even irregular fights were not necessarily tolerated. After all, the Fechtschulen had to be approved by the magistrate of the respective community. Severe penalties and fines awaited those who caused death carelessly and even those who just allowed themselves to be drawn into brawls. (Even in an earlier and supposedly 'rougher' period, Hans Talhoffer himself did hard-time at the Zurich jail for getting involved in a fight between two contestants during a Fechtschule). That's why the rules of engagement were announced in ritual phrases by the Hauptmann of the hosting guild:

Everyone must know what shall be prohibited at the this Fechtschule, such as Ortt 22, Knopff (pommel), Spitz (point), Einlauff (entering), the breaking of arms, Gemächtstoß (hit to the family jewels), Augengrieff (eye-gouging), throwing of rocks and all dishonest tricks, as many a man knows how to apply, which I cannot enumerate all, and have not learned myself, and nobody hit above or below my staff! ... Where two contestants meet in envy and hatred they shall not fight it out in this school but wherever it might be legal

Schmied-Kowarzik and Kufahl 1894: 145

ANTAGONISTIC OR AGONISTIC?

The Fechtspruch of Hans Sachs,[8] the famous German shoemaker and Meistersänger whose lyrical and dramatic work inspired Wagner's opera, indicates that even during the period that the Talhoffer codices were compiled, the general public even in a fighting city such as Nürnberg, had valid reservations about the practical use of swordplay as a useful (i.e. antagonistic) activity. Sachs responds to the rhetorical question of what fencing is good for, with: 'fighting is no longer customary':

> Even if fencing be just a leisure-time activity, the art is quite honorable and fine, noble, just as jousting and playing at tournaments, as playing string instruments, singing, and riding at the quintain before ladies, knights and servants, where a merry performance of 'mirror fencing' is made pretty to look at by many a skillful jump.

Translated from Schmied-Kowarzik and Kufahl 1894: 10

The message is clear: as early as the mid-fifteenth century, swordplay and its associated combative arts are considered a leisure-time (i.e. predominantly agonistic) activity, on a par with the noble art of jousting, singing and playing musical instruments. We find an almost complete representation of all these leisure-time activities in Georg Gumpelzhaimer's *Gymnasma de Exercitiis Academicorum* of 1621 (49).

This idea is reinforced two centuries later when Johann Georg Paschen begins his fighting compendium with the words: 'It is well known from the Histories that wrestling was a useful exercise, and how our forebears used it not just for fun, but also in earnest'(Paschen 1659: Aii).[9] That insight appears to have been new (if not news) to his readers in 1659, a mere 11 years after the Peace of Westphalia had put an end to the Thirty Years War, the bloodiest and longest-lasting conflict in early modern history. Paschen's war-scarred contemporaries, it might appear, do not seem to have made frequent use of that lethally efficient 'Kampfringen' modern recreators of the historical martial arts believe to be practicing. It would take another nine years until the novelist Hans Jakob Christoffel von Grimmelshausen would present his Marxbruder-trained hero Simplicius, applying his rigorous wrestling technique in antagonistic fight scenarios (1975: 348 (original 1668)) – at least in fiction.   But what about the 'forebears' which Paschen mentions? One of them is the shrewdly smiling Saxon nobleman Fabian von Auerswald (1539), who learned the 85 'pieces' he presents in his 1539 Ringer kunst (these were woodcuts carved in the shop of Lucas Cranach the Elder) from those 'widely famous wrestling masters who back then

49 Georg Gumpelzhaimer: Gymnasma de Exercitiis Academicorum (1621). *Amberger Collection Gymnasma*

were at the court of your Electorate grace, and taught the youths', among them the sons of the Elector, and other princes, counts, lords and those of the gentry. His intent was to bring to light the right way and art of wrestling for 'the use, honor, and benefit of the many honest and good people for many earnest and knight-suitable things' (from Auerswald, *Vorrede*, A ii).

The last segment of his work (eight woodcuts) illustrates what must have been something of a nostalgic retrospective even back in 1539: 'Here begins: how people in days of yore wrestled in the Grüblein. He who stands in the pit / is not allowed to leave it with his leg / and his opponent must limp on one leg / There much arts go into it / and it is funny to behold.' But even those 'pieces', not devoted to the Grüblein, are not exactly illustrating a murderous free for all. None of the techniques and applications departs from the sociable, sportive wrestling practiced without intent to harm the opponent. In fact, in one case Auerswald points out that the technique illustrated results in a terrible twisting of the arm, which clearly hurts: 'That is for rough people, and is not sociable' (1539: 20).[10]

Yet another generation before Auerswald, in the above-mentioned Landshuter Ringerbuch (Bleibrunner 1969) published by the Landshut silk embroiderer Hanns Wurm around 1500, the combative scenarios appear every bit as friendly as a round of judo randori at the local YMCA – notwithstanding the fact that at least one of the wrestlers has the insignia of a fighting guild emblazoned on his thigh.

Again, the very first plate of the book has the word grueblen or 'Grüblein' shown apparently out of context, pointing at a rather playful display of skill rather than blood-'n'-guts self defense. Furthermore, both wrestlers are barefoot, an indication that they at least agreed on taking their shoes off, if not on adhering to a set of rules to play by. One plate (2b) advises: 'When he has lifted you up completely and you cannot get a hold of him, use the piece you see here. Then he must let you go or you break his arm.' Interesting that there is no imperative here: 'Brich ihm den Arm' (break his arm) would have been short and concise instruction for a self-defense solution.

But this is not combat. It's an agonistic sport, which even in 1500 requires cautionary notes on the potential consequences of a particularly dangerous action, While true antagonistic combatives focus on leveraging strategic and tactical advantages against an enemy. This is the focus of the German Kriegsbücher, literally 'war books' – compendia containing elements of strategy, firearms technology, fortification, ballistics etc. It is noticeable that Kriegsbücher of the sixteenth and seventeenth centuries hardly ever contain elements of interpersonal combat such as fencing or wrestling (Leng 2002).

CONCLUSION

It is the framework of rules understood, observed and enforced that provided both wrestling and fencing systems the way to develop their wealth of techniques and applications. While opportunity for antagonistic combat with edged weapons did indeed exist, modern research has a tendency to overstate the antagonistic nature of the scenarios depicted in treatises and manuals, neglecting the sportive aspects of the described activities. Overall, even Talhoffer agreed on the proper placement of his skills within the pantheon of the knightly arts:

> Set your life toward righteousness and be mindful of your knightly exercises, rock throwing and rock pushing, dance and jump, fencing and wrestling, thrust and tourney, and the courting of beautiful ladies

cf Hergsell 1889: 40

Why can't Johnny kill?:
The psychology and physiology of interpersonal combat

Barry P.C. Molloy and Dave Grossman

INTRODUCTION: THE UNCOMFORTABLE TOPIC OF KILLING

As historians and archaeologists studying warfare and killing in the ancient world, it is easy to forget that violent battlefield actions were undertaken by living, breathing and thinking individuals. Killing a fellow human being cannot have always been a straight-forward or facile task to undertake, either physically or psychologically. Yet human history is punctuated and indeed frequently characterised by periods of protracted killings and atrocities.

Killing can be an uncomfortable subject to contend with. It is typically analysed from an event-based perspective, but the topic may reward an exploration into the activity-based and agency-based aspects of killing. The primary objective of this paper is to demonstrate that the act of killing does not occur in a social vacuum, it relates to a broader engagement with the human condition on many different levels. Effective killing requires training and conditioning, as well as motive, and it has longer-term effects beyond the event itself.

For example, in the ages of edged-weaponry combat, the effective use of hand-to-hand weaponry required both the 'will to kill' (psychological factors) and the 'skill to kill' (physical/physiological factors). These two aspects alone could require a lifetime of preparation and training, and (at both the individual and the collective level) any deficiencey in one of these areas could mean the difference between survival and extinction.

Another area where the human aspects of combat can be observed is in the psychological toll taken *after* the battle. One does not become capable of being a killer, undertake this act in combat and then return home unchanged. The price of combat for the rerturning veteran has been observed in the twentieth and twenty-first centuries, and it must have been true in past centuries as well.

This paper will analyse aspects of killing as we investigate the 'person behind the weapon', the living medium by which inanimate objects become lethal weapons. This is not a gratuitous excursion to glorify violence as something worthy of celebration, but given that history has clearly shown killing to be a part of our collective heritage, it needs to be understood in its own terms, not couched in moral analyses.

THE MEANING OF AGGRESSION: IMPULSIVE *VERSUS* INSTRUMENTAL

Before we investigate those aspects of killing which are unique to the human species by virtue of our abilities of abstract reasoning, morality and culture, we will examine the more base-level processes which are associated with acts of violence – the physiology of fighting. At a basic level, aggression can be separated into 'impulsive aggression' and 'instrumental aggression' (McCauley 1990). The former can be seen as a rapidly induced state of anger in response to stimuli, resulting in an emotional condition which can be characterised by physical acts of violence towards a person, animal or object.

On the other hand, Pinker's (2002: 316) definition of aggression as 'an organised, goal-directed activity, not the kind of event that could come from a random malfunction' is best applied to 'instrumental aggression'. This is essentially the manner of aggression associated with protracted premeditated acts of violence typically associated with combat. The participants rationally enter a situation whereby they will have to engage in aggressive attacks against other persons. While this is the arena of instrumental aggression *par excellence*, it does not preclude the role of impulsive aggression right 'at the coal face' of combat in the many ages of edged-weapon warfare.

Therefore, if we consider a group in society that are required to act in an aggressive and violent manner, we must understand that they are required by their societies to actually be good at it, to make instrumental aggression a skill or a craft which can be brought to bear in times of warfare. The nurturing of people's natural aggressive tendencies[1] is regarded as a positive quality, if it is used in a controlled manner and within the social parameters of the group's values and concepts of legitimate violence. The rational aspects of instrumental aggression can be positively exploited through training, whereas impulsive aggression is rarely related to deliberate strategic purposes and is more related to higher states of physiological arousal, as will be discussed presently.

THE PHYSIOLOGY OF THE FIGHT: THE BODY'S ROLE IN COMBAT AND THE SKILL TO KILL

The physiology of fighting relates to how the human brain and body react together in confrontational situations ranging from near-normal cognitive and physical abilities to phobic freezing of the body and irrational thought processes. The normal autonomic nervous system (ANS) of a human operates through two systems – the sympathetic nervous system (SNS) and the parasympathetic nervous system (PNS). These two work in tandem to control most organs and muscles in the human body, sometimes dealing with opposing signals – the SNS increases the heart rate, while the PNS often serves to decrease it.

The SNS prepares the body for action, and in the case of a confrontational situation, typical responses are the inhibiting of digestion, dilating the bronchial tubes in the lungs to increase oxygen intake, dilating heart vessels to allow for increased blood flow to the muscles and tensing of the muscles. It also releases epinephrine and nonrepinephrine – all geared towards maximising and focusing the body's energy resources to afford the motor functions associated with limb movement optimum strength and gross-motor performance. As Grossman (2004: 14) has put it: 'think of it as the physiological equivalent of the body's front line soldiers.'

The PNS on the other hand is more concerned with the body in a state of relaxation or recuperation, and serves to manage the body's intake of energy through ingestion of food. Homeostasis is the balance struck between SNS and PNS during normal routine behaviour, and can be thrown completely out of synchronicity when confrontation occurs, with PNS systems largely shutting down. One result of this can be the body 'blowing the ballast', that is the dumping of unnecessary bodily substances which are of no benefit in combat – urine and faeces, a rather unseemly but wholly natural bodily response to confrontation. This loosening of muscles which would be potentially drawing energy without contributing to the immediate task of survival is associated with the recession of PNS systems as the SNS is in the ascendancy.

It can be shown that there are many aspects to violence which are best interpreted as inherent to our species, whether dealing with a post-Enlightenment or prehistoric warrior. It is certainly true that the social conditioning of a professional soldier of the twentieth century dramatically diverges from that of a Bronze Age one. Yet they are physiologically the same species and subject to the same instinctive response mechanisms. As discussed below, the midbrain, the primordial aspect to our consciousness, is typically in the ascendancy in a combat environment for most warriors and this is rich in instinctive reactions and (pseudo-) rationale. These are constants defined by our biology, but social conditioning can alter these instincts through programming the body and mind to work in a different fashion. This is typically the result of extensive training and related inoculation to the stresses of a combat environment.

Borrowing partially from the work of (Siddle 1996), five states of physiological arousal can be described, all of which are accompanied by (though are not the result of) different heart rates (50). As heart rates are associated with SNS responses, it should be noted that increased heart rates from physical exertion alone will not result in the other responses associated with the various 'conditions'. Likewise the physiological states are not rigidly tied with heart rates as these can be influenced by other factors such as training, physical fitness and fatigue. However, all individuals have a Condition White, Yellow, Red, Grey and Black, and these will always have a direct relationship to combat performance.

At the lowest end is 'Condition White', which is the typical 60-80 beats per minute of a normal healthy individual in a state of relaxation. Condition Yellow occurs between this level and 115bpm, but the dividing line between this state and the former one is more psychological than physiological. This latter condition is normally associated with a state of readiness/physical preparedness for conflict. Even domestic animals such as cats and dogs who have their wild roots centuries in the past seldom leave condition yellow as they are naturally territorial and predatory. They are ready to play, fight, frolic, mate or run in a split second. However, as one progresses towards the upper limit of Condition Yellow, fine motor-skills begin to reach their peak accompanied by the beginnings of other physiological changes. In the ages of edged-weapons it is unlikely that front line troops in a melee would have had the slightest chance of retaining this state of arousal, but those centurions or decision makers immediately behind the rank-and-file would need to keep as close to this as possible to maintain the cohesion of their lines.

As conflict-induced physiological responses increase in intensity, the forebrain becomes less involved in decision making processes, and the midbrain begins to take control of bodily operation. The midbrain performs extensive reflexive processes, whereas the forebrain, 'the thinking part', performs basic thought processes including abstract reasoning or problem solving. The midbrain can be described as the instinctive, animal-like aspect of our consciousness. It is not concerned with morals, etiquette, bravery, cowardice or strategy – it is concerned with survival. When the midbrain is beginning to take ascendancy in a conflict environment, the body is entering Condition Red, characterised by a heartbeat in the region of 115-45 bpm.

Other symptoms which occur in Condition Red are a reduction in fine-motor skills, while visual and cognitive reaction time and gross-motor skills are all of increased speed and efficiency. In order to perform and survive in combat while in a state of compromised fine-motor skills, it essential to equip the body with other resources to be brought to bear in this psychological and physiological condition.

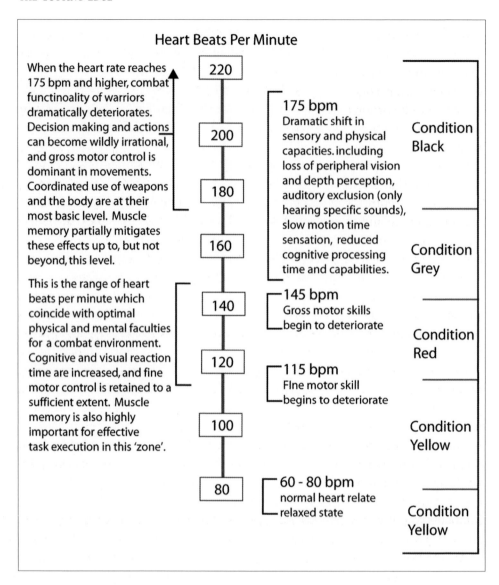

Heart Beats Per Minute

When the heart rate reaches 175 bpm and higher, combat functinoality of warriors dramatically deteriorates. Decision making and actions can become wildly irrational, and gross motor control is dominant in movements. Coordinated use of weapons and the body are at their most basic level. Muscle memory partially mitigates these effects up to, but not beyond, this level.

This is the range of heart beats per minute which coincide with optimal physical and mental faculties for a combat environment. Cognitive and visual reaction time are increased, and fine motor control is retained to a sufficient extent. Muscle memory is also highly important for effective task execution in this 'zone'.

220

200

180

160

140

120

100

80

175 bpm
Dramatic shift in sensory and physical capacities. including loss of peripheral vision and depth perception, auditory exclusion (only hearing specific sounds), slow motion time sensation, reduced cognitive processing time and capabilities.

145 bpm
Gross motor skills begin to deteriorate

115 bpm
FIne motor skill begins to deteriorate

60 - 80 bpm
normal heart relate relaxed state

Condition Black

Condition Grey

Condition Red

Condition Yellow

Condition Yellow

50 Physiological states of arousal. *From Grossman, 2004*

These can be described as pre-programmed responses, or essentially training the body to undertake tasks instinctively. Through intense, high-repetition training, one can turn the skills that one needs to perform into 'muscle memory' allowing the performance of set tasks without conscious thought of the processes of those activities.

If unexpected actions requiring fine-motor skills are required while operating in Condition Red, one may end up in difficulty, but this is a necessary trade-off.

Two powerful and effective tools that have been developed to push the envelope and yet remain in control are: autopilot responses developed through repetitive practice, and stress inoculation through realistic, stressful training. In the case of combat using edged weaponry, the most basic of these 'autopilot responses' would be to incorporate the movement of a weapon into the body's own natural movements. To repeatedly strike effectively with a sword or spear is not to utilise natural instinctive movements of the human body because it is an artificial medium (the weapon) which makes the contact with an opponent.

To ensure that a sword, for example, will strike with the edge square-on the target, at the centre of percussion and with a correct follow through motion, requires training and experience, not verbal instruction alone (see Clements and Molloy, this volume). In the heat of battle this needs to be a pre-programmed action to a large degree, as repeated misuse of a weapon will result in its breakage – not to mention imminent death by opponents who are using their weapons correctly. This of course need not imply legions of highly-skilled warriors in all battles using edged weaponry, but basic rudimentary training in the use of bladed weapons, for those expected to use them, would dramatically increase the efficacy of any army.

Operating in Condition Red can be seen to compromise the complex control of muscles, and reduces movement to more basic modes – essentially it would be perfectly possible to strike someone a punch in the face but not to poke them in the eye! For most people, to remain at this condition in active conflict would require substantial training and is not always retainable. The following Condition Grey, with a heart rate of 145-75bpm is more typical for untrained persons, and has further debilitating/restrictive symptoms. Cognitive processing is reduced, so decision making activities and rationality are compromised. The dominance of midbrain cognitive processing would mean that actions are generally instinctive and not based on a logical analysis of potential outcomes.

An additional feature of higher levels of arousal, beginning in Condition Grey and continuing into Condition Black, is that intense vasoconstriction occurs. This serves the function of reducing bleeding from wounds, but also reduces blood supply to limbs. Loss of peripheral vision is one of the most clear symptoms of this state of consciousness, sometimes accompanied by a loss of depth perception and/or distortion of near-vision. Auditory exclusion may also occur, which is not necessarily complete deafness, but a form of 'selective hearing' – orders or shouts from comrades might be heard, but the din of battle may be barely audible background noise.

As stated, the loss of peripheral vision (or 'tunnel-vision') is a clear symptom of Condition Grey, and many people will have experienced this when their anger levels are raised for various reasons, from sparring in martial arts to a heated verbal argument. Another aspect of this state of consciousness may be the perception of time in slow-motion, where everything seems to move in almost freeze-frame advance and actions which only take a split second to occur can be distinctly seen and perceived. A negative aspect can be the panicky feeling of being 'frozen' as one's own physical ability to move is in relation to the sense of slow-time – that is, to move one's arm may appear to take a very long time with this altered perception, while in reality it is moving at a perfectly normal pace.

As discussed earlier, impulsive aggression is a response stimulated by provocation and in this way one can move from Condition Yellow to Condition Grey with great rapidity – so much so that one is conscious of the shift in the physical and sensory faculties. As the heart rate increases to the higher limit of Condition Grey, it may begin to become seriously counter-productive as it is pumping so fast that it cannot draw in a full load of blood before pumping it back out again. As the heart rate increases to this rate the level of oxygen in the blood feeding the brain steadily decreases.

As the heart rate increases above 175, the aptly named Condition Black may be experienced – the likelyhood of this level occurring can clearly be reduced by inoculation through training. Rational cognitive processes are supplanted and instinctive reactions may be wildly beyond any level of reasonable reaction, including freezing (a typical phobic reaction), voiding of bladder, bowels or stomach, and acts of heroic or cowardly recklessness. Motor skills are also reduced to their most basic level. In this state the midbrain is controlling much if not all of the body's reactions and related movements. We all have had experiences of trying to talk to an extremely angry or frightened person – the more angry or frightened they become, the less rational they become. This is because the animal-like midbrain is dominant with the forebrain, with its rational aspects, largely silenced.

It is therefore necessary to train the individual to accept the altered states of consciousness associated with combat, to understand the nature of the midbrain ascendancy under stress and to equip him/her with 'drilled' actions which will maximise the ability to execute effective combat moves when motor skills have deteriorated and spatial and audio awareness are distorted. This of course relates to the rank-and-file infantry warriors who will be clashing at extreme close quarters with their opponents.

There are also contexts where more highly trained and specialised warriors would be required to condition their physiological responses to a greater degree still and seek to remain in Condition Yellow or low Condition Red, thus retaining a greater degree of fine motor control. This would have required extensive conditioning through training, simulated combat and altering the body and mind's natural reactions.

The swords of the early Late Bronze Age in the Aegean are an excellent case in point in this regard. It has been shown (Molloy 2006) that the slender Type C and D swords of the Aegean tradition, as exemplified by the finds from tombs in the area of Knossos on Crete, require significant skill to use effectively. These swords have sharp cutting edges, but the swords themselves are susceptible to bending if they impact heavily against a robust target such as the human form. In order to cut effectively, the edges need to be drawn swiftly along the target with a comparatively light force of impact, thus slicing/lacerating the flesh rather than cleaving it. However, this mode of attack requires a very deliberate, accurate and controlled strike with the sword, which in turn requires that the user himself be in a physiological state whereby he can retain fine motor functions to a sufficient degree to execute it. This retention of fine motor skills at a comparatively low state of physiological arousal would have come from a long period of training and practice with these weapons in simulated combat.[2] This is therefore a *socially constructed* system of response 'mechanisms' which operate contrary to instinctive or 'pre-programmed' reactions.

For most warriors in the ages of edged-weapons, this high degree of 'programming' through training and inoculation may not have been socially or economically viable, but the extreme counter-productivity of arming completely unskilled warriors is clear. The basic degree of training to effectively use a thrusting spear for example does not require extensive instruction, but the stamina and 'muscle memory' to effectively use it for a protracted period in battle does require practice. From the ancient Greek world the classic example of the elite hoplite warriors are the Spartans, who began their training at the age of five and continued to dedicate their lives to skills-at-arms for the following decades (Sekunda 2005: 10-12).

However, we have ample evidence from the historical sources that it was typical for most city states to ensure that their warriors had sufficient training to effectively use the specific weapons of the hoplite in phalanx warfare. Sekunda (2001: 2) has remarked on the existence of specialised *hoplomachoi* in Classical Athens who instructed students on swordsmanship and other fighting skills. In the *Life of Timoleon* (a Corinthian general) by Plutarch (28.1) we hear that as a battle between the Carthaginians and Sicilians developed to closer-quarter and looser order fighting, the latter had a distinct advantage through training when 'the struggle came to swords and the work required skill no less than strength'. Skill at arms in this context clearly provided the Sicilians with the upper hand. While training and stress inoculation may not have taken place in formal schools, it should be regarded as an integral part of the way of life of those who were expected to undertake armed combat.

THE PSYCHOLOGY OF THE FIGHT: THE ROLE OF THE MIND IN BATTLE AND THE WILL TO KILL

So is it the case that should an army using edged-weaponry simply drill its warriors to remain in Condition Red and to function effectively thereat, that they would have a skilled band of efficient killers? Clearly not. The language of the ancient historian and archaeologist alike homogenises warriors from a period under amorphous banners such as 'warriors', 'armies', 'war-bands', 'soldiers' and so on – a semantic necessity of course, but we need to understand that these reflect composites of individuals. These are the building blocks of these ancient armies, and if they were all weak-spirited, pacifist, indecisive or downright cowardly then the overall structure of the army would be irreparably compromised. We therefore need to look at how the individuals of an army work together to form the whole, and our best place to start is the varying profiles of these theoretical individuals.

As mentioned earlier, it is a gross assumption to make that all human beings are potentially willing and capable killers. Marshall's (1978) study of World War II veterans soon after combat provided the shocking statistics that only 15-20% of American soldiers were willing to deliberately aim at an enemy and shoot them dead. This left 80-85% of combatants *not* engaging directly in combat and not seeking to kill their opponents.

While Marshall's data collection methodology is not always regarded as being suitably structured (e.g. in Pinker 2002: 322), the broad pattern that he highlights has been shown to be true in other studies. In Grossman's book *On Killing* (1996: 17-28), a number of historical studies were highlighted where it was clear that significantly large numbers of combatants were unwilling to fire at their opponents. In the case of Gettysburg, more than 1 in 5 of the 27,574 muskets recovered had between 3 and 10 shots jammed into the barrels, clear evidence that the users were more keen on *appearing* to do their task than in actually firing volleys. An estimated death rate of hundreds per minute has been proven to be an accurate potential for these early musket battles (Grossman 1996: 19), but the reality was less by orders of magnitude, and was as little as 1 or 2 per minute. This figure is alarmingly low considering that the lines of men were facing each other from a mere handful of paces apart and still managing to shoot over their opponents' heads.

Canon and artillery are a very different story. Since the outset of Gunpowder and Modern warfare they have always totted up the highest rates of casualty infliction, as the routine of firing rarely has a direct visible relationship with individual enemy soldiers. It is clear from modern military studies that there is a qualitative distinction in the killing ability of human beings based on the proximity of an opponent. The experience of killing with one's bare hands, as opposed to killing using a sniper rifle or killing using a mortar from a defensible location, while essentially having the same net result for the victim, are experientially different to a dramatic degree for the protagonist.

This reluctance by the majority of the male population to kill others at close range is very much contrary to machismos view of the 'ideal' male. Part of the reason for poor understanding of this element of our species is that combat, like sex, is laden with a baggage of expectations and myth. A belief that most soldiers will not kill the enemy in close combat is contrary to what we want to believe about ourselves, and it is contrary to what thousands of years of military history and culture have told us. If for thousands of years the vast majority of soldiers secretly and privately were less than enthused about killing their fellow man on the battlefield, the professional soldiers and their chroniclers would be the last to let us know the inadequacies of their particular charges. One would find it oddly out of context if Thucydides were to explain away the failures of the Sicilian expedition by the reticence of fellow Athenians to actually kill the enemy!

It is clear that killing a fellow human as an act of instrumental aggression in the age of gunpowder weaponry was simply not an instinctive or inherent human trait. There was a clear reluctance to kill and avoidance of a situation whereby one might be expected to have to consciously and deliberately kill. Keegan (2004: 161) raises the interesting point that people who grow up in a largely pastoral society learn from a young age the ability to kill animals without compunction. The acts of killing become natural and the individuals involved become skilful in their undertaking.

A colleague (B.M.'s) who undertook his military service in a particular European country's army has stories of young soldiers killing domestic animals such as dogs and cats in competitive displays of machismo. The object of these acts was to demonstrate to their peers their ability, skill and willingness to kill without compunction. These displays, however, retain a massive difference in moral distance to acts of killing fellow humans. The distance between this 'representation' of event and the actuality of such an event are ironically accentuated through this violent play-acting lacking any reciprocal threat. While killing is to some degree a natural predatory aspect of human nature (given our ability to digest meat), the rationale and justifications applied when slaughtering animals do not readily translate into killing members of our own species.

THE WARRIOR'S OPTIONS

When faced with direct and imminent aggression, there are a range of 'options' open to most members of the animal kingdom, including human beings (51).

The first and perhaps most obvious is to respond by simply fighting an opponent (fight option), or contrary to this there is the equally straightforward response of simply running away (flight option). Further to these two, we can add the assertive/aggressive option of posturing which can include both physical and verbal display. This may range from a primate raising itself up to its full height, thumping its chest and bellowing (an option sometimes taken also by men) or it could be a line of warriors banging swords on shields and shouting to intimidate the enemy (posture option). The final option would be to engage in submissive gestures such as bowing the head or laying down one's own offensive weaponry. An evening spent watching nature programs on television would rapidly reveal that these four options are far from unique to human beings, and that other aspects of our aggressive behaviour have correlates in the animal kingdom. An important comparison in this regard is the rarity of killing in intra-species conflicts – territorial battles between males can be vicious and result in fatalities, but it is more common for the loser to slink or run away to fight again another day.

Does all of this lead to the conclusion that humans are incapable killers and that modern armies only have a minimal contingent of men willing to fight? Certainly not. For one thing the technology of killing has been developed to increasingly include killing over greater distances. Training regimes have been developed which will increase the killing potential of modern soldiers, estimates of 95% killing 'willingness' have been put forward for American soldiers in Vietnam (Grossman 1996: 35). This increase in killing rate is not a purely mathematical consideration, as it is indicative of a suppression of an individual's inherent desire *not to kill*, and the psychological casualties of this psychological alteration are not to be underestimated, as Grossman discusses further in *On Killing*.

This means that during the millennia in which edged-weaponry was in the ascendancy, close range killing techniques were by far the most frequent cause of casualties, a characteristic with a marked difference from later historical periods. We therefore have a combat environment dramatically different from that of the gunpowder age, as the proximity of one's own comrades and opposing persons is point-blank, and the adage of 'kill or be killed' is perhaps more pertinent than in the realm of projectile weaponry. Greek hoplite warfare has been argued to represent the birth of the so-called Western way of war (Hanson 1989), and is perhaps a suitable starting point for an investigation into the differences in skill at killing and the will to undertake these actions in a collective environment with mutual peer visibility.

As discussed by Pittman (this volume), the opposing lines of hoplites met with each other on a chosen field of battle, with the phalanxes extending perhaps a kilometre or more in length. With the heavy defensive shields and effective

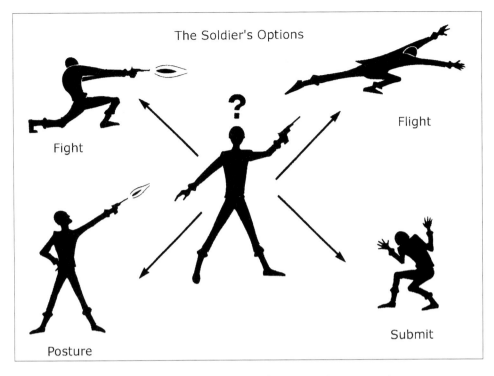

The Soldier's Options

Fight

Flight

?

Posture

Submit

51 The warrior's options : Fight, Flight, Posture and Submit. *From Grossman, 1996*

armour it would have proved very difficult to accurately land a strike capable of killing an opponent in this environment and consequently brute force was a contributory factor in the breaching of opponents' lines. This is not to suggest that it was a harmless pushing contest, but as discussed by Molloy (2006) if each man were to kill an opponent only every 15 minutes or so, this could result in casualty rates of 50% or more in a mere hour of combat. From historical sources such as Thucydides, Herodotus and Xenophon, there are no references to casualty figures of this scale in typical Greek versus Greek combat (of course the figures cited for the Persian wars are higher but more questionable).

We can therefore see that from this earliest historical period in Europe killing rates were not excessively high and that battle was not a bloody free-for-all as characterised by modern cinema. The reputed Spartan phrase of 'come home with your shield or on it' is perhaps characteristic of this situation as the shield is the weapon which is used to hold the structure and defensibility of one's line as opposed to the tool used to kill opponents. The exiled Spartan king Demaratos, when asked why it was more shameful to return without one's shield than one's helmet or cuirass replied: 'Because the latter they put on for their own protection, but the shield for the common good of the whole line.' (Plutarch

Moralia. 220 A cf Sekunda 2005: 26). It was more important not to endanger one's comrades by cowardice or negligence than it was to actively kill opposing soldiers. Indeed repeatedly seeking to strike and kill opponents for hours-on-end in group combat would rapidly exhaust a warrior and, counterproductively, increase the risk of being killed and/or weakening one's own line.

When the integrity of a line crumbles or a rout occurs, the dynamic of killing is rapidly altered and the ability to kill opponents increases exponentially as the chase instinct takes effect. While posturing, fighting or even submission have a direct engagement with the enemy, flight has a negative relationship as the engagement is broken and the killing distance consequently increased. Add to this the impersonal aspect of not being able to see an opponent's face or eyes and the fact that a human-being's offensive capabilities are geared towards the front of the body – a fleeing opponent is somewhat de-personalised and does not represent a direct threat.

In the *Iliad* (Book XIV) we hear that Ajax is a particularly keen pursuer of the routed Trojans: 'there was none so speedy of foot as he, to follow men fled, when Zeus sent terror among them'. A very early pictorial scene of a possible rout is dated to the fifteenth century BC and comes from identical sealings from Knossos and Aghia Triada on Crete (*52*). The osteological evidence for the skeletons recovered from the Battle of Towton indicates that many of them were killed when fleeing, or at least from behind (Novak, 2000). Another pattern from this collection of skeletal material is the degree of overkill found on victims, some having as many as 10 peri-mortem wounds, further examples of this overkill are known from Ireland (Sikora & Buckley, 2003) and Crete (MacGeorge 1984, 1988; Arnott 1999). These were clearly inflicted when the threat represented by the enemy had been neutralised but the physiological state of the assailant led to frenzied (essentially unnecessary/irrational) attacks on a defeated foe.

The reticence to kill fellow humans appears to be intrinsic to most members of our species and while it is well documented in modern times, casualty figures from historical sources from earlier periods support this contention. While mutual peer visibility and extreme proximity in edged-weapon combat is likely to increase the potential for an individual to kill, it does not and cannot be taken to suggest that all of those involved in these battles sought to kill opponents. The known mortality rates simply do not support this. The fundamental principal in edged-weapon combat was the maintenance of the cohesion of one's line of battle while trying to disrupt the integrity of the enemy's line. This would clearly involve killing, but the *majority* of the time an individual would be seeking to literally stay on his feet and maintain his guard, to defend against opposing combatants. When an opening was created, even briefly, this was the time when one may *choose* to strike.

52 Image from clay sealings found at Knossos and Aghia Triada on Crete depicting warrior (probably armed with a sword) chasing down another male figure. This could be interpreted as symbolising a rout in progress. *Sketch by B.P.C. Molloy after CMS II.6 15*

We must be acutely aware that battles were not a five minute set-piece but protracted events typically lasting many hours with perhaps more than one single engagement (rallied troops, use of reserves or specialised troop types etc.). The maintenance of relative order (and organisation) amidst chaos was of prime importance, not brute force or vein heroics. As the dynamic of a battle shifts, especially in the case of a rout, the killing potential is dramatically increased and it appears that the ferocity of attacks can also increase in these instances. As discussed above, the 'excitement' at seeing the enemy fleeing when in a heightened physiological state is likely to trigger instinctive midbrain responses of pursuit.[3] This may also account for the apparent barbarity enacted in some cases.

CONCLUSION: ARCHAEOLOGY'S ROLE IN THE STUDY OF KILLING

Killing in combat in ancient times, like later times, would have been undertaken with relative ease by some warriors, while others may have taken on more severe psychological effects from the experience. When we discuss a natural reluctance in most humans to kill members of our own species, it is clearly not a denial that this all too frequently occurs; rather we seek to explore the humanity of this experience. It is perhaps ironic that fictitious narratives of killing are so prevalent in our popular culture, almost to the same level as sexual fiction and/or pornography, yet factual explorations of the nature and reality of the former appear more uncomfortable and infinitely more rarely than the latter.

This shroud of myth and mystery that surrounds killing is still firmly in place; unlike sex, it is not a 'taboo' subject that can be liberalised or legitimately experienced by interested parties due to its illicit nature being part of the very fabric of our societies. *If* it is a repeatedly occurring human action, taking place all around the world on a daily basis, yet vilified by most world cultures, *then* we must continue to explore it as part of human nature, despite it being abhorrent to most. Archaeology is a discipline well located in the humanities and social sciences to investigate this topic since we have a great breadth of time and cultures to draw our data from, as has been discussed throughout this volume.

This chapter has been concerned with the functional aspects of how human beings operate in a combat environment, physically and emotionally, and also with what it 'means' to kill another person(s).[4] Killing is not to be understood merely in the short-term limited environment of the act or event, but as part of a broader pattern of human consciousness, development and nature.

We should not underestimate the importance that the act of killing can have on the trajectory and policy of a society where the elite were (at least in part) characterised by their warrior identity. Some were willing killers, some postured as such, some had killed and incorporated the trauma of this experience into their nature. There would have been veterans who had never killed and those who had yet to kill: all were part of this same group. The dynamic relationships that this would develop in a peer-group with the same social expectancies of killing, could potentially have had a very significant impact on socio-political dynamics.

The control of legitimate violence by a polity's leadership was manifested through this group, and this control would have a reciprocal relationship with social policies with regard to undertaking acts of legitimate violence. In this regard, the act of killing is clearly not an incidental event in the life of a warrior, but a potentially transformative event with potentially longer term personal effects. Warfare and killing represent a dynamic in social interaction which should not be interpreted solely in an event based military-historical mould, but need to be understood as lived-experiences which shaped the social and moral perceptions of past human beings.

Endnotes

CHAPTER 1

1   The status of *infames* in Roman society was attributed to certain classes of people who were denied most political and social rights and could not own property. They were regarded as being 'without status', and were frequently slaves. While gladiators were of this class and therefore held no official status in Roman social structures, if they gained fame and popularity this could win them wealth, social standing in keeping with their fame and eventually even their freedom.

CHAPTER 3

1   Melankomas' story is curiously similar to the nineteenth-century Chinese story of the bout between the two boxers, Dong Haichuan and Guo Yunshen. These two boxers are historically attested characters. Their bout is, however, probably more legendary. The story runs: Guo Yunshen, of the Xingyi, Form and Mind style, challenged Dong Haichuan, of the Bagua, Eight Trigram style. They fought for three days with Dong successfully evading all Guo's attacks. On the third day, Dong took the offensive and so thoroughly defeated Guo, though without injuring him, that the two men became friends and their students learned each others' styles.

2   I am especially grateful to Stephen Logan and Patrice Pujol for enthusiastically participating in this research, bruises notwithstanding.

3   I am grateful to the Irish Institute of Hellenic Studies at Athens for hosting a demonstration as part of their Ancient Olympics Day-school in Dublin in 2004.

CHAPTER 7

1   Further work carried out since the replica was completed has allowed me to suggest the actual lengths of rod required to both span the haft and produce the heads (O'Flaherty, 2002). In addition, a rereading of the analyses carried out by Penniman and Allen (1960) suggests that one head of the rivet may have been pre-formed by heating and forging before insertion into the blade/haft, and once inserted the other end was closed cold against the haft. I have also suggested that the rivet holes through the shaft may have been counter-sunk, which would have eased the production of domed heads.

CHAPTER 8

1   This issue is also addressed for Aegean weaponry in Molloy, B.P.C. Forthcoming.
2   I am very grateful to Dr Tony Kenny for facilitating me for these tests and to Mr. Ciaran Flanagan for assisting in the testing and documentation.
3   It is noteworthy that this latter culture had shields of as widely varying sizes as we find in the Bronze Age (see Underwood, this volume). We know from the historical record that there was a variety of forms of combat practiced by these Anglo-Saxon warriors, dependent on the social context (Pollington 1996, Underwood 2001).
4   Of slightly later date: one is Late Bronze Age and two are early Iron Age in date.
5   Indeed Krisitansen (2005) makes a compelling case for judiciously using such textual evidence in certain circumstances.
6   For example, changes in settlement pattern from Middle to Late Bronze Age take place over a protracted period of time and do not coincide directly with the adoption of the new swords.
7   For discussions on the typologies of Late Bronze Age swords see Eogan (1965); Colquhoun and Burgess (1988), Bridgford (2000) and Molloy (2006).
8   The device consisted of a bar of c.8mm cross-section acting as an anvil, and a similar bar gripped in the device above this. The latter bar was struck on the end by a hammer as the sword was fed between the two, thus producing a neat bevel and an effectively hammered edge. While the device is clearly unhistorical in its design (being of steel!), it is the only technique tried in research to date (see O'Faolain and Northover 1998 and Bridgford 2000) which has successfully hardened a blade's edges. It is possible therefore that the technique, as opposed to the device itself per se represents many elements of the Bronze Age craftsman's technique of working the edges (but using bronze and wooden tools).
9   'Broken' in this context means allowed loose and free movement for a brief moment.

CHAPTER 9

1   In the language of archery, 'back' is the side of the bow showing away from the archer and onto the target, while 'belly' or 'face' is the side which the archer is facing at.
2   This means that the tips (the very ends of a bow) have been bent under dry heat or steam so that they point away from the archer and onto the target.
3   The limbs are the working parts of a bow; here the bow bends when the string is drawn. A reflexed handle is curved like the letter C, where the ends of the handle region point away from the archer; a deflexed handle is curved just the other way round. The same holds for the limbs (the working parts atop and below the riser), they can be straight, deflexed or reflexed on an unstrung bow. Reflexed tips are usually called 'recurves', and the respective bows are called 'recurve bows'.
4   The draw weight is the power which is needed to draw the string, the draw length is the distance between the string at the point where the arrow is nocked and either the outer or the inner side of the handle. In our first experiments, we defined the draw length with the outer side of the riser as the starting point, but since 2005, we define the draw length as the distance between the string and the inner side of the handle. If the bow is braced but not drawn, then in this case the draw length of zero directly is the brace height. The first definition of the draw length was standard for the FITA (the world association fot target archers) and that is the reason why we used it, but now also the FITA prefers the second definition or a slight variation of it: to compute the draw length of one definition from the other one, they agreed that the draw length according to the new definition (from the inner part of the riser) is the draw length according to the old definition (from the outer part of the riser) diminished by 3.2 cm which is the average distance between the outer side of the riser and the arrow rest or the deepest inner point of the riser for most modern target bows.

5 Bows with heavier weight have to be used together with thicker and therefore heavier arrow
   shafts, thus delivering a blow with a higher impulse to the target. The reason for English archers
   to use longbows with draw weights of about 68kp may have been to be able to penetrate plate
   armour or literally to 'blow' a rider from his horse. But probably, this tactic was effective only
   against a bulk of people where no aiming was necessary.

CHAPTER 11

1 This type of arrow is commonly considered to be extremely effective against the metal armour
   (cf. Buchholz 1962: 27 with n.104). The modern experiments tried by Pope (1962: 56-8) with
   heavy bodkin-pointed arrows showed that even an armour of sheet steel, not to mention bronze,
   would not be sufficient protection against them.
2 For instance, the above mentioned warrior burial with the bronze helmet in Tomb V at the New
   Hospital site yielded also a long one-piece spearhead of type Hi (Höckmann 1980: 145 (H 21);
   Avila 1983: 133 no.866) and a short sword of type Di (Sandars 1963: 147; Macdonald 1984: 73 (Di
   9).
3 In previous reconstructions of the Dendra armour (see also figure 1) these triangles were usually
   placed on the chest. However, experiments with a full scale replica of the armour showed that
   they probably served as a protection for the armpit (Wardle 1988: 475).
4 Only one greave could be restored from numerous fragments of bronze sheet from the cuirass
   tomb (cf. Fortenberry 1991, who suggested the use of a single metal greave as a symbol of status),
   although there are still remaining plenty of bronze pieces which may have belonged to the
   second greave (Verdelis 1977: 45).
5 A LH IIIC bronze plate from a scale corslet found at Mycenae (Catling 1970) and a similar
   plate from a PG tomb at Lefkandi (Popham & Sackett 1980: 251, Pl. 110.59, 37 & Pl. 239) remain
   unique in the Aegean.

CHAPTER 12

1 Because of this last text, Hils attributes the manuscript to Von Danzig, and it is widely known
   by his name, but there is no convincing proof that he made the compilation, and the name is
   problematic because it means that we have two 'Von Danzig' texts on armoured combat – one by
   Peter von Danzig, the other almost certainly not by him. It is probably best in this case to refer to
   the codex as the Starhemberg manuscript, after its earliest known owner.
2 On the 'Ringeck' Fechtbuch (Dresden, Sächsische Landesbibliothek Mscr. Dresd. C 487), see Hils
   1985: 54-7 (no.16). The text is edited in Wierschin 1965: 87-166; translated in Tobler 2001. On the
   'Lew' Fechtbuch (Augsburg, Universitätsbibliothek Cod. I.6.40.3) see Hils 1985: 32-4 (no.5). With
   these as with other Fechtbücher, naming is problematic, and cannot be taken as ascriptions of
   authorship.
3 The 'Thwart Cut' (Zwerchhaw) is a technique in which the combatant rotates the weapon
   overhead like the blade of a helicopter.
4 Although the Starhemberg text is certainly the best surviving copy, the Lew version seems to have
   been the most widely influential, as most subsequent copies derive from this version.
5 Known manuscripts from before 1500 include Hils nos.2, 5, 11, 14, 16, 17, 20, 21, 24, 25, 26, 27,
   28, 31, 32, 33, 35, 42, 43, 44, 46, 47, 48, 49, 50 and 53; and the Bologna Paulus Kal manuscript
   (University of Bologna A.III. Append. Mss. 1391; see Welle 1993: 241).
6 Manuscripts produced after 1500 include Hils nos.1, 3, 6, 7, 8, 9, 10, 12, 13, 15, 18, 19, 22, 29, 34,
   38, 39, 40, 45, 51, 52, 54, 55; the Solothurn Fechtbuch of c.1506-25 (see Studer c.1991); the early
   sixteenth-century copy of Hils no.20 at the Metropolitan Museum of Art, New York (26.236; see

LaRocca 1998: 4); and a Fechtbuch of c.1508 in the Scott Collection, Glasgow (E.1939.65.341; see Anglo 2000: 359 and pl. 18-21). Printed works include Auerswald (1539); the 'Egenolph' Fechtbuch (4 eds. c.1531-58); Gunterrodt (1579); the Landshut Ringbuch (c.1500; ed. Studer c.1991); Meyer (1570 and 1600); Paurenfeindt (1516); the Strassburg Ringbuch (c.1510-12); Sutor (1612); Verolinus (1679); and two anonymous wrestling books published in Munich c.1500 (Anon c.1500 a & b).

7 For example, compare Starhemberg seq. 62v.2 (armoured longsword); Meyer 2006: seqs. 3.10r.3 (dagger), 3.30r.2 (quarterstaff).

8 Important sources on longsword technique include the Starhemberg commentaries, fol. 9v ff.; Lew fol. 1r ff.; Ringeck fol. 10v ff.; Speyer fol. 5r ff.; Mair (Vienna MS) fol. 1.1r ff.; Meyer 2006: bk. 1. Also important is the Munich manuscript of Lecküchner's treatise on the Messer, which incorporates many of the Liechtenauer longsword techniques.

9 Important sources on armoured combat include Gladiatoria fol. 1v ff.; the Starhemberg commentaries on Liechtenauer (Starhemberg fol. 53r ff.); Hundfeld (Starhemberg fol. 87r ff.); Liegnitzer (Starhemberg fol. 73r ff.); Von Danzig (Starhemberg fol. 108r ff.); sources on mounted combat include the Starhemberg commentaries (Starhemberg fol. 39v ff.); Mair (Vienna MS) fol. 2.28or ff.

10 Important sources on dagger include Liegnitzer (Starhemberg fol. 85r ff.), Hundfeld (Starhemberg fol. 94r ff.); Mair (Vienna MS) fol. 1.190r ff.; Meyer 2006: bk. 3; sources on wrestling include Ott (Starhemberg fol. 100v ff.); Auerswald 1539; Mair (Vienna MS) fol. 2.2or ff.

11 Important sources on the *Messer* and *dusack* include Speyer fol. 5r ff.; Mair (Vienna MS) fol. 1.97r ff.; Meyer 2006: bk. 2.

12 Important sources on staff weapons include Mair (Vienna MS) fol. 1.155r ff.; Meyer 2006: bk. 3.

13 Important sources on dueling weapons include Talhoffer (Hergsell 1887: pl.104 ff. and 242 ff.); Von Eyb, fol. 45r ff.; Mair (Vienna MS) fol. 2.206r ff.

14 It should be noted that this binary distinction, while schematically useful, actually represents two poles on a graduated spectrum of violence. A skilled practitioner would be able to judge the level of earnestness in his opponent, and respond with an appropriate level of violence: for multiple legal and social reasons, one would not wish to kill someone when injuring would be sufficient, or to injure them when subduing would be sufficient.

15 Strikingly, there is little explicit reference to warfare as a context, but it is clearly one of the possible applications of Liechtenauer's techniques, mentioned in line six of his longsword verses.

16 This interpretation naturally presumes that the sequences were actually intended for physical practice. In some cases, Mair's techniques can be traced to earlier documentary sources that were clearly being reconstructed by Mair and his team – perhaps history's earliest example of experimental archaeology.

17 For example, the techniques known as mutieren, duplieren and the Krumphaw are given only on the left side in Ringeck (24r ff.), but on both sides in Starhemberg (16r ff.), Lew (12r ff.) and Speyer (17v ff.).

18 Other circumstances might also be invoked to account for the absence of long-range sparring techniques, for example situations with limited room for motion (such as a barroom brawl), or where there are multiple potential attackers in the vicinity (as in a street ambush), both of which can be well attested in medieval legal records. Also relevant is the applicability of such techniques in armoured combat, where similar techniques are well documented in the treatises, and where the substantial protection to the limbs as well as the additional weight carried by the combatant would encourage entry into close distance. The unarmoured longsword techniques in the Liechtenauer system are similarly lacking in sparring-type attacks to the arms, but here the issue may be the configuration of the weapon and body: the longer blade and two-handed grip may again encourage attacks to the body.

CHAPTER 14

1   Woudt's latinised name 'J(ohann) C(ornelius) Woudanus' appears on the Glasgow print, along with the name of 'bibliopol[us]' (bookseller) And[reas] Cloucg.

2   Van Ceulen had been granted permission to keep a fencing school in a hall below the university library as early as 1594. He was succeeded by Dirck van Sterbergen.

3   The other dominant fraternity of amateur fencers, the Freifechter von der Feder, officially organised around 1570, wasn't granted a coat of arms or the lucrative imperial teaching privileges until Emperor Rudolph II did so on 7 March 1617.

4   Schmidt 1749: [2r] 'Ein rechtschaffener Fecht-Meister [wird] niemal die unchristliche Intention bey sich hegen, seine Scholaren zu unrechtmŠssigen GezŠncke und SchlŠgereyen, noch weniger zu vorsetzlichen Duellen anzureitzen.'

5   Self-published manuscript by Roland in Edinburgh in the mid-nineteenth century.

6   The scenarios depicted in these various manuscripts by Talhoffer are of such different characters that they have yet to be analysed in detail.

7   A bloody hit received in a duel or Mensur that was at least an inch (2.5cm) long and caused blood to flow. This would be sufficient to terminate a fight until the first third of the nineteenth century, after which the termination of a duel or Mensur for medical reasons was delegated to the attending physicians.

8   Sachs was born on 5 November 1494 in Nürnberg, one of the centers of German fighting guild activity. He was a contemporary of Emperor Maximilian I (whose love for the European combatives is as well documented as his visits to Nürnberg) and a fellow citizen of Albrecht Dürer who himself tried his hand at editing the Codex Wallerstein in 1512. Sachs died on 19 January 1576 in Nürnberg. His literary activity covered the period from 1514-69. By 1567, he had written 4,275 master-songs, 208 dramas, 1,558 comic stories, histories, comparisons, allegories, visions, lamentations, street and tavern songs, as well as dialogues. One of them is this Fechtspruch.

9   Original: 'Was das Ringen vor ein nützliches Exercitium, und wie es unsere Vorfahren nicht allein im Schertz / sondern auch in Ernst gebraucht haben / Solches ist auß denen Historien bekannt.'

10 'Das gehŠrt fur grobe Leute / und ist nicht Geselliglich.'

CHAPTER 15

1   For a discussion of aggression as a 'natural' human emotion see below and Pinker (2002: 316).

2   That they were combat-worthy and effective weapons has been discussed at length in Molloy's unpublished PhD thesis (2006).

3   Hence the well known tactic of feigning a rout to draw an opposing line into disarray.

4   These themes are explored more completely by Grossman in On Killing (1996).

Bibliography

Åkerström, Å. 1987. *Berbati 2. The Pictorial Pottery* (Acta Instituti Atheniensis Regni Sueciae 36, 2). Stockholm.

Allely, S., Baker, T., Comstock, P. Hamm, J. *et al.* 1992. *The Traditional Bowyer's Bible (Vol. I-III)*. Bois d'Arc Press, New York.

Amberger, J. 1999. *The Secret History of the Sword. Adventures in Ancient Martial Arts*. New York.

Anglo, S. 1989. 'How to Win at Tournaments: The Techniques of Chivalric Combat' *Antiquaries Journal LXVIII*.

Anglo, S. 1991. '*Le Jeu de la Hache*: a fifteenth-century treatise on the technique of chivalric axe combat' *Archaeologia,* Vol. CIX.

Anglo, S. 2000. *The Martial Arts of Renaissance Europe*. New Haven and London.

Anon. (*c.*1500a). *Das ist ain hybsch ring byechelin*. Munich: Hans Sittich.

Anon. (*c.*1500b). *Hye in disem büchlin findt man die recht kunst und art des Ringens*. Munich: n. p.

Anon. *La noble science des joueurs d'espee* (1538). Antwerp: Guillaume Vorsterman.

Anon. The 'Strassburg Ringbuch' (*c.*1510-12). Strassburg: Matthias Hupfuff.

Asbell, F. 2000. 'Die Sache mit dem Zuggewicht oder, Was in Männerköpfen so abgeht'.

Traditionell Bogenschießen 18 (2000): 37-9 (translated from: Bow Weight and the Macho Head Trip, *Bowhunter* February 2000).

Von Auerswald, F. 1539. *Ringerkunst: fünff vnd achtzig stücke.* Wittemberg: Hans Lufft.

Aurigemma, S. 1926. *I Mosaici di Zliten*. Roma.

Avila, R.A.J. 1983. *Bronzene Lanzen- und Pfeilspitzen der griechischen Spätbronzezeit* (Prähistorische Bronzefunde V.1). Munich.

Barber, M. 2003. *Bronze and the Bronze Age*. Gloucestershire.

Barrett, J.C. 1993. *Fragments from Antiquity: An archaeology of social life in Britain 1900 − 1200 BC*. Oxford.

Barton, C.A. 1993. *The Sorrows of the Ancient Romans. The Gladiator and the Monster*. Princeton.

de Becker, G. 1997. *The Gift of Fear*. New York.

Becker, K. and Riesch, H. 2002. Untersuchungen zu Metallurgie und Effizienz merowingerzeitlicher Lamellenpanzer. *Archäologisches Korrespondenzblatt* 32.4, 597-606.

Beckhoff, K. 1963. Die eisenzeitlichen Kriegsbogen von Nydam. *Offa (Berichte und Mitteilungen aus dem Schleswig-Holsteinischen Landesmuseum für Vor- und Frühgeschichte in Schleswig, dem Landesamt für Vor- und Frühgeschichte von Schleswig-Holstein in Schleswig und dem Institut für Ur- und Frühgeschichte an der Universität Kiel)* 20, 39-48.

Bell, M.J.V. 1965. 'Tactical reform in the Roman Republican army', *Historia* 14. 404-22.

Bergman, C.A., McEwen, E., Miller, R.L. 1982. Experimental Archery Projectile Velocities and Comparison of Bow Performances. *Antiquity* 62, 658-70.

Bisel, S.C. & Bisel, J.F. 2002. 'Health and nutrition at Herculaneum. An examination of human skeletal remains', in Feemster Jashemski, W. & Meyer, F.G. (eds.), *The Natural History of Pompeii*, Cambridge. 451-75.

Bishop, M.C. 1990. 'On parade: status, display and morale in the Roman army', in Vetters & Kandler 1990. 21-30.

Bishop, M.C. 2002. *Lorica Segmentata* I. *A Handbook of Articulated Roman Plate Armour*, Journal of Roman Military Equipment Studies Monograph Series 1, Chirnside.

Bishop, M.C. & Coulston, J.C.N. 2006. *Roman Military Equipment from the Punic Wars to the Fall of Rome*, Oxford.

Bivar, A.D.H. 1972. 'Cavalry tactics and equipment on the Euphrates', *Dunbarton Oaks Papers* 26. 273-91.

Blackwell, E. A. 1734. *Complete System of Fencing: or, The Art of Defence, In the Use of the Small-Sword*, (Williamsburg: William Parks) Williamsburg: Colonial Williamsburg Printing and Post Office.

Bleibrunner, H. (ed.). 1969. *Das Landshuter Ringerbuch: Ein farbiges Blockbuch aus dem Jahre 1500.* Munich: Süddeutscher Verlag.

Blyth, P. H. 1980. 'Ballistic properties in ancient Egyptian arrows', *Journal of the Society of Archer-Antiquaries* 23. 34–9.

Boardman, J. 1991. 'The sixth century poster and painters of Athens and their public', in Rasmussen, T. & Spivey, N. (eds.), *Looking at Greek Vases*, 79-102.

Borchhardt, J. 1972. *Homerische Helme. Helmformen der Ägäis in ihren Beziehungen zu orientalischen und europäischen Helmen in der Bronze- und frühen Eisenzeit.* Mainz a. Rhein.

Bottini, A., Egg, M., Hase, F. W. von, Pflug, H., Schaaff, U., Schauer, P. & Waurick, G. 1988. *Antike Helme. Sammlung Lipperheide und andere Bestände des Antikenmuseums Berlin*, Mainz.

Bourke, J. 2000. *An intimate history of Killing.* London.

Bouzek, J. 1985. *The Aegean, Anatolia and Europe: Cultural Interrelations in the Second Millennium B.C.* Prague.

Bradley, R. 2005. *Ritual and domestic life in prehistoric Europe.* London.

Brandherm, D. 2003. *Die Dolche und Stabdolche der Steinkupfer- und der älteren Bronzezeit auf der Iberischen Halbinsel.* Prähistorische Bronzefunde, VI, Band 12.

Bridgford, S. 1997a. 'Mightier than the pen? An edgewise look at Irish bronze age swords.' In Carman, J. (ed) 1997. *Material harm: archaeological studies of war and violence.* Glasgow. 95-115.

Bridgford, S. 2000. *Weapons Warfare and Society in Britain: 1250 – 750BC.* Unpublished PhD thesis, University of Sheffield.

Brown, M.A. & Powell, T.G.E. (eds.), *The European Community in Later Prehistory: Studies in Honour of C.F.C. Hawkes.* London. 33-50.

Bruck, J. 1999. Ritual and Rationality: some problems of interpretation in European Archaeology. *European Journal of Archaeology* 2(3). 313-44.

Buchholz, H.-G. 1962. 'Der Pfeilglätter aus dem VI. Schachtgrab von Mykene und die helladischen Pfeilspitzen,' *Jahrbuch des Deutschen Archäologischen Instituts* 77: 1-58.

Buchholz, H.-G., Jöhrens, G., Maull, I. 1973. *Jagd und Fischfang.* (Matz, F., Buchholz, H.G. (eds.): *Archaeologia Homerica, Vol. II.J*). Herbig, Vandenhoeck & Ruprecht, München.

Buchli, V.A. 2000. 'Interpreting material culture: The trouble with text' in Thomas, J. (ed.) *Interpretive archaeology.* Leicester, 363-76.

Bulanda, E. 1913. *Bogen und Pfeil bei den Völkern des Altertums.* Alfred Hölder K.U.K. Hof- und Univer sitätsbuchhandlung, Wien – Leipzig.

Burgess, C. and Gerloff, S. 1981. *The dirks and rapiers of Great Britain and Ireland.* PBF IV 7. Munich.

Burton, R. 1884. *The Book of the Sword.* (Dover reprint 1988).

Campbell, B. 2002. *Warfare and Society in Imperial Rome, c. 31 BC-AD 280*. London.

Carman, J. (ed.) 1997 *Material Harm – archaeological studies of war and violence*. Glasgow.

Carman, J. and Harding, A. (eds.). 1999. *Ancient Warfare*. Sutton Publishing.

Carman, J. and Carmen, P. 2005. 'War in prehistoric society: modern views of ancient violence', in Parker-Pearson, M. and Thorpe, I.J.N. (Eds.). *Warfare, Violence and Slavery in Prehistory*. Oxford. 217-25.

Càssola Guida, P. 1973. *Le armi difensive dei Micenei nelle figurazioni* (Incunabula Graeca LVI). Rome.

Castle, E. 1885. *Schools and Masters of Fencing*. (Dover reprint 2003).

Castle, E. 1911. 'Fencing' from the 'Scholar's edition' *Encyclopedia Britannica*.

Catling, H.W. 1970. 'A Bronze Plate from a Scale Corslet Found at Mycenae,' *Archäologischer Anzeiger*, fasc. 4: 441-9.

Catling, H.W. 1977. 'Panzer', in *Kriegswesen*, Teil 1: *Schutzwaffen und Wehrbauten* (Archaeologia Homerica I E.1), eds. H.-G. Buchholz and J. Wiesner, pp. E74-E118. Göttingen.

Cernenko, E.V., Gorelik, M.V. 1983. *The Scythians 700–300 BC*. 'Men at Arms' Series Vol. 137. Osprey.

Chagnon, N.A. 1967. 'Yanomamö social organisation and warfare.' In Fried, M., Harris, M. and Murphy, R. (eds.) *War: the anthropology of armed conflict and aggression*. New York. 109-59.

Champollion, J. F. 1835. *Monument de L'Egypte et de la Nubie*. De M. Guizotet de m. Thiers Ministeries de l'Instruction Publique et de l'Interieun. 4 Volumes (1972 reprint).

Charron, B. 2002. *Italian Medieval Swordsmanship the Flos Duellatorum of Fiore Dei Liberi: Facsimile and Translation; Interpretations*. Chivalry Bookshelf.

Chenorkian, R. 1988. *Les Armes Metalliques dans l'art protohistorique de l'Occident Mediterranean*. Paris: editions du C.N.R.S.

Cichorius, C. 1896-1900. *Die Reliefs der Traianssäule*. Berlin.

Clements, J. 1997. *Renaissance Swordsmanship: The Illustrated Use of Rapiers and Cut-and-thrust Swords*. Paladin.

Clements, J. 1998. *Medieval Swordsmanship: Illustrated Methods and Techniques*. Paladin.

Cochavi-Rainey, Z. 1999. *Royal Gifts in the Late Bronze Age. Fourteenth to Thirteenth Centuries BCE*. Bengurion University of the Negev Press.

Cohen, R. 2002. *By the Sword*. London.

Coles, J.M. 1962. 'European Bronze Age shields', *Proceedings of the Prehistoric Society 28*. 156-90.

Colquhoun, I. and Burgess, C. 1988. *The swords of Britain*. PBF IV 5. Munich.

Connolly, P. 1981. *Greece and Rome at War*. London.

Connolly, P. 1989. 'Greece and Rome', in Cope, A. (ed.). *Swords and Hilt weapons*. London. 20-9.

Connolly, P. 1991. 'The Roman fighting technique deduced from armour and weaponry', in V. Maxfield and M.J. Dobson, *Roman Frontier Studies 1989*. Exeter. 358-63.

Connolly, P. 1997. '*Pilum, gladius* and *pugio* in the Late Republic', *Journal of Roman Military Equipment Studies 8*. 41-57.

Connolly, P. 2000a. 'The reconstruction and use of Roman weaponry in the 2nd century BC', *Journal of Roman Military Equipment Studies 11*. 43-6.

Connolly, P. 2000b. 'Experiments with the *sarissa* – the Macedonian pike and cavalry lance – a functional view.' *Journal of Roman Military Equipment Studies 11*. 103-12.

Connolly, P. 2003. *Colosseum. Rome's Arena of Death*. London.

Cope, A. (ed.) 1989. *Swords and Hilt Weapons*. London.

Cornell, T., Rankov, B. & Sabin, P. (ed.). 1996. *The Second Punic War. A Reappraisal*. London.

Coulston, J.C. 1985, 'Roman archery equipment', in Bishop, M.C. (ed.). *The Production and Distribution of Roman Military Equipment*. Oxford. 220-366.

Coulston, J.C. 1986. 'Roman, Parthian and Sassanid tactical developments', in Freeman, P. & Kennedy, D. (ed.), *The Defence of the Roman and Byzantine East*, Oxford, 59-75.

Coulston, J.C.N. 1990. 'Later Roman armour, 3rd-6th centuries AD', *Journal of Roman Military Equipment Studies 1*, 139-60.

Coulston, J.C.N. 1998. 'Gladiators and soldiers: personnel and equipment in *ludus* and *castra*', *Journal of Roman Military Equipment Studies* 9. 1-17.

Coulston, J.C.N. 2001. 'The archaeology of Roman conflict', in Freeman, P. M. W. and Pollard, A. (eds.), *Fields of Conflict: Progress and Prospect in Battlefield Archaeology*, Oxford. 23-49.

Coulston, J.C.N. 2003a. 'Tacitus, *Historiae* I.79 and the impact of Sarmatian warfare on the Roman empire', in von Carnap-Bornheim, C. (ed.), *Kontakt - Kooperation - Konflikt: Germanen und Sarmaten zwischen dem 1. und 4. Jahrh. n. Chr.*, Marburg. 415-33.

Coulston, J.C.N. 2003b. 'Overcoming the barbarian. Depictions of Rome's enemies in Trajanic monumental art', in. de Blois, L., Erdkamp, P., Hekster, O., de Kleijn, G. & Mols, S. (eds.), *The Representation and Perception of Roman Imperial Power*, Amsterdam, 389-424.

Crouwel, J.H. 1981. *Chariots and Other Means of Land Transport in Bronze Age Greece* (Allard Pierson Series 3). Amsterdam.

Čugunov, K.V., Parzinger, H., Nagler, A. 2003. Der skythische Fürstengrabhügel von Arzhan 2 in Tuva (Vorbericht der russisch-deutschen Ausgrabungen 2000–2002). *Eurasia antiqua* 9. 113-62.

Davies, N. de G. 1930. *The Tomb of Kenamun at Thebes*. The Metropolitan Museum of Art, New York. Volume 1.

Dempsey, J. 1950. *Championship Fighting: Explosive Punching and Aggressive Defence* Centerline Books.

DeMarrais, E., Godsen, C. (Eds.). 2004. *Rethinking Materiality: The Engagement of Mind with the Material World*. Cambridge.

Dickinson T. and Härke H. 1992. 'Early Anglo-Saxon Shields', *Archaeologia*, 110.

Dillon, T. 1916. 'Armour and Weapons' in *Shakespeare's England - An account of the Life & Manners of his Age. Volume I*. Oxford.

Divale, W. 1973. *War in Primitive Society*. Santa Barbara.

Dobres, M.A. 2000. *Technology and social agency*. Oxford.

Dobres, M.A., and Robb, J. 2000. *Agency in Archaeology*. London.

di Donato, F. 1994. The Egyptian double-curved bow, *Journal of the Society of Archer-Antiquaries* 37. 42–4.

Dörnhöffer, F. 1909. *Albrecht Dürers Fechtbuch*. Vienna and Leipzig.

Draeger, D. & Smith, R. 1981. *Comprehensive Asian Fighting Arts*. Kodansha Europe.

Drews, R. 1993. *The End of the Bronze Age: Changes in Warfare and the Catastrophe ca. 1200 BC*. Princeton University Press.

Dwyer, B. 2003. Scythian-Style Bows Discovered in Xinjiang. *Journal of the Society of Archer Antiquaries* 48. 71-82.

Eckhardt, H. 1991. Der schwirrende Tod – Die Bogenwaffe der Skythen. In: Rolle, R. (Hrsg.): *Gold der Steppe Archäologie der Ukraine*. Wachholtz-Verlag, Neumünster. 143–149.

Eckhardt, H., 1996. *Pfeil und Bogen – Eine archäologisch-technologische Untersuchung zu urnenfelder- und hallstattzeitlichen Befunden* (Reihe 'Internationale Archäologie', Band 21). Verlag Marie Leidorf, Espelkamp.

Edge, D. 1999. *Arms & Armor of the Medieval Knight*. Brompton Books.

Edmonds, M. and Thomas, J. 1987. 'The archers: an everyday story of country folk.' In Brown, A.G. and Edmonds, M.R. (eds.) *Lithic analysis and later British prehistory*. British Archaeological Reports (British Series) 162. Oxford. 187-99.

Elton, H. 1996. *Warfare in Roman Europe, AD 350-425*. Oxford.

The 'Egenolph' Fechtbuch (?c.1535). *Der Altenn Fechter anfengliche Kunst*. Frankfurt-am-Main: Christian Egenolph.

English, F.L. 1930. 'The Exterior Ballistics of the Arrow'. *Journal of the Franklin Institute* 210. 805-819.

Eogan, G. 1965. *Catalogue of Irish Bronze Swords*. Dublin.

Espérandieu, E. 1907-66. *Recueil général des bas-reliefs, statues et bustes de la Gaule romaine*. Paris.

Evans, A. 1935. *The Palace of Minos at Knossos*. Vol. IV. London.

Fairbairn, W.E. 1943. *Get Tough*. Colarado.

Ferguson, R.B. and Whithead, N.L. (eds.). 1992. *War in the Tribal Zone. Expanding states and indigenous warfare*. Santa Fe.

Ferris, I.M. 2000. *Enemies of Rome. Barbarians Through Roman Eyes*. Stroud.

Feugère, M. 1994. *Casques antiques. Les visages de la guerre de Mycènes à la fin de l'empire romain.* Paris.

Ferguson, R.B. and Whitehead, N.L. (eds.). 1992 *War in the Tribal Zone. Expanding states and indigenous warfare*. Santa Fe: School of American Research Press.

Fiorato, V., Bolyston, A. & Kunsel, C. (eds.) 2000. *Blood Red Roses: the Archaeology of a Mass Grave from the Battle of Towton AD 1461*. Oxford.

Florescu, F.B. 1965. *Das Siegesdenkmal von Adamklissi Tropaeum Traiani*. Bonn.

Forgeng, J. L. 2003. *The Medieval Art of Swordsmanship: A Facsimile and Translation of Europe's Oldest Personal Combat Treatise, Royal Armouries MS I.33*. Leeds and Union City.

Forgeng, J. L. 2006. *Hans Lecküchner's Art of Falchion Combat (1482)*. Texas.

Fontijn, D. 2005. 'Giving up weapons', in Parker-Pearson, M. and Thorpe, I.J.N. (Eds.). *Warfare, Violence and Slavery in Prehistory*. Oxford 2005. 145-55.

Fortenberry, D. 1991. 'Single Greaves in the Late Helladic Period', *American Journal of Archaeology* 95: 623-7.

Fraia, G. di & d'Oriano, M.R. 1982. 'Scheletri sulla battigia', *Archeologia Viva* 1.9. 18-25.

Frenz, H.G. 1992. *Corpus Signorum Imperii Romani, Deutschland* II.7. *Germania Superior. Bauplastik und Porträts aus Mainz und Umgebung*. Mainz.

Futrell, A. 1997. *Blood in the Arena. The Spectacle of Roman Power*. Austin.

Fyllingen, H. 2003. 'Society and Violence in the Early Bronze Age: An analysis of human skeletons from Nord-Trondelag, Norway', *Norwegian Archaeological Review. Vol. 36 No.1*. 1-17.

Franceschetti, A. 1978. 'Armi e guerra in testi micenei,' *Rendiconti della Accademia di archeologia, lettere e belle arti (Napoli)* 53: 67-79.

Fried, M., Harris, M. and Murphy, R. 1967. War: *The Anthropology of Armed Conflict and Aggression*. New York.

Gabelmann, H. 1971. *Antiken aus dem Akademischen Kunstmuseum Bonn (Reihe: Kunst und Altertum am Rhein 19)*, Rheinland-Verlag, Düsseldorf.

Garbsch, J. 1978. *Römische Paraderüstungen*. München.

Gardiner, F. N. 1930. *Athletics of the Ancient World*. Oxford.

Gilchrist, R. 2003. 'Towards a social archaeology of warfare' in *World Archaeology* 35. 1-6.

Gilliver, C.M. 1999. *The Roman Art of War*. London.

Gladiatoren 2002. Gladiatoren in Ephesos. Tod am Nachmittag. Wien.

Godehardt, E., Leeuw, A., Jaworski, J. 2006. *Penetrating Power of Ancient Bows with Low Draw Weight*. In: Sekunda, N. (ed.): *Proceedings of the 1st Conference on Hellenistic Warfare, Torun 2003* (forthcoming)

Godfrey, J. 1747. *Treatise upon the Useful Science of Defence*. London.

Goldsworthy, A.K. 1996. *The Roman Army at War, 100BC-AD200*. Oxford.

Golvin, J.C. & Landes, C. 1990. *Amphithéâtres et gladiateurs*. Lattes.

Grant, M. 1971. *Gladiators*. Harmondsworth.

Greenhalgh, P. 1973. *Early Greek Warfare: Horsemen and Chariots in the Homeric and Archaic Ages*. Cambridge.

Greenhalgh, P. 1980. 'The Dendra Charioteer', *Antiquity* 54, no. 213: 201-5.

Gregori, G.L. 1989. *Epigraphica Amphitheatrali dell' Occidente Romano*, II. *Regiones Italiae VI-XI*. Roma.

Griffiths, W.B. 2000. 'Re-enactment as research: towards a set of guidelines for re-enactors and academics' in *Journal of Roman Military equipment studies* 11, 135-39.

Grossman, D. 1996. *On Killing*. New York.

Grossman, D. with Christensen, L.W. 2004. *On Combat*. New York.

Guilaine, J. and Zammit, J. 2001 *Le Sentier de la Guerre – Visages de la violence préhistorique*. Éditions de Seuil, Paris.

à Gunterrodt, H. (1579). *De veris principiis artis dimicatoriæ tractatus brevis, ad illustrissiumum principem Joannem ducem Megapolensem*. Wittenberg: Mattheus Welack.

Hain, J.R. 1989. Fatal Arrow Wounds. *Journal of Forensic Sciences* 34.3. 691-3

Hackett, J. (ed.) 1989. *Warfare in the Ancient World*. London.

Hamilakis, Y., Pluciennik, M. and Tarlow, S. (eds.). 2002. *Thinking through the body, archaeologies of corporeality*. Kluwer Academic.

Hamilakis, Y. 2002 'Experience and corporeality', in Hamilakis, Y. Pluciennik, M. and Tarlow, S. (eds.). *Thinking through the body, archaeologies of corporeality*. Kluwer academic. 99-103.

Hamilton, T.M. 1982. *Native American Bows*. Missouri Archaeological Society Publications, Columbia.

Hanson, V.D. 1989. *The Western Way of War. Infantry Battle in Classical Greece*. Oxford.

Harbison, P. 1969a. *The Daggers and the Halberds of the Early Bronze Age in Ireland*. Prahistorische Bronzefunde, Abteilung VI: Band 1. Munich.

Harding, A. 1999. 'Warfare: a defining characteristic of Bronze Age Europe?', in Carmen, J. and Harding, A. (eds.). *Ancient Warfare*. Gloucestershire. 157-75.

Hardy, R. 1992. *Longbow*. Patrick Stephens, Sparkford Nr Yeovil.

Harris, H.A. 1964. *Greek Athletes and Athletics*. Greenwood Press.

Hart, E. 1994. An arrow case and arrows from ancient Egypt, *Journal of the Society of Archer-Antiquaries* 37. 4-8.

Healy, M. 1991. *The Ancient Assyrians* 'Elite' Series, Vol. 39, Osprey.

Healy, M. 1992. *New Kingdom Egypt* 'Elite' Series, Vol. 40, Osprey.

Hedges, R.E.M., Housley, R.A., Ramsey, C.B., and Van Klinken, G.J. 1991. Radiocarbon dates from the Oxford AMS system: *Archaeometry* date list 23. *Archaeometry* 33. 121-34.

Hergsell, G. 1887. *Talhoffers Fechtbuch aus dem Jahre 1467*. Prague: J.G. Calve.

Hergsell, G. 1889a. *Talhoffers Fechtbuch (Gothaer Codex) aus dem Jahre 1443*. Prague: author.

Hergsell, G. 1889b. *Talhoffers Fechtbuch (Ambraser Codex) aus dem Jahre 1459*. Prague: author.

Hergsell, G. 1890. *Livre d'escrime de Talhoffer (manuscrit d'Ambras) de l'an 1459*. Prague: author.

Hergsell, G. 1893. *Livre d'escrime de Talhoffer (Codex de Gotha) de l'an 1443*. Prague: author.

Hergsell, G. 1894. *Livre d'escrime de Talhoffer de l'an 1467*. Prague: J. G. Calve.

Herity, M. and Eogan, G. 1977. *Ireland in Prehistory*. London.

Hickman, C.N. 1929. Velocity and Acceleration of Arrows. Weight and Efficiency of Bows as Affected by Backing of Bow. *Journal of the Franklin Institute* 208. 521-37.

Hickman, C.N. 1937. The Dynamics of a Bow and Arrow. *Journal of Applied Physics* 8. 404-9.

Hickman, C.N. 1959. Ancient Composite Bows. *Journal of the Society of Archer Antiquaries* 2, 21.

Higgins, G.J. 1933. The Aerodynamics of an Arrow. *Journal of the Franklin Institute* 216. 91–101.

Hill, J.M. 1986. *Celtic Warfare 1595-1763*. Edinburgh.

Hiller, S. & O. Panagl. 1976. *Die frühgriechischen Texte aus mykenischer Zeit*. Darmstadt.

Hils, H-P. 1985. *Meister Johann Liechtenauers Kunst des langen Schwertes*. Frankfurt am Main and New York.

Höckmann, O. 1980. 'Lanze und Speer im spätminoischen und mykenischen Griechenland,' *Jahrbuch des Römisch-Germanischen Zentralmuseums Mainz* 27: 13-158.

Höckmann, O. 1987. 'Lanzen und Speere der ägäischen Bronzezeit und des Übergangs zur Eisenzeit,' in Buchholz, H.-G. *Ägäische Bronzezeit*. Darmstadt. 329-58.

Hodder, I. 2000. 'Agency and individuals in long-term processes' in Dobres, M.A. and Robb, J. (Eds.). *Agency in Archaeology*. London. 21-33.

Hood, M.S.F. & de Jong, P. 1952. 'Late Minoan Warrior-Graves from Ayios Ioannis and the New Hospital Site at Knossos,' *The Annual of the British School at Athens* 47: 243-77.

Humble, R. 1980. *Warfare in the Ancient World*. London and New York.

Hutchinson, R.W. 1956. 'A Late Minoan Tomb at Knossos', *The Annual of the British School at Athens* 51: 68-83.

Hutton, A. 1892. *Old Sword Play*. (Dover reprint 2002).

Ilkjaer, J. 1997. 'Gegner und Verbündete in Nordeuropa während des 1. bis 4. Jahrhunderts', in A. Nørgård Jørgensen & B.L. Clausen (ed.), *Military Aspects of Scandinavian Society in a European Perspective, AD 1-1300*. Copenhagen. 55-63.

Inosanto, D. 1998. *Filipino Martial Arts*. Los Angeles.

Jacobelli, L. 2003. *Gladiators at Pompeii*. Los Angeles.

James, S. 2004. *Excavations at Dura-Europos, 1928 to 1937, Final Report VII, The Arms and Armour, and other Military Equipment*. London.

Jørgensen, L., Storgaard, B. & Gebauer Thomsen, L. (eds.) 2003. *The Spoils of Victory. The North in the Shadow of the Roman Empire*. Copenhagen.

Junkelmann, M. 1986. *Die Legionen des Augustus. Der römische Soldat im archäologischen Experiment*. Mainz.

Junkelmann, M. 2000a. *Das Spiel mit dem Tod. So kämpften Roms Gladiatoren*. Mainz.

Junkelmann, M. 2000b. 'Gladiatorial and military equipment and fighting technique: a comparison', *Journal of Roman Military Equipment Studies* 11. 113-17.

Junkelmann, M. 2000c. *Römische Helme. Sammlung Axel Guttmann* VIII. Mainz.

Karasulas, A. 2004. *Mounted Archers of the Steppe 600 BC–AD 1300* 'Elite' Series Vol. 120, Osprey.

Karger, B., Sudhues, H., Kneubuehl, B.P., Brinkmann, B. 1998. Experimental Arrow Wounds: Ballistics and Traumatology. *The Journal of Trauma: Injury, Infection and Critical Care* 45.3. 495–501.

Keegan, J. 1994. *A History of Warfare*. Pimlico.

Keeley, L. 1996. *War before civilisation*. Oxford.

Kendall, T. 1974. *Warfare and Military Matters in the Nuzi Tablets*. Unpublished PhD Thesis, Brandeis University.

Kendall, T. 1981. *Gurpisu sa aweli*: the helmets of the warriors at Nuzi, in Morrison, M. A. and Owen, D. I. (eds.) *Studies in the Civilizations and Cultures of Nuzi and the Hurrians*. Winona Lake, Indiana, Eisenbrauns.

Keppie, L. 1984. *The Making of the Roman Army from Republic to Empire*. London.

Kilian, K. 1982. 'Mycenaean Charioteers Again', *Antiquity* 56, no. 218: 205-6.

Klopsteg, P.E. 1987. *Turkish Archery and the Composite Bow*. Butler & Tanner and Simon Archery Foundation, London (3rd ed., 1st ed. dated 1934).

Köhne, E. & Ewigleben, C. 2000. *Gladiators and Caesars*. London.

Kooi, B.W. 1981. On the Mechanics of the Bow and Arrow. *Journal of Engineering Mathematics* 15.2. 119–45.

Kooi, B.W. 1983. On the Mechanics of the Bow and Arrow. PhD Thesis, Rijksuniversiteit, Groningen.

Kooi, B.W. 1991a. 'Archery and Mathematical Modelling'. *Journal of the Society of Archer Antiquaries* 34. 21-9.

Kooi, B.W. 1991b. On the Mechanics of the Modern Working-Recurve Bow. *Computational Mechanics* 8. 291–304.

Kooi, B.W. 1993. On the Mechanics of Some Replica Bows. *Journal of the Society of Archer Antiquaries* 36. 34.

Kooi, B.W. and Sparenberg, J.A. 1980. 'On the Static Deformation of a Bow'. *Journal of Engineering Mathematics* 14.1. 27-45.

Kopytoff, I. 2000. 'The cultural biography of things', in Thomas, J. (ed.). *Interpretive archaeology*. Leicester. 377-93.

Kristiansen, K. 1999. 'The emergence of warrior aristocracies in later European prehistory and their long-term history', in Carmen, J. and Harding, A. *Ancient Warfare*. Gloucestershire. 175-91.

Kristiansen, K. 2002. 'The tale of the sword – swords and swordfighters in Bronze Age Europe', in *Oxford Journal of Archaeology 21 No.4*. 319-332.

Kristiansen, K. and Larsson, T.B. 2005. *The rise of Bronze Age society*. Cambridge.

Kusudo, K. 2004. 'Notion of Swordmanship by P.H. Mair (1517-1579).' In *Local Identity and Sport: Historical Study of Integration and Differentiation. Proceedings of the 6th ISHPES Seminar, Kanazawa, Japan 2002*. Hideaki Okubo (ed.). Sankt Augustin: Academia Verlag. 181-85.

Lafaye, G. 1896. 'Gladiator', in C. Daremberg & E. Saglio (ed.), *Dictionionaire des Antiquités Grecques et Romaines d'apres les textes et les monuments*, II. Paris. 1563-99.

La Regina, A. (ed.) 2001. *Sangue e Arena*. Milano.

LaRocca, D. J. 1998. *The Academy of the Sword: Illustrated Fencing Books 1500-1800*. New York.

Leng, R. 2002. *Ars belli: Deutsche taktische und kriegstechnische Bilderhandschriften im 15. und 16. Jahrhundert*. Wiesbaden: Reichert Verlag.

Lepsius, C. R. 1842-5. *Denkmaeler Aegypten und Aethiopian*. Volumes 5 and 6.

Lorimer, H. 1950. *Homer and the Monuments*. London.

Louwe Kooijmans, L.P. 1993. An Early/Middle Bronze Age multiple burial at Wassenaar, the Netherlands. *Analecta Praehistorica Leidensia* 26. 1-20.

Macalister, R.A.S. 1928. *The Archaeology of Ireland*. London.

Macdonald, C. 1984. 'Aegean Swords and Warrior Graves. Their Implications for Knossian Military Organization', in J. Driessen & C. Macdonald, 'Some Military Aspects of the Aegean in the Late Fifteenth and Early Fourteenth Centuries B.C.,' *The Annual of the British School at Athens* 79: 56-74.

Maedebach, H. 1968. *Die Fechtkunst 1500-1900, Grafik und Waffen*. Coburg: Kunstsammlungen Veste Coburg.

Mair, P. H. 2006. *Treatise on the Martial Arts (c. 1550)*. Vol. 1: *Frontmatter, Longsword, Dusack*. Edited and translated by Forgeng, J.L.; Tsay, J.; Lord, J. and Delaney, L. Union City.

Malafouris, L. 2004. 'The cognitive basis of material engagement: where brain, body and culture conflate', in DeMarrais, E., Godsen, C. and Renfrew, C. (Eds.) 2004. 53-63.

Mallory, J.P. and McNeill, T.E. 1991. *The Archaeology of Ulster from Colonization to Plantation*. Belfast.

Marcotty, Th. 1997. *Bogen und Pfeile*. Herbig, München (reprint, 1st ed. dated 1958).

Marlow, W.C. 1981. Bow and Arrow Dynamics. *American Journal of Physics* 49.4. 320-33.

Marshall, S.L.A. 1978. *Men against fire*. Gloucester Massachusetts.

McCauley, C. 1990. 'Conference overview', in Haas, J. (ed.). *The Anthropology of war*. Cambridge. 1-26.

McDermott, B. 2004. *Warfare in ancient Egypt*. Stroud, Sutton.

McDonald, W.A. & Wilkie, N.C. (eds.) 1992. *Excavations at Nichoria in Southwest Greece*. Vol. II: *The Bronze Age Occupation*. Minneapolis.

McEwen, E., Bergman, C.A., Miller, R.L. 1991. Early Bow Design and Construction. *Scientific American* (June). 50-6.

Mclean, T. *The English at Play in the Middle Ages*. Kensal Press

McLeod, W. 1960. 'An Unpublished Egyptian Composite Bow in the Brooklyn Museum' in *Journal of the Society of Archer-Antiquaries* 3. 11-17.

McLeod, W. 1964. 'Tutankhamun's composite bows' in *Journal of the Society of Archer-Antiquaries* 7. 16-19.

McLeod, W. 1969. 'Egyptian composite bows made in Asia' in *Journal of the Society of Archer Antiquaries* 12. 19-23.

McLeod, W. 1970. *Composite Bows from the Tomb of Tutankhamun (Tutankhamun's Tomb Series, Vol. III)*. Oxford.

McLeod, W. 1982. *Self bows and other archery tackle from the tomb of Tutankhamun*. Oxford, Griffith Institute.

McLeod, W. 1995. Woods used in Egyptian bows and arrows, *Journal of the Society of Archer-Antiquaries* 38. 7-9.

Meyer, J. 1570. *Gründtliche Beschreibung der freyen ritterlichen unnd adelichen Kunst des Fechtens in allerley gebreuchlichen Wehren mit vil schönen und nützlichen Figuren gezieret und fürgestellet. Durch Ioachim Meyer, Freyfechter zu Strassburg*. Strassburg: printed by Thiebolt Berger.

Meyer, J. 1600. *Gründtliche Beschreibung der freyen Ritterlichen und Adelichen Kunst des Fechtens in allerley gebreuchlichen Wehren, mit schönen und nützlichen Figuren gezieret und fürgestellet*. Augsburg: printed by Michael Manger for Elias Willer.

Meyer, J. 2006. *The Art of Combat: A German Martial Arts Treatise of 1570*. Transl. Jeffrey L. Forgeng. London.

Miller, R.L., McEwen, E., Bergman, C.A. 1986. Experimental Approaches to Ancient Eastern Archery. *World Archaeology* 18.2. 178-95.

Molloy, B.P.C. 2004. 'Experimental combat with Bronze Age weapons', in *Archaeology Ireland, Vol. 17 No. 4*. 32-4.

Molloy, B.P.C. 2006. The role of combat weaponry in Bronze Age societies: The cases of the Aegean and Ireland in the Middle and Late Bronze Age. Unpublished PhD thesis, University College Dublin.

Molloy, B.P.C. Forthcoming (a). 'Thrusting too much? Aegean Swordsmanship in the Bronze Age.'

Molloy, B.P.C. Forthcoming (b). 'Martial Arts and Materiality: Locating the warrior in prehistoric society'.

Morris, C.E. and Peatfield, A.A.D. 2002. 'Feeling through the body: Gesture in Cretan Bronze Age religion', in Hamilakis, Y. Pluciennik, M. and Tarlow, S. (eds.). *Thinking through the body, archaeologies of corporeality*. Kluwer academic. 105-115.

Mount, C. 1991. Early Bronze Age burials – the social implications. *Archaeology Ireland* 5(2). 21-3.

Nardoni, D. 1989. *I gladiatori romani*. Roma.

Niemeier, W-D. 1982. 'Mycenaean Knossos and the Age of Linear B,' *Studi Micenei ed Egeo Anatolici* 23: 219-87.

Oakeshott, E. 1960. *The Archaeology of Weapons – Arms and Armour from prehistory to the Age of Chivalry*. Boydell Press.

Oakeshott, E. 1980. *European Weapons and Armour, From the Renaissance to the Industrial Revolution*. London.

O'Faolain, S. 2004. *Bronze artefact production in Late Bronze Age Ireland*. Oxford.

O'Faolain, S. and Northover, J.P. 1998. 'The technology of Late Bronze Age sword production in Ireland', *The Journal of Irish Archaeology IX*. 69-88.

O'Flaherty, R. 2002. *A consideration of the Early Bronze Age Halberd in Ireland – Function and Context*. Unpublished Doctoral thesis, University College Dublin.

O'Flaherty, R. (forthcoming) A weapon of choice – experiments with a replica Irish Early Bronze Age halberd. *Antiquity*.

O'Flaherty, R., Rankin, B., and Williams, L. 2002 Reconstructing an Irish Early Bronze Age halberd. *Archaeology Ireland* 16 (No.3). 30-4.

O'Kelly, M.J. 1989. *Early Ireland*. Cambridge University Press.

O'Meara, J.J. 1951. *The first version of the Topography of Ireland by Giraldus Cambrensis*. Dundalk.

O'Riordain, S.P. 1937. The halberd in Bronze Age Europe. *Archaeologia* 86, 195-321.

Osborne, R. 1998. *Archaic and Classical Greek Art*. Oxford.

Osgood, R. 1998. *Warfare in the Late Bronze Age of North Europe*. British Archaeological Reports International Series 694.

Osgood, R. and Monks, S. 2000. *Bronze Age Warfare*. Sutton Publishing.

Parker Brewis, W. 1923. 'The sword in Great Britain', in *Archaeologia 23*. 253-65.

Parker-Pearson, M. and Thorpe, I.J.N. (eds.) 2005. *Warfare, Violence and Slavery in Prehistory*. Oxford.

Paulsen, H. 1995. Bögen und Pfeile. In: Bemmann, G., Bemmann, J. (Hrsg.): *Der Opferplatz von Nydam. Die Funde aus den älteren Grabungen: Nydam I und Nydam II (Band 1: Text)*. Wachholtz-Verlag, Neumünster, pp. 387 427.

Paurenfeindt, A. 1516. *Ergrundung ritterlicher Kunst der Fechterey*. Vienna.

Partridge, R.B. 2002. *Fighting Pharaohs*. Manchester.

Peatfield, A.D. 1999. 'The Paradox of Violence: Weaponry and Martial Art in Minoan Crete', in Laffineur, R. (ed.). *Polemos*. Liege. 67-74.

Penniman, T. and Allen, I. 1960. A metallurgical study of four Irish Early Bronze Age ribbed halberds in the Pitt Rivers Museum, Oxford. *MAN* 60. 85-9.

Persson, A.W. 1931. *The Royal Tombs at Dendra near Midea*. Lund.

Persson, A.W. 1942. *New Tombs at Dendra near Midea*. Lund.

Petculescu, L. 1990. 'Contributions on Roman decorated helmets and breast-plates from Dacia', in Vetters & Kandler, 1990. 843-54.

Pflug, H. 1988. 'Helm und Beischiene eines Gladiators', in Bottini, 1988. 365-74.

Pfuhl, E. & Mobius, H. 1977. *Die ostgriechischen Grabreliefs*. Mainz.

Pini, I. 1975. *Kleinere griechische Sammlungen* (Corpus der minoisch-mykenischen Siegel V). Berlin.

Plass, P. 1995. *The Game of Death in Ancient Rome. Arena Sport and Political Suicide*. Madison.

Poliakoff, M. 1987. *Combat Sports in the Ancient World: Competition, Violence, and Culture*. Yale University Press.

Pollington, S. 1996. *The English Warrior from earliest times to 1066*. Norfolk.

Pollock, F. 1911. 'Swords' from the 'Scholar's edition' of the *Encyclopaedia Britannica*.

Pope, S.T. 1962. *Bows and Arrows*. Berkeley – Los Angeles (reprinted 1972).

Popham, M.R. & Sackett, L.H. 1980. *Lefkandi I: The Iron Age* (BSA Supplement XI). Oxford.

Porter, J. 1995. 'Anglo-Saxon Riddles', Hockwold-cum-Wilton.

Potter, D.S. 2004. *The Roman Empire at Bay, AD 180-395*. London.

Prebble, J. 1967. *Culloden*. Harmondsworth.

Raddatz, K. 1963. Pfeilspitzen aus dem Moorfund von Nydam. *Offa (Berichte und Mitteilungen aus dem Schleswig-Holsteinischen Landesmuseum für Vor- und Frühgeschichte in Schleswig, dem Landesamt für Vor- und Frühgeschichte von Schleswig-Holstein in Schleswig und dem Institut für Ur- und Frühgeschichte an der Universität Kiel)* 20. 49-56.

Raftery, J. 1942 A bronze halberd from Carn, Co. Mayo. *Journal of the Galway Archaeological and Historical Society*. 54-6.

Ramsey, W.G. 1989. *Middle Bronze Age weapons in Ireland*. Unpublished PhD thesis, Queens University Belfast.

Ramsey, W.G. 1995. 'Middle Bronze Age metalwork: Are artefact studies dead and buried?', in Waddell, J. and Shee-Twohig, E. (eds.). *Ireland in the Bronze Age*. Dublin. 49-62.

Randsborg, K. 1999. 'Into the Iron Age: a discourse on war and society'. in J. Carmen and A. Harding (eds.), *Ancient Warfare*. Stroud.

Rawlings, L. 1996. 'Celts, Spaniards and Samnites: warriors in a soldiers' war'. in Cornell, 1996. 81-95.

Reindl, H. 1996a. 'Wie hätten Sie's denn gern? Hart oder weich?' *Bogensport Magazin* 2.2. 12-15.

Reindl, H. 1996b. Wie weit die Pfeile fliegen. *Bogensport Magazin* 2.3, 46-9.

Renfrew, C. and Zubrow, E.B.W. (eds.). 1994. *The Ancient Mind. Elements of cognitive archaeology*. Cambridge.

Rich, J. and Shipley, G. (eds.). 1995. *War and Society in the Greek world*. London.

Richardson, T. 2001. 'Preliminary thoughts on the Roman armour from Carlisle', *Royal Armouries Yearbook* 6. 186-9.

de Ridder, A. 1915. *Les bronzes antiques du Louvre* II. *Les instruments*. Paris.

Riesch, H. 1999. Untersuchungen zu Effizienz und Verwendung alamannischer Pfeilspitzen. *Archäologisches Korrespondenzblatt* 29.4. 567-82.

Riesch, H. 2001a. Die Pfeilspitzen der Merowinger. *Traditionell Bogenschießen* 19. 18-21

Riesch, H. 2001b. Alamannische Pfeile und Bogen. In: Hörnig, A. (Hrsg.): *Das Bogenbauer-Buch*. Verlag Angelika Hörnig, Ludwigshafen. 143-9.

Riesch, H. 2002. *Pfeil und Bogen zur Merowingerzeit – Eine Quellenkunde und Rekonstruktion des frühmittelalterlichen Bogenschießens*. Karfunkel-Verlag, Wald-Michelbach.

Ritchie, W.F. & J.N.G. 1985. *Celtic Warriors*. Aylesbury.

Rees, G. 1993. The Longbow's Deadly Secrets. *New Scientist* (June). 24-5.

Robarchak, C. 1986. In *Papers presented to the Guggenheim Foundation Conference on the Anthropology of War*. Santa Fe.

Robert, L. 1940. *Les gladiateurs dans l'Orient grec*. Paris.

Robinson, H.R. 1975. *The Armour of Imperial Rome*. London.

Robson, B. 1997. *Swords of the British Army: the Regulation Patterns, 1788-1914*. London.

Roland, G. *An Introductory Course of Fencing*. Edinburgh: self-published.

Roth, F. 1917. *Die Chroniken der schwäbischen Städte: Augsburg. 7 Bd*. Die Chroniken der deutschen Städte vom 14. bis 16. Jahrhundert. 32. Bd. Hg. durch die Historische Kommission bei der Bayerischen Akademie der Wissenschaften. Leipzig: Verlag von S. Hirzel. Studer, Charles (c.1991). *Das Solothurner Fechtbuch*. Solothurn: Zentralbibliothek.

Sabbatini Tumolesi, P. 1980. *Gladiatorum Paria. Annunci di spettacoli gladiatori a Pompei.* Roma.

Sabbatini Tumolesi, P. 1988. *Epigraphica Amphitheatrali dell' Occidente Romano,* I. *Roma.* Roma.

Sabin, P. 1996. 'The mechanics of battle in the Second Punic War' in Cornell, 1996. 59-79.

Sabin, P. 2000. 'The Face of Roman Battle', *Journal of Roman Studies* 90. 1-17.

Sage, M. 1996. *Warfare in Ancient Greece: a source book.* London.

Sandars, N.K. 1961. 'The First Aegean Swords and their Ancestry', *American Journal of Archaeology* 65: 17-29.

Sandars, N.K. 1963. 'Later Aegean Bronze Swords,' *American Journal of Archaeology* 67: 117-153.

Santosuosso, A. 1997. *Soldiers, Citizens and the Symbols of War.* Boulder.

Savignoni, L. 1904. 'Scavi e scoperte nella necropoli di Phaestos,' *Monumenti Antichi* 14: 501-666.

Schmied-Kowarzik, Josef and Kufahl, Hans. *Fechtbüchlein,* Leipzig: Philipp Reclam, n.d. [1894]

Schmidt, J.A. 1749. *Gründlich lehrende Fecht-Schule, oder Leichte Anweisung, aud Stoss und Hieb sicher zu fechten; nebst einem curieusen Unterricht zum Voltigieren und Ringen, mit vielen saubern dazu dienlichen Kupfern versehen.* Nürnberg: bey Endterischen Consorten und Engelbrechtts Wittwe.

Schnurbein, S. von 1979. 'Eine hölzerne Sica aus dem Römerlager Oberaden', *Germania* 57. 117-34.

Sde-Or, I., and Yanilov, E., 2001. *How to Defend Yourself against Armed Assaults.* Tel Aviv.

Sekunda, N. 1986 *The Ancient Greeks.* 'Elite' Series, Osprey.

Sekunda, N . 1992. *The Persian Army 560–330 BC* 'Elite' Series, Vol. 42, Osprey.

Sekunda, N. 2000. *Greek Hoplite, 480-323 BC: Weapons, Armour, Tactics.* 'Elite' Series, Osprey.

Sekunda, N. 2001. 'The Greek Hoplite 480 – 323BC', *Osprey Military Journal 3.1*

Shackley, M. 1986. 'Arms and the man: 14th century Japanese swordsmanship illustrated by skeletons from Zaimokuza, near Kamakura, Japan', *World Archaeology* 18.2. 246-54.

Sharples, N. 1991. Warfare in the Iron Age of Wessex. *Scottish Archaeological Review* 8. 79-89.

Silver, G. 1933. *Paradoxes of Defence* (1599) cf Shakespeare Association Facsimile No. 6. Oxford.

Sim, D. & Ridge, I. 2002. *Iron for the Eagles. The Iron Industry of Roman Britain.* Stroud.

Snodgrass, A.M. 1964. *Early Greek arms and armour.* Edinburgh.

Snodgrass, A.M. 1965. 'The Linear B Arms and Armour Tablets Again,' *Kadmos* 4: 96-119.

Snodgrass, A.M. 1967. *Arms and Armour of the Greeks.* London.

Snodgrass, A.M. 1971. 'The First European Body-Armour', in Boardman, J., Brown, Snodgrass, A.M. 1999. *Arms and Armour of the Greeks.* (2nd edition) Maryland.

Speidel, M.P. 1992. *The Framework of an Imperial Legion.* Cardiff.

Sulimirski, T. 1970. *The Sarmatians.* London.

Starr, R. F.S. 1939. *Nuzi. Volume 1: Text.* Harvard University Press.

Stephenson, I.P. 2002. *The Anglo-Saxon Shield.* Stroud.

Stirland, A.J. 2001. *Raising the Dead: The Skeleton Crew of King Henry VIII's Great Ship the Mary Rose.* Wiley, Chichester.

Stodiek, U., Paulsen, H. 1996. *'Mit dem Pfeil, dem Bogen …' Technik der steinzeitlichen Jagd.* Isensee, Oldenburg.

Stoylov, S.P., Nsanzabera, J.C., Karenzi, P.C. 1972. A Demonstration of Momentum Conservation Using Bow, Arrow, and Ballistic Pendulum. *American Journal of Physics* 40. 430-2.

Strickland, M., Hardy, R. 2005. *The Great Warbow.* Sutton Publishing, Phoenix Hill.

Sudhues, H. 2004. *Wundballistik bei Pfeilverletzungen.* Dissertation, Institut für Rechtsmedizin der Universität, Münster.

Sutor, J. 1612. *New kunstliches Fechtbuch.* Frankfurt-am-Main: Johann Bringern.

Taracha, P. 1989. 'Dating the Cheek-Piece of a Helmet from Ialysos, Rhodes,' *Archeologia Warszawa* 40: 9-13.

Taracha, P. 1992. 'Wagenkämpfer aus Knossos und Dendra: Zur Rolle der Bogenwaffen im späthelladischen Griechenland,' *Archeologia Warszawa* 43: 121-3.

Taracha, P. 1993. 'Weapons in the Shaft Graves of Mycenae: Aspects of the Relative Chronology of Circle A and B Burials', *Archeologia Warszawa* 44: 7-34.

Taracha, P. 1996. 'Mycenaean Bronzes from Biliotti's Excavations at Ialysos, Rhodes, Revisited', *Aegean Archaeology* 3: 87-94.

Taracha, P 1999. 'Reconstructing the Dendra Panoply,' *Archeologia Warszawa* 50: 7-11.

Taracha, P. 2004. 'From Dagger to Sword. Some Reflections on the Development of Early Swords in the Aegean, Anatolia and the Levant,' *Archeologia Warszawa* 55: 7-18.

Talhoffer, H. 2000. *Medieval Combat. A Fifteenth-Century Illustrated Manual of Swordfighting and Close-Quarter Combat*. Edited and translated by Rector, M. London: Greenhill Books.

Tarassuk, L. and Blaire, C. 1979. *Complete Encyclopedia of Arms & Weapons*. Bonanza Books.

Technau, W. 1931. Eine Schale des Onesimos in Berliner Museum. *Mitteilungen des Deutschen Archaeologischen Instituts (Roemische Abteilung, München)* 46. 189-97.

Thibault, G. 1628. *Académie de l'Espée, ou se demonstrent par reigles mathématiques, sur le fondement d'un cercle mystérieux, la théorie et pratique des vrais et jusqu'à present incognus secret du maniement des armes, à pied et à cheval*. Leyden: Elzeviers.

Thordeman, B. 1939. *Armour and the Battle of Wisby 1361*. Stockholm.

Tobler, C. 2001. *Secrets of German Medieval Swordsmanship*. Union City, California.

Tölle-Kastenbein, R. 1980. *Pfeil und Bogen im antiken Griechenland (Reih, Pfeil und Bogen in der Geschichte', Band 1)*. Duris, Bochum.

Treherne, P. 1995. The warrior and his beauty: the masculine body and self identification in Bronze Age Europe. *Journal of European Archaeology* 3.1. 105-44.

Tuijn, C., Kooi, B.W. 1992. The Measurement of Arrow Velocities in the Students' Laboratories. *European Journal of Physics* 13. 127-34.

Turney-High, H.H. 1949. *Primitive War*. Columbia.

Ulbert, G. 1974. 'Straubing und Nydam. Zu römischen Langschwertern der späten Limeszeit', in G. Kossack & G. Ulbert (ed.), *Studien zu Vor- und Frühgeschichtlichen Archäologie. Festschrift für Joachim Werner zum 65. Geburtstag*, München, 197-216.

Underwood, R. 1999. *Anglo-Saxon Weapons & Warfare*. Stroud.

Vandenabeele, F. 1978. 'L'idéogramme de l'armure sur une tablette en Linéaire B de Tirynthe,' *Bulletin de Correspondance Hellénique* 102, fasc. 1: 25-39.

Väyda, A. 1976. *War in Ecological Perspective*. New York.

Ventzke, W. 1986. 'Der Schuppenpanzer von Kamid el-Loz' in Hachmann, R. (ed.) *Kamid el-Loz 1977–81, Bericht uber Ergebnisse der Ausgrabungen in Kamid el-Loz in den Jahren 1977 bis 1981*, Bonn, Dr. Rudolph Habelt GMBH.

Verdelis, N.M. 1967. 'Neue Funde von Dendra', *Mitteilungen des Deutschen Archäologischen Instituts. Athenische Abteilung* 82: 1-53.

Verdelis, N.M. 1977. 'The Metal Finds,' in Åström, P. and Verdelis, N.M. *The Cuirass Tomb and Other Finds from Dendra: The Chamber Tombs* (Studies in Mediterranean Archaeology 4/1). Göteborg. 28-50.

Verolinus, T. 1679. *Der Künstliche [sic] Fechter, oder, Dess Weyland wohl-geübten und berühmten Fecht-Meisters Theodori Verolini kurtze jedoch klare Beschreibung und Aussweisung der Freyen Ritterlichen und Adelichen Kunst des Fechtens im Rappier, Dusacken und Schwerd*. Würzburg: Joann Bencard.

Vetters, H. & Kandler, M. (eds.) 1990. *Akten des 14. internationalen Limeskongresses 1986 in Carnuntum*. Wien.

Waddell, J. 1998. *The Prehistoric Archaeology of Ireland*. Galway University Press.

Wagner, E. 1967. *Cut and Thrust Weapons*. London.

Wagner, P. and Hand, S. *Medieval sword and shield: The combat system of Royal Armouries MS I.33*. California.

Wardle, D.E.H. 1988. 'Does Reconstruction Help? A Mycenaean Dress and the Dendra Suit of Armour,' in French, E.B. & Wardle, K.A. (eds.), *Problems in Greek Prehistory: Papers Presented at the Centenary Conference of the British School of Archaeology at Athens, Manchester, April 1986*. Bristol. 469-76.

Warry, J. 2001. *Warfare in the Classical world*. London.

Waurick, G. 1988. 'Römische Helme', in Bottini, 1988. 327-64.

Wassmannsdorff, K. 1870. *Sechs Fechtschulen (d.i. Schau- und Preisfechten) der Marxbrüder und Federfechter aus den Jahren 1573 bis 1614; Nürnberger Fechtschulreime v. J. 1579 und Rösener's Gedicht: Ehrentitel und Lobspruch der Fechtkunst v. J. 1589*. Heidelberg: Karl Groos.

Van Wees, H. 2004. *Greek Warfare: Myth and realities*. Duckworth.

Welch, K. 1994. 'The Roman Arena in Late Republican Italy: a new interpretation', *Journal of Roman Archaeology* 7. 59-80.

Welle, R. 1993. *'...und wisse das alle höbischeit kompt von deme ringen': Der Ringkampf als adelige Kunst im 15. und 16. Jahrhundert*. Pfaffenweiler: Centaurus.

Wheeler, E. 1979. 'The Roman legion as phalanx', *Chiron* 9. 303-18.

Wiedemann, T. 1992. *Emperors and Gladiators*. London.

Wierschin, M. 1965. *Meister Johann Liechtenauers Kunst des Fechtens*. Munich.

Winkler, M.M. (ed.) 2004. *Gladiator. Film and History*. London.

Wise, T. 1981. *Ancient Armies of the Middle East*. Man-at-Arms 109, Osprey.

Xenaki-Sakellariou, A. 1985. *Hoi thalamotoi tafoi ton Mykenon. Anaskafes Ch. Tsounta (1887-1898)*. Paris.

Yadin, Y. 1963. *The Art of Warfare in Biblical Lands in the Light of Archaeological Discovery*. London.

York, J., 2002, 'The life cycle of bronze age metalwork from the Thames', *Oxford Journal of Archaeology* 21 No.1. 77-92.

Verfasserlexikon, 1985. *Die deutsche Literatur des Mittelalters: Verfasserlexikon*. Berlin, New York: Walter de Gruyter.

Zhmodikov, A. 2000. 'Roman Republican heavy infantry in battle (IV-II centuries BC)', *Historia* 49. 67-78.

MANUSCRIPTS

The 'Döbringer' Fechtbuch (1389). Nuremberg, Germanisches Nationalmuseum Cod. Ms. 3227a. Hils no. 41.

Gladiatoria (c.1425). Krakow, Biblioteka Jagiellonska Ms. germ. quart. 16. Hils no. 28. Lecküchner, Johannes (?c.1480). Heidelberg, Universitätsbibliothek Cod. Pal. Germ. 430. Hils no. 24.

Lecküchner, Johannes (1482). Munich, Bayerische Staatsbibliothek Cgm 582; translated in Forgeng 2006. Hils no. 33.

The 'Lew' Fechtbuch (c.1450). Augsburg, Universitätsbibliothek Cod. I.6.40.3. Hils no. 5.

The 'Ringeck' Fechtbuch (c.1425). Dresden, Sächsische Landesbibliothek Mscr. Dresd. C 487. Edited in Wierschin 1965: 87-166; translated in Tobler 2001. Hils no. 16.

The 'Starhemberg' Fechtbuch (1452). Rome, Biblioteca dell'Academica Nazionale dei Lincei e Corsiniana Cod. 44 A 8 (Cod. 1449). Hils no. 42.

The 'Speyer' Fechtbuch (1491). Salzburg, Universitätsbibliothek M. I. 29. Hils no. 43.

Talhoffer, Hans (1459). *Fechtbuch*. Royal Library Thott 290 20. Copenhagen. Hils no. 27.

von Eyb, Ludwig (1500). Erlangen, Universitätsbibliothek B 26. Hils no. 17.

Index